# Hypnotherapy Revealed

## HYPNOTHERAPY TRANCE SCRIPTS

by Dan Jones

Connect with Dan Jones:
www.DanJonesHypnosis.com

Twitter: @AuthorDanJones

Third Edition 2020

Published by Dan Jones

Copyright © Dan Jones 2011

First and second edition released as *Advanced Ericksonian Hypnotherapy Scripts*

Daniel Jones asserts the moral right to be identified as the author of this work

ISBN 979-8643817659

THIRD EDITION

For Graham

Hypnotherapy Revealed Series

# Contents

# INTRODUCTION

Since getting involved in the field of hypnosis over 25 years ago I have been fortunate enough to have helped people with a wide range of problems from clients who want to quit smoking to people with anxiety and depression and pretty much everything in between.

In the early days I used to get a client's history and information about the problem and what they would like as the solution then by the time they came for the first session I would have written a script and developed treatment ideas to use with the client in their session. Before the second session I would have contact with the client by phone to see how they were getting on and what changes they had noticed, what improvements and what they still wanted to improve. From this information by the second session I would have written a second script for the client to help them to continue moving forward.

Writing all of these scripts became quite time consuming so I began to purchase books of scripts. None of these scripts matched my clients exactly but they gave me ideas which I could use to mix and match and get ideas from for individuals I was working with.

I stopped using scripts about a year into seeing clients, but still think they have their place as all Hypnotherapists are unique and some like scripts to help formulate ideas before client sessions, whereas others aren't so keen on the use of scripts. My view is that therapists should at most only use scripts to develop ideas and as a learning aid perhaps when they are starting out, they shouldn't be reading scripts verbatim to clients because no client will match any script, each client is a unique individual and therapists should be paying attention to the client, not a sheet of paper. Scripts are best used for ideas by those who have already trained as a professional hypnotherapy practitioner to work without scripts. The concern of doing things the other way around, learning a little and then relying on scripts first, is that scripts can become a crutch which can be difficult to let go of. Any legitimate hypnotherapy practitioner qualification will teach you how to work without needing hypnotherapy scripts because you will be learning to work with clients rather than learning how to read to clients. I think it is interesting that hypnotherapists are just 'talking therapists' like any other counsellor, psychotherapist or cognitive-behavioural practitioner, if they have been properly trained then they will have been trained in some form of counselling or psychotherapy and how to use hypnosis as an adjunct to that therapy, so they should be suitably qualified, just like any other practitioner of that therapy to work with clients without scripts. Hypnotherapy seems to be the only field where its practitioners seem to hunt out scripts to inform what to say to clients, other counsellors and psychotherapists don't ask for counselling or psychotherapy scripts, yet the only difference between what a hypnotherapist is doing and what a counsellor or psychotherapist is doing should be that the hypnotherapist is doing the same, plus hypnosis. Hypnosis is really easy to do and doesn't require a script, but to see how different hypnotic techniques and language patterns can be integrated into counselling or psychotherapy it can be helpful for the beginner to read scripts and see how the author of the scripts combines hypnosis and therapy. You may also find research papers when searching for evidence-based ways to work with clients. Some of these papers may share about the use of hypnosis in the treatment of various problems and may state the effectiveness of that treatment. The research often uses a standardised approach so that each of the people taking part in the study would have received the same therapy. In these situations, it can be helpful to know what that approach was, what wording or structure was used so that you know for example that if you use the same approach as they used it you should get similar results. If a study said that 75% of those taking part in the study got better and everyone received the same approach and same wording, then you should be able to replicate these results and help 75% of your clients who present with that problem by just using that approach the same as was used in the research.

All the scripts in this book are based on my interpretation of an Ericksonian approach to hypnotherapy. The Ericksonian approach was covered in my last book. The approach isn't about always being covert and indirect or all about using stories and metaphors and complex hypnotic language. It's about getting the balance right and using what is right for the individual client you are working with, as mentioned in my last book *Hypnotherapy Revealed: The Ericksonian Approach*, the Ericksonian approach isn't therapy or hypnosis, but can be used as a way of approaching how you do therapy or hypnosis. Erickson frequently used direct suggestion and direct inductions. The Ericksonian Approach is about taking what works with each client. If the client needs to be worked with in a direct manner then do this, if they need to be worked with indirectly use this. Usually it will be a balance of direct techniques and indirect techniques. Although the scripts in this book are based on the style of Milton Erickson MD, the fact that they are scripts means that they aren't truly Ericksonian, as the Ericksonian approach is about observing the client in front of you and utilising your observations towards a goal.

From over 25 years' experience, the way I work with clients' often starts with indirect techniques to prime ideas, concepts and mental processes and begins to activate these without the client realising that this is what I am doing so they don't resist it and then moving on to being more direct with indirect techniques being used to compliment the direct work. Because this is how I naturally work, this is what the scripts in this book are like. The scripts are also based on my approach to therapy. The Ericksonian approach isn't therapy, it is an attitude to how to work with clients, what I use predominantly in therapy is cognitive-behavioural approaches, solution focused, motivational interviewing and human givens.

Since teaching hypnosis to others, I have been repeatedly asked if I can create scripts for other therapists that they can use with their clients. Everything I'm sharing with you in this book has been used effectively with my own clients and with clients of others. Many of the scripts are based on the wording I have used with my own clients. The book was initially released in 2009 as *Advanced Ericksonian Hypnotherapy Scripts*. It quickly became a number one hypnosis and hypnotherapy bestseller, the second edition which released in 2011 included significant additional content bringing the book up to over 100 hypnotherapy scripts consisting of inductions, deepeners and therapy scripts and two additional sections, one teaching Ericksonian hypnotic language patterns and one teaching how to structure therapy sessions to help the reader better understand the scripts and how they fit in the wider context of the therapy the reader will be doing with their clients. This third edition has been written to fit within my new *Hypnotherapy Revealed* hypnotherapy books series and includes additional hypnotic inductions bringing the total to 88 inductions. Not all of these inductions are fully scripted word for word because they are inductions where you are carrying out behaviours or having to respond to the client, so what you get is the structure of the induction and guidance on what you need to do when using the induction and there is additional information about the evidence for treating various conditions and the therapeutic scripts have been updated. Although I teach hypnotic language patterns and structuring therapy sessions, it is best to have read my previous two books to gain greater understanding about hypnosis and how it works. Without this understanding some of the inductions may seem too easy or 'not enough words' to work. For example, the structure of the *push down on my hand induction* is that you tell the client that when you say 'sleep' they can close their eyes and relax deeply into hypnosis. You then ask the client to push down on your hand, you tell them to push harder and harder (until you see them go inside their mind to say to themselves that they can't push any harder), then you pull your hand away, click your fingers and say sleep.

Every time I have ever done this induction, what I described above is exactly as I have done it. What I do next will vary depending on the way each client responds, but I have never done the above induction with someone I have prepared or as a re-induction process, I have done it as described with people I have hypnotised before and people I have never hypnotised. Usually I have done the induction in front of audiences of students where I ask for anyone to come up to the front for me to do the next demonstration with.

Obviously, being the instructor and given the setting, this increases the likelihood of whoever sits in the demonstration chair responding better than average, but it isn't the case that I am just choosing highly hypnotisable people to work with.

I mention this induction as an example of the type of thing which complete beginners can read the description of and feel that there is no way it could work, they don't believe it would work and will say they don't understand how it could work. There are many inductions like this, that to the untrained eye, on paper can appear like there is no way they could work. My previous books teach how the different inductions work.

I was initially reluctant to write a book of 'scripts' but as time went on I realised that many hypnotherapists in training and newly qualified hypnotherapists found the use of scripts to learn from and get ideas from; especially scripts they knew worked, gave them confidence and this confidence influenced their effectiveness with clients.

One of the reasons for being reluctant to write a book of scripts is that it may encourage people to stop paying attention to clients and to stick rigidly to what is written in the script as if it is 'the truth' and the way you have to do things.

From this concern I have decided to include a little more information rather than just the scripts to encourage people; especially those new to the field of hypnotherapy that are perhaps going through training to look at the client as a whole and integrate the scripts into how you work with clients rather than have the script as the starting point and trying to make clients fit the scripts.

As well as hypnotic induction scripts there are also therapeutic scripts to address different issues clients may present with in therapy. All of the therapeutic scripts are things I've used successfully during the 'hypnosis' part of sessions with clients. Most issues clients present with involve them having to develop doing different behaviours in the future, so it is common in my work with clients for me to transition from what you may read in the therapeutic scripts into having the client do some mental rehearsal of the new way they want things to go in the future before they exit hypnosis. I usually follow this up towards the end of the session by setting tasks for the client to do between sessions to take the change work out of the therapy room and into the client's life. If you are using this book for self-hypnosis, it is useful to treat yourself as if you are a therapy client, so include mental rehearsal and set yourself therapeutic tasks, don't just expect change to happen magically without the need for taking an active role in your own personal development.

I hope you enjoy this book and find the scripts, strategies and ideas helpful in your work creating positive change in people's lives. If you find this book helpful, it would be highly appreciated and valued if you could write a review, or create your own self-hypnosis YouTube videos from the scripts and share them (if you let me know about your self-hypnosis videos on my Facebook page (www.facebook.com/DanJonesHypnosis) I can share them with others).

Before embarking on using any of these scripts in your own private practice there are some useful pointers to keep in mind:

1. **Some clients come to therapists because they have been told to; not because they**

**have chosen to.** With these clients they are more likely not to carry out any tasks set and may come in with such a strong mind-set that they don't need your help or don't want to change or that they want the therapy to fail so that they can say they 'tried' hypnosis and it didn't work, or they don't see that there is a problem. With these clients it is difficult to help them to change using a script because they have no intention of changing. A large number of these people can be helped with hypnotherapists that are not using scripts but instead are responding moment by moment to the client as an individual. It doesn't mean that in the future these clients couldn't come back to you to be helped when they are ready it's just now isn't the right time for them.

2. **You don't 'fix' clients they 'fix' themselves.** You are a guide for your client. If they come to you seeking help, you can give them ideas and information but for them to change they need to do the work. For example, if you set a task and they don't carry it out that is their choice. For lasting change, the client needs to feel empowered and in

control of their own situation not reliant on a therapist so they need to do the work.

3. **Change isn't always instant.** For lasting change, oftentimes other things need to happen outside the therapy room. For example, someone may want to quit smoking but may smoke when they get stressed. They may expect 'you' to stop them smoking instantly but the thing causing them stress may not yet be dealt with or they may not have mastered relaxing in a new way. This can all take time and so if they just quit at the end of the session they are likely to fail because once they get stressed they will resort to what they know and start smoking again. If on the other hand they practice a relaxation technique and also deal with the situation that is causing them stress then they will be in a better place to quit. In many cases the client may not get the result until months later when the time is right. I worked with someone that had a fear of success and had a dream about what she wanted to do. It was going to take some hard work on her part to make the dream a reality and her fear of success

came from a lack of confidence which was due to a lack of knowledge and skill about what she needed to know. After the session she didn't think things had changed; a few weeks later she still maintained 'it didn't work' because she was still nervous about the success she wanted. She then 'forgot' about our session and just carried on with her life; following her dream; learning more and becoming more skilled. Then a year later a friend of hers contacted me and told me she is living her dream. It all played out as I had expected. She went through all the stages I had expected and built on all the seeds sown in the single hypnotherapy session that we had had. I had explained to her friend just after the session what I had done (they were a hypnotherapist in training and observed the session for training purposes and we discussed the session afterwards) and what I expected to happen. The one thing I couldn't answer was how long it would take her to go through all the necessary stages as she would have to find opportunities to attend courses and learn new things.

4. **The scripts in this book are best used as guides.** Every client is an individual so the best way to use and read the scripts is to keep the essence of the script whilst adapting the wording to suit each client. You can also mix and match scripts to include what would be best suited to the client you are working with. If a specific suggestion, metaphor, induction or task seems like it would be good for a client you can use it and edit it into the 'main' script you are using.

5. **Make sure your client understands what hypnosis is and how it works.** Make sure they understand hypnotherapy isn't a 'quick fix' therapy. I often ask clients how quickly they expect the changes to take before they begin to notice the improvements. This gives me the opportunity to discuss any unrealistic expectations they may have. If I know a client is unlikely to be a non-smoker instantly because they have other issues to sort out and they tell me they expect to instantly be a non-smoker then I would discuss this with the client until we get some agreement on how long it is likely to

realistically take, what stages the client may well go through and if they may have any relapses I will discuss with them how it is okay to have a few relapses, what they can learn from them and how they can get back on track again to move on. I talk about how in the session we lay down new patterns of responding in the brain and that these new patterns need strengthening and reinforcing to make them become habitual and some of the patterns may need specific events to happen before they become active. I often mention that sometimes suggestions and ideas need time to seep through from outside of their awareness to in their awareness because they need time to be understood and incorporated fully before they can be used.

## How to induce a hypnosis

Hypnosis is induced by focusing attention (it could be on a spot on the wall, or on a thought, or on a rhythm, or on almost anything else).

Hypnosis or trance states can be induced in many different ways:

- By confusion followed by a solid suggestion (utilising the orientation response).

- Pattern interruption, (like handshake inductions) these trigger the orientation response by creating confusion as the correct pattern isn't happening so the client takes their cue on what to do next from the hypnotist.

- Shock inductions (like stage hypnotists frequently do, these set off the orientation response requiring a clear suggestion to follow).

- Relaxing the muscles (which are part of the process for falling asleep and accessing the rapid eye movement (REM) and non-rapid eye movement (NREM) states and it is also something to focus attention on).

- Deepening rhythmic breathing (part of the process towards accessing the REM and NREM states and focusing attention).

- Visualisation (part of falling asleep and dreaming – accessing the REM state).

Everyone uses hypnosis all of the time. When people think about winning the lottery and what they would do with the money, they are visualising which induces a light trance. Smokers may go into a trance when they focus on the cigarette they are having and they take deep breaths as they allow their muscles to relax. When people have cravings, they enter a trance as they become so intensely focused on what they crave. When people get angry they focus on what is causing the anger. When people get depressed they focus on worrying and negative thoughts.

## Hypnosis CAN be induced in pretty much anyone

If you hypnotise people using a scripted or structured induction then that induction is likely to have varied results depending on who is being hypnotised. Some people will respond well, but others may not respond at all because the script or structured induction isn't right for them. Often in hypnosis research structured inductions are used so that researchers can properly evaluate and evidence the effectiveness of an approach. If they tailored the approach to each research subject then they wouldn't be researching the effectiveness of a specific approach because they varied the approach with each person.

Using the same approach on everyone doesn't work because people are all different. For example, some people might feel uncomfortable with an induction that guides them down in an elevator so they won't engage with it, but that same person may love sailing and if the hypnotist has them imagine what it is like to sail and focuses on the experience of sailing then the person may become deeply absorbed in this experience and increase their responsivity. So, to be able to hypnotise pretty much anyone the hypnotist needs to tailor what they do to the individual client, this goes for the approach used and to the way the approach is used, like the pacing of the induction, the voice used, how silence is used, how hypnotic language is used or not used.

My first book in the *Hypnotherapy Revealed* series covered how to do hypnosis and the second book taught the Ericksonian approach. Both of these books go into far more detail than we are going into here, so are useful to read for those who want to dive into how to do hypnosis and how the Ericksonian approach works, reading those books will give you a greater understanding of the scripts in this book.

Some types of induction are:

- Conversational (overt & covert)

- Pattern interrupt

- Embedded-meaning/metaphorical

- Confusion

- Directive

## Conversational Inductions

Conversational inductions are induction's that initially start with an ordinary conversation. They involve embedding suggestions and utilising on-going experiences or events to induce hypnosis. It could be embedding suggestions in a conversation or feeding back what a client says to deepen their experience.

## An example of an overt conversational induction

As you *sit back and begin to feel comfortably relaxed (embedded commands in italics)*, I would like you to *let those eyes gently close*...that's it (acknowledging the client closing their eyes)...recognising that with those eyes closed you can *drift pleasantly inside*, accessing memories, past experiences or other meaningful events when *you feel good*...now you can *take a few deep, refreshing breaths* and as you release those breaths you can *drift even more deeply into hypnosis*...etc.

## Pattern Interrupt Inductions

A pattern interrupt induction is where you interrupt a clients' pattern of behaviour. This triggers a response in the client for them to want to complete or have a resolution to the pattern. Clients will often take the lead of the therapist at this point just to get a resolution to the incomplete pattern. This could be interrupting someone mid-sentence, it could be interrupting a handshake or any other automatic behaviour.

## *An example of a pattern interrupt induction*

Interrupting the pattern of a handshake example:

"Hi, I'm Dan (hand goes out; clients hand comes to meet it. I take it with my opposite hand, raise it with the palm facing the clients face then slowly start moving their hand toward their face)…and as that hand continues to move closer to your face all by itself you can begin to notice the change in the focus of your vision…and as the vision changes you can notice how heavy those eyelids are getting…and you don't have to go all the way into hypnosis until that hand comfortably touches the face…" etc.

## Metaphorical and Embedded-Meaning Inductions

Metaphorical and embedded-meaning inductions use patterns within stories to convey what is expected of the client, for example the metaphor of walking down stairs could be used to give the pattern for going deeper into hypnosis, or the metaphor of looking out from the top of a mountain could be used to give the pattern of gaining new perspective on a problem. It is common to also embed suggestions within the induction.

## An example of a metaphorical induction

Take a moment to close your eyes and with your eyes closed you can *begin to relax* and as you relax you can have a sense that you *go on a journey* one day and as *you take this journey*, you are walking out through the woods and while you walk through the woods, you can wonder about different things, you can wonder about what it is you have got to do later, you can wonder about a conversation you had earlier or the previous day, you can wonder about someone you are going to see later in the week and a part of you can also be aware of, the sounds around you, also aware of the feeling of each footstep you take as you walk through the woods and aware of the sounds of the rustling leaves and noticing the dancing light, as it shimmers through the trees.

And while you are out on this nice, relaxed walk, you are searching for a lake, you have never visited this lake before, you have been told that if you come out into this wood you can discover a lake, a lake that will help *you find some inner discovery* and you can be curious what inner discovery you can get by finding this lake. So, as you continue walking, you notice rabbits hopping around, you notice birds flying, you notice butterflies and bees going about their daily business; popping in and out of different flowers.

And you don't know what kind of inner discovery you are going to gain at the lake and what it is about the lake that will help *you find that inner discovery*, you just know it is what you have been told. So, you walk along the path *going deeper* into the woods and as *you go deeper and deeper* into the woods, so *you relax more with the experience*, that kind of daydream relaxation that you have, as you are walking along, where your mind is wandering and feeling pleasant, where the day just *feel so pleasant,* that you just *feel so relaxed.* And while you wander along you hear someone further along the path, so you keep walking, you are curious who that person is going to be and as you get closer you can hear their voice speaking louder.

And then as you approach you notice, a man dressed in nondescript clothing, a man who can just blend in anywhere, he even seemed to almost blend in here, if it wasn't for his talking. And because you are walking through the woods and there is only you and this man, it is only polite to say hello, as you walk past. And as you walk past and you say hello, so the man responds to you. "Do you know where you are going here in the middle of nowhere?" The man asks.

You think you understand what the man says as you experience a little confusion and you tell him yes, you are trying to find the lake and he responds "Yes, you are trying to find the lake and the lake is in the middle of nowhere and nowhere is where you are going and you will know where you are going when you discover that nowhere is here and here in the middle of nowhere is nowhere. And some people try to travel to somewhere and other people try to travel to anywhere, but you're not trying to go somewhere or anywhere, you are here nowhere and as you walk around here nowhere, you should be able to find the lake you are looking for. Because the lake you are looking for is nowhere, but in your mind." And with that, the man began to walk away leaving you feeling a little confused.

And so, you continue to *walk along the path* looking for the lake and you don't know where you are going exactly, but you know that you will find the lake *following this path*. So you continue looking along the path, *going deeper* into the woods and as *you relax deeper and deeper* into the woods, so the, woods appear to, become thicker and denser and that makes them become slightly darker which helps you to notice as you turn a corner on the path, that there is a clearing off in the distance which is much brighter over there and you don't pick up the pace or speed up in anyway just because *you notice the clearing*, but you now know where you are going. You are confident that in that clearing you will find the lake that you are searching for. And as you walk along towards that clearing, so you have the words of that man going around in your head. Nowhere, somewhere, anywhere. You think to yourself quizzically. Nowhere, somewhere, anywhere.

You don't know exactly what he was on about, but in the same way when you meet someone and you can't remember their name but you know you know their name and the harder you try to remember their name, the harder it becomes to remember and then you just put it out of your mind and you carry on with other things and their name springs up in your mind a little while later, you know the same thing will probably happen here and if you carry on with the journey and you put what that man said out of your mind, the answer will spring up in mind when the time is right, there is no need to try and force it, the answers will come through when the unconscious has worked it out enough to let you know.

## Directive Inductions

Directive inductions are directly telling a client what you want them to do, part of the challenge with them is that some people can feel the hypnotist is being controlling or forceful. There is also a greater chance of the induction mismatching the clients' experience. If you say "your eyes don't work" and the client tries to open their eyes and succeeds, then you were wrong and this doesn't match the clients' experience and can impact on future success with the client.

## An example of a directive induction

I'm going to shake your hand three times…the first time your eyes will get tired…let them…the second time they'll want to close…let them…the third time they'll lock and you won't be able to open them…want that to happen, and watch it happen…now…1…2…now close your eyes…now 3…and they're locked and you'll find they just don't work, no matter how hard you try…the harder you try the less they'll work…test them and you'll find they won't work at all…

## Confusion Inductions

Confusion inductions can be done in many ways, I used some confusion in the metaphorical induction example above. Confusion is often used to some extent in most inductions, but you can build an induction entirely around confusion, rather than just adding confusion into the induction. When someone is confused, they seek clarity and are more likely to accept the way out of confusion offered by the hypnotist as long as it isn't done to the extent that they get annoyed and decide to escape the confusion themselves, for example, by walking away.

## An example of a confusion induction (used within a story)

One afternoon a woman set out looking for her friend's house. She was tired and not really paying attention until she got halfway there and realised she'd lost her way. She checked her map for directions, holding her bag in her right hand using her left hand she lent right down and left her drink on the ground right by her left foot. Then reaching right across her side with her left hand to the right pocket of her bag she discovered the map wasn't there so she took her left hand out of the right pocket deciding the pocket must be wrong and that one of the pockets left must be right. She checked one of the pockets left which wasn't right and then another pocket she thought must be right leaving only one left when she discovered that wasn't right either. She now knew it must be in the pocket left which was on the right-hand side of the bag. She was convinced this pocket left must be right. She checked the pocket discovering the pocket left was indeed right and took out the map. She then lent right down and with her left hand picked up the drink stood right up and left on the *rest* of her journey.

## Naturalistic inductions

Probably the easiest way for a beginner to induce hypnosis in someone is to use a naturalistic approach. A naturalistic approach involves talking about everyday trance states. As you talk to a client about everyday trance states they will be familiar so will rapidly start to enter trance. If you do this utilising hypnotic language the effects will be even greater.

To focus attention you can have clients talking about something that they are interested in. In the old day's hypnotists would tell the client what to think and what to focus on. To induce a trance you need to focus attention but it doesn't matter what you focus that attention on. That is one of the beauties of naturalistic inductions. Hypnotists used to use swinging watches, stroking, telling the client to look at a spot or a candle. Modern day hypnotists get clients to focus on issues, thoughts, comments, or even the process of their problem. One quick way to hypnotise a smoker for example, is to ask them to tell you the process they go through when they smoke.

It can be helpful to utilise naturalistic phenomena. Almost anything can be used to achieve goals. If you want to lead to a trance state you can use naturalistic phenomena leading to trance, like sleep, day-dreaming, a leisure activity. If you wanted to evoke a hypnotic phenomenon then you can use examples of times that they have happened naturally like numbness – sleeping on an arm or holding snow, or amnesia – forgetting someone's name or being interrupted mid-sentence.

Creating responses this way will then come from within the client so they will be more powerful. It is completely different telling someone to laugh uncontrollably than reminding them of times they found themselves laughing uncontrollably.

You can encourage the client to talk about something they enjoy doing that makes their mind wander and as they talk about it they will begin to go back into that same state of mind again. When you hypnotise someone, you want to communicate in a way that will encourage automaticity rather than conscious effort or control. There isn't really such a thing as a conscious mind and unconscious mind as often talked about, but these ideas can work well when doing hypnosis. The reality is that there are things we are consciously aware of and things we aren't consciously aware of. We have some processes which are unconscious processes, like our blinking, cell division, heart beating, and things which we may or may not be conscious of like certain memories, feelings and sensations. We don't have two minds, but have one brain. I prefer the term non-conscious, simply to refer to what someone isn't consciously aware of and rather than use the term conscious mind, I prefer conscious awareness – those things which in this moment you are aware of. When you are communicating in a way that encourages automaticity, what you are doing is communicating in a way that conveys that you aren't asking a client to do something with volition but instead for them to be a curious observer about what is happening.

There is a difference between saying "I want you to lift up your right arm" and saying "I wonder how that right arm will lift?" or "And you can just let that right arm lift in its own way". The second and third sentences encourage the idea that the arm will move without the client taking a conscious role in lifting the arm, but rather that they will be an observer of the arm lifting. In reality conscious control, or free will is an illusion, everything happens automatically, but we give ourselves the illusion that we had conscious involvement in some things. The conscious experience of deciding to do something is just a retrospective experience, by the time we experience a decision to act, we have already decided to act in a particular way. With hypnosis, you are encouraging behaviours and thoughts to happen just like normal, but in a way that the client doesn't give themselves the feeling that they did the behaviours. An example could be that if you told someone to block balls being thrown at them, they would feel like each move to block the balls was a conscious choice, they would think "the ball was coming at me so I decided to move my arm to block the ball". The ball is coming at them and they feel like they intentionally move to block each ball. If you did the same experiment but didn't give any instructions, you just started throwing balls at the person, they would still move to block the balls the same, but wouldn't have the experience of deciding to move to block each ball, their arms would be coming up automatically in both cases.

## *Other useful ways for beginners to induce hypnosis and do effective therapy*

- **Encourage someone to talk about their problem without using words relating to the problem, then use this to help do treatment.** This can allow you to work completely metaphorically. You can use the metaphor clients give for their problem and then just get them to play out the metaphor to a positive conclusion in the clients' mind.

- **Utilise everything don't think of anything as failure.** If a client doesn't give the response that you expect, then utilise what they do give you and acknowledge that what they are doing is what they need to do to achieve the desired goal. For example: If a client says that they can't relax enough to go into hypnosis, then say something like "How did you know that you needed to have a little tension there to be able to do good effective change work?"

- **Time your rhythm to the rhythm of the clients breathing.** This is probably one of the easiest ways to increase your effectiveness at altering someone's state. If you match their breathing and talk with the client's outbreath you can begin to slow your breathing down and begin to slow down what you say and they will begin to relax deeper. This is because breathing is such a fundamental part of life that if you match it you quickly begin to build rapport with the client non-consciously.

- **Use fractionation.** Fractionation is a technique where you take the client in and out of trance repeatedly which deepens the trance each time they enter the trance. This can be done simply by asking the client to open their eyes then close their eyes again and perhaps suggesting they "go deeper". Or you could ask them to recall something; then bring them back to the room; then again have them recall something and keep repeating this. Fractionation was created because hypnotists noticed that each time clients came into a session and were hypnotised they went deeper and responded faster than they had done on previous sessions. It was realised that they didn't need to have a big gap between sessions, the same thing occurred if the client was repeatedly hypnotised during one session.

- **Feedback what the client says as suggestions.** For example:

Client: 'My left hand feels heavier than my right'

Therapist: 'Your left hand feels heavier than your right!'

By doing this you are telling the client true statements; which helps to deepen their state and you are utilising on-going behaviour and comments to lead to the desired outcome.

- **Take the client to the future to when they no longer have the problem and ask 'what happened that helped you?'** The psychiatrist Milton H Erickson MD would often have clients imagine they are in the future after they have overcome their problem and while in the future, he would ask them what had happened that helped them to successfully move on from the problem. After he did this and they told him how they got better, he would bring them back to the present and guide them to do the therapy they had suggested.

## *An Introduction to Ericksonian Language Patterns*

In my book *Hypnotherapy Revealed: The Ericksonian Approach* I go into more detail about the Ericksonian approach and Ericksonian hypnotic language patterns, but for those who haven't read the previous two books in the series, *An Introduction to Hypnotherapy* and *The Ericksonian Approach* I wanted to give an overview of some of the language patterns that are used throughout the scripts in this book so that as you read them, you have an idea of how they are being used and why.

### Agreement set

The agreement set is a language process that gets agreement from the client. This agreement deepens rapport and makes it less likely that the client will disagree in the future as they are in a pattern of agreement. It also builds client responsiveness.

The usefulness of this is that if the client is in a state of mind where they are agreeing to what you are saying and they are being responsive, then when you say something that the client may not entirely have agreed with previously they are more likely to do so now.

You can get agreement by having the client say or think yes or no. For example, you could be recapping information on a referral form with the client. "So, your name is… and your address is… and your date of birth is…" and that has already got three agreements when they tell you that information is correct. It is three agreements whether they verbalise their answers or not. The agreement can be implied. The therapist could say those statements as if to themselves recapping what is on the referral form, rather than to the client for a response. Getting a 'no' response can also be agreement, for example, saying to a client "you wouldn't expect to go into hypnosis until you are ready?" Which is likely to get a 'no' response but that 'no' mean 'yes I agree with you'.

Any time you are going to say something you want agreement with, it is best to say two or three things first that you know they will agree with to pace the client. Make sure these things are truisms. So, you may say "you have come here today…and you would like me to help you…and you've been relaxing for a little while now… (all truisms getting 'yes responses') and you can make the necessary changes in your own unique way (likely to also be agreed with in context with the other yes's but not necessarily a true statement, you are leading the client)".

## Linking Suggestions

Linking suggestions are suggestions that build on each other. They link things together that may not always be connected in reality; making it seem like because one thing has happened or is true the next thing should also then happen or be true.

The two main types of linking suggestions are compound suggestions and contingent suggestions. With compound suggestions often, the linking is done with an 'and' or with a pause and the first part is a truism 'pacing' statement whilst the second part doesn't necessarily have to be true but it leads. To start with it is often best to use pacing and leading truisms and then pacing truisms and leading with things which are likely to be true or undeniable. As far as possible use things that are true or undeniable. Sometimes this can just come down to a slight change of wording. If you say "you will relax" this may or may not be true, you could say "you will relax" and they may not relax. If you say "you can relax" this is true, everyone can relax, but in the context of a hypnosis session there is an increasing likelihood that they will take this as a presented idea to relax and they relax, but if they don't relax nothing has been lost because you never said they had to relax and because the hypnotist is responsive to the client, if the client doesn't relax when this idea has been presented then they are likely to pace what the client is doing and lead this and stop the focus on relaxation.

One thing I find clients often say is that their experience is like a gentle journey. This is because, with compound suggestions, almost every sentence from first meeting the client, to the client saying goodbye is like one continuous sentence from wakeful awareness, into hypnosis and back to wakeful awareness.

Example compound suggestions:

"You are looking at me and you can relax"

"You can relax and think of memories from the past"

"You can be thinking of memories from the past and wonder what you can learn from them"

As you may have noticed above you can also use compound suggestions to guide people from external reality to internal reality. Above I started with what I could see (they are looking at me - which also means they are focusing externally). Then I mentioned they can relax which begins to direct their focus internally. Then thinking of memories deepens the focus on the internal reality and less on external reality. Then finally had them wonder what they can learn from this which increases the focus on having to now find something to learn.

With contingent suggestions the linking is often done with a time-based word like 'before, during, after, as, while'. Like with compound suggestions they often start with truisms and then lead the client in a specific direction (pacing and leading). Another pattern that can be used is 'Don't...until' which works well for people that are more likely to be resistant. With this pattern you are giving the client permission not to do something now, or for something not to happen now, but implying it will happen at some point in the future. It can give an illusion of choice and freedom. For clients who don't like being told what to do, they often do what they have been told not to do sooner because you told them not to do something now.

Example of contingent suggestions:

"You are reading this book as you hear your internal dialogue"

"As you hear your internal dialogue you can be curious about what you will be learning"

"Before that curiosity can deepen into unconscious learning you can read some of the scripts in this book"

"Don't let full unconscious learning happen until you have finished reading"

Or creating a contingent suggestion out of the compound suggestion used before:

"As you look at me, you can relax"

"As you relax, you can think of memories from the past"

"As you think of memories from the past you can wonder what you can learn from them"

## Embedded commands and suggestions

Embedded commands and suggestions are where part of the communication is marked out for the client to pick up on and respond to non-consciously. This could be done with a gesture, a head movement, a tonal shift, or a touch. As long as the marking out is done consistently the client will pick up on it, ideally non-consciously.

Some example of embedded commands could be (*embedded commands in italics*):

"I don't know whether...*you will discover*...that...*you relax deeply*...as you listen to my voice...or whether ...*you will discover*...that...*you become more fully absorbed in your internal experience with each out breath*..."

"Someone asked the other day how...*you go into hypnosis*...I began explaining to them the process of how...*you go into hypnosis*...I explained that firstly the client will be looking at me while I talk to them and probably won't notice at first how...*the breathing begins to slow down*...and as they...*begin to relax*...I continue talking to them and they...*go into hypnosis easily and effortlessly*..."

"I remember travelling on a plane and discovering how high up we went...it was so difficult not to just...*close your eyes and fall asleep*...with the sounds in the cabin and the lights turned down...I couldn't help myself...*drifting off*..."

What you probably notice is that the embedded commands in the examples above are surrounded by linking suggestions and agreement and truisms.

## Double binds

Double binds are a class of language pattern where you are offering illusory choices to the client. It doesn't matter which choice they follow the outcome will still be the desired one. With double binds the outcomes are non-conscious so the client has little chance to sabotage it. Whereas binds are a conscious choice which can easily be sabotaged.

Bind: "Which chair do you want to sit in to go into hypnosis?"

Double Bind: "I wonder whether you will sit in one of the chairs, remain standing, or do something different as you drift into hypnosis?"

The client can easily avoid being caught in the bind by standing or lying on the floor or just flatly deciding "I'm not going into hypnosis (or "I don't want to be hypnotised")".

The double bind leaves it open for almost any response to occur for the person to enter hypnosis. "do something different" could mean almost any response; and "as you" being used instead of "to" means it is going to happen the question isn't if it will happen, it is what will you be doing whilst hypnosis is developing.

Clients can still decide that they don't want to be hypnotised and could walk away, but if they are engaging it doesn't sound so forceful or manipulative and because it focuses on curiosity about how hypnosis is going to happen, rather than whether hypnosis is going to happen, most people engage with the curiosity.

Some more examples of double binds:

"I wonder whether you go deeper into hypnosis with the sound of my voice or the spaces between my words?"

"Which hand do you think will lift as you drift into hypnosis or do you think neither hand will move?"


## Metaphors

Metaphors, stories and analogies are a useful tool in hypnotherapy because they allow the hypnotherapist to prime for things to take place and to lay down and work with the pattern of the problem and solution. For example; if you want an arm levitation you can prime it in advance by talking about being desperate to politely get attention in class at school or reaching up to put shopping away or hailing a taxi or stopping a bus. All of these stories seed or prime the client with the idea of arm levitation making them more likely to do it as those patterns in the mind are activated.

If you wanted to help someone forget pain you could talk to them about being in a cinema and needing the toilet as they enter but getting so engrossed in the film they forget they need the toilet. Or having fun playing as a child and not noticing any bumps and bruises or cuts until later when you are home. Again, these stories then activate related processes.

Stories also allow you to lay down future useful patterns. If the answer to the problem is to be patient you can tell a story that gives this message. If the answer to a problem is to relax you can lay down this pattern. You could lay down a 'relax' pattern by talking about a stick floating on a river that gets wider and wider and as the river gets wider, so the water slows down and isn't as rough and the stick floats slower and more gently. Or you could talk about a friend that had a situation at work that really was annoying them and how they overcame this. This second option would mirror the client's situation and offer a potential solution or way of approaching the situation. You can also talk about past successes you've had with other clients in similar situations and what they did to move on.

## Presuppositions

Presuppositions are where you assume that something will be happening. This can be done overtly or ideally more covertly. For example; if you say "I wonder how you will go into hypnosis today?" you are implying the client will go into hypnosis You are expecting it. All you are asking is how that will happen not whether it will happen or not. The therapist can say things like "before you make those changes, I just wanted to ask you a few more questions" which implies that the client will be making the changes. Generally, when done conversationally and in-line with what client's want and in a way that doesn't have them feel negatively manipulated, client's go along with the presuppositions and focus on the rest of what has been asked, so in the first sentence they focus on the curiosity about how hypnosis will occur, in the second sentence they focus on agreeing to be asked a few more questions and on then answering those questions.

## *Structuring a Therapy Session*

The model I use or keep in mind when I am doing hypnotherapy sessions is the RIGAAR model, developed by Joe Griffin and Ivan Tyrrell within Human Givens Therapy.

The idea of the RIGAAR model is that it gives a structure to work from. It is a structure that includes the areas that you will need to cover when you are working with a client, but not all of the parts have to be done in order, and often you may be doing many parts of the RIGAAR model simultaneously. The idea is that you aim to do all of the parts to gain the best results. This is a hypnotherapy scripts book and so some readers may be wondering why there needs to be a section on structuring therapy sessions and may have been wondering why I have covered how to induce hypnosis and information about hypnotic language patterns etc., the reason is that what you do with the hypnotherapy script doesn't happen in isolation from the therapy and scripts aren't just about the words on the page, but also about how you present those words to the client and what words you choose to use. Hypnotherapy isn't just reading a script that suggests the problem away and then hoping that the client no longer has the problem, hypnotherapy is psychological therapy that is tailored to the individual client, utilising hypnosis.

This is where RIGAAR is helpful, as it gives you a framework for what you are doing and can help you to see where the 'hypnosis' fits in the hypnotherapy. Even if you are using the scripts for self-hypnosis, RIGAAR is helpful.

RIGAAR starts with **Rapport Building**, this is essential and does have to be done right from the beginning and maintained until the end. Next comes **Information Gathering**, this again will be done throughout because client's will always be giving you information, whether it is about what they like or dislike or about an interest or any number of other useful bits of information and about how they are responding to the ongoing experience. Clients will be giving you plenty of information about the structure of the problem and potential solutions and important information about their problem and solutions.

The next stage in RIGAAR is **Goal Setting**; this will be done fairly early on depending on your questioning but will become clearer and more specific as you gather further information, for any therapy or coaching you need to know what the goal of the therapy or coaching is. In the goal setting stage, you want to know what the client wants, rather than what they don't want and how they will know when they have got this. Then comes **Agreeing a Strategy**, this may be done with or without the client's knowledge. Really it is a stage for clarifying what they want and what the steps are to achieving that.

The next stage is **Accessing Resources**; again, this will take place throughout as the client offers different resources to you, and as you discover or notice resources, but you may well also be intentionally eliciting certain resources. If a client needs to be confident in a situation then the therapist may access times the client has felt and experienced confidence, if they need to be assertive, then the therapist may help the client find and access times they have been assertive. If they need to be able to quit something and stay stopped then the therapist may help the client to find times they have done this in the past. The therapist could access resources like the fact the client has friends, or a job, or goes for walks, or has a hobby, whatever is relevant and could be used for helping the client with their presenting problem.

Lastly is **Rehearsal**, this stage is where you help the client to imagine the future positively with their desired goals and perhaps on stages leading to the desired outcome. This may be done to some extent throughout the whole process but is definitely an important part to fully do at the end so that the client can leave having clearly practiced a preferred future. It is this rehearsal stage that is where you will do the 'hypnosis'. This is where you will have the client mentally rehearse changes and whilst they are in a focused, relaxed, receptive state of mind you can present the 'hypnotic script' information to the client when their mind is most primed to receive it. This is the time when you may explain to the client that you will guide them into a state of mind where they can rehearse future success, recap useful information from the session and where you will present useful ideas and information to them that will help them to move forward. You may then do the induction part of the script, followed by the 'therapeutic script' or the mental rehearsal (the order you do these will depend on your preference as a therapist and what is the best order for your specific client), then the 'exiting trance script'.

Following all of the stages of RIGAAR the therapist would round up the session, perhaps setting tasks based on what has emerged in the session of things the client can do between this session and the next, also checking in with the client to see how they are, to see that they know what their next steps are and check that they are okay to leave the session (not drowsy or in an emotionally difficult place, etc).

# UNDERSTANDING THE SCRIPTS IN THIS BOOK

Before we move on to the scripts themselves I would just like to take some time to explain about how to read the scripts to your clients; how they are written; and how to practice 'saying' the script in the most effective manner.

'…' – When reading the hypnotherapy scripts, you will notice that I have added in '…'s between certain words and phrases. These dots indicate a pause in your speech. If the pause is for more than a few seconds I will usually give a suggested pause duration in brackets. This doesn't have to be stuck to rigidly. The best way to know how long to pause is to watch the client. If the pause is recommended to last for more than a few seconds you can judge how long the individual you are working with might need to do the internal work required of them during that pause. If it is quite a long suggested pause like a minute or more then you can pause for much longer than this if it necessary. I usually pause until I see physical signs of a shift in internal focus for example noticing movement or a change in breathing or skin colour. Where the pause maybe 5 or 6 seconds I mark this with an extra set of '…'s.

*'Italics'* – Words and sentences that are written in *'italics'* should be given added emphasis. You can practice what works best for you when adding this emphasis. Some people like to speak a little softer as they say these words or sentences others like to change their tone of voice a little up or down; and some people like to speak them with more clarity or slowing down their rate of speech on these words and sentences. The words and sentences that you emphasise stick in the mind of the listener like a deeper level of communication. These become embedded commands or suggestions that often go unnoticed consciously by the client yet they pick up on

the pattern and so take on board these marked out words and phrases as an additional layer of communication.

Another way of adding this emphasis is to move your head as you talk so that the location of your voice is different when emphasising words and sentences compared to when you are communicating more to the clients' consciously. The head movements could be leaning slightly to one side as you give the suggestions, or if you are reading the script to the client you could look up when giving the suggestions.

The scripts often include information that is designed to prime the client for what is to come or to activate a specific mental process prior to requiring it. This can be done using metaphors or examples or even provoking internal wonder around an idea. By priming clients before needing a response from them you increase the likelihood of them responding to what you are doing.

The best way to practice how to read hypnotherapy scripts effectively is to record yourself reciting the scripts and then listen to the recordings. You can then make adjustments to get it just right.

These adjustments will make it just right for you and not necessarily for the client but they will begin to give you practice of adapting how you say the scripts and what definitely doesn't work for you. For example, most people like scripts to be relaxing and to make them feel calm. This involves speaking with a calm voice and speaking slowly and gently and giving the client time to respond. Silence is an important part of doing hypnosis. When you listen to tracks you make you can adjust how long your periods of silence are and see what works best for you to allow you to keep up with the track. When you are face to face with a client you can observe them closely and watch for relaxation and tension and adjust your speed accordingly. You can do the same with silences. You can remain silent until you notice subtle signs of movement. These are often cues to let you know they have now done any internal work asked of them and are ready for the next step.

As you hypnotise people and give therapeutic suggestions clients become more responsive and enter a state of heightened awareness. In this state they pick up on your thoughts and emotions (although they may not be consciously aware of this). Because of this you need to be congruent in what you say and do. If you want them to relax you need to relax and speak in a relaxing tone of voice. If you want them to exit trance you need to begin to be fuller of energy, and speaking in an increasingly wide-awake lively manner. If you want them to be curious or excited you need to get into a curious or excited state first and convey this through your voice.

Because clients enter a heightened state of awareness you need to believe 100% in what you are saying and doing. If you have any doubt then this doubt will be communicated in your voice and in the way you present yourself which will add doubt to the client and make the work you do less effective, so approach everything you do with a sense of expectation. Expect that the client has the skills and abilities to succeed. If you believe in the client they can begin to believe in themselves.

The next chapter will include a selection of hypnotic inductions and deepeners that you can use with your clients.

Many people wonder about how deep the client has to be; whether they were in a trance or not and whether they fell asleep in the session or not (which in my experience is very rare. I used to think people were falling asleep but they always came out of hypnosis on cue and 'got better'. I then realised they just became so absorbed in the experience they appeared asleep. On rare occasions people have fallen asleep but it has always been people that were desperate for sleep that perhaps had insomnia and never seemed to be able to relax enough to sleep well until they were hypnotised. For these people their brain clearly prioritised sleep above any work we were going to do together).

The depth of trance in therapeutic hypnosis isn't much of an issue. The most important thing is focus and response attentiveness. That is; you are looking for the client to be following your lead and focusing on what you are wanting them to focus on. As you talk with the client you can notice whether they are responding to you or not. You can see if they are nodding to things you say; notice whether they are focusing on you or looking around the room and fidgeting; etc. If they aren't focusing well you can be direct in getting their attention by suggesting they look at you uncross their legs and put their feet flat on the floor (or any other change of posture that you can suggest). You can reflect back what they say and ask them 'is this correct' so that they have to pay attention to what you are saying. You can talk softer and quieter so that they have to pay closer attention to hear you. All of this will increase the focus and response attentiveness of the client.

In hypnosis it is helpful to see nothing is failure just something else to utilise. That doesn't mean things always work, but it is more helpful thinking this because then you are more likely to try to use responses you get, rather than give-up when you get undesired or unexpected responses. If for example a client opens their eyes and they weren't supposed to then you can suggest "that's right" acknowledging that they have just done the right thing by opening their eyes. And then follow that with a suggestion for eye closure and going deeper. If they say they don't feel comfortable closing their eyes or they keep opening their eyes then you can suggest "or would you prefer to look up at that spot on the wall and keep those eyes wide open as I talk to you". This instantly utilises the fact the client doesn't want to close their eyes and instead of thinking you are failing or that they are being a difficult client you are focusing their attention and if they look at that spot on the wall and keep their eyes open they are also then being responsive to you again.

As you hypnotise people it is usually best to speak slowly and clearly in time with the clients breathing so that you talk as they breathe out and you breathe in as they breathe in. This is especially useful as you guide the client into hypnosis. As you guide them out of hypnosis it is useful to speak on the clients in-breath so that they pick up on the different pattern. Generally, I like to try to stick to speaking on the client's outbreath throughout the induction and 'therapy' part of the session. I don't use scripts, part of the reason for this is that there is very little distinction in the work I do between induction and therapy. I don't normally do formal inductions, so often the client doesn't know when the hypnosis begins or when the therapy begins and I respond to the ongoing feedback and behaviour of the client so I don't know what I will be saying or doing from moment to moment as it is all dependent on the client sitting in front of me.

In the next chapter you will notice that the inductions and deepeners are broken into sections; induction introduction; type of client; induction; deepener. With your clients you can just suggest they close their eyes and then just take an induction from the induction section. Or you can make it a little more specific by including an introduction section and targeting the type of client you are working with and if you want to you can include a deepener before moving onto the 'therapeutic section' where you can select one of the scripts and finally the exiting hypnosis stage.

By breaking down the scripts into parts like this means that if you know of specific inductions you like from other books or courses or that the client likes, or if you are comfortable just responding to the client in front of you, you can use those instead and just add in the therapeutic section from this book.

Many of the scripts follow on from scripts from the previous section where possible. You can change the wording if you decide not to include scripts from certain sections or feel slightly different wording would work best for your specific client. For example, the inductions don't usually mention closing the eyes because this is often in the induction introduction so if you skip the introduction then you can ask the client to close their eyes before reading the induction, and some inductions involve closing the eyes as a key part of the induction, or involve having the eyes open to do the induction, so the wording would need to be altered to account for this if you use an introduction. Likewise, all the inductions end in the same way so they can flow into the next stage. Again, you can change this if you have a preferred way of doing things.

Each individual induction element may appear short, but it is just an element. On average in an hour or two hour long therapy session the 'hypnosis' part is likely to be about 15-20 minutes long. It could be longer or shorter depending on individual clients and circumstances but this would be an average length for the hypnosis element. This 20-minute 'inner-work' process matches the 20-minute rest phase of our Basic Rest and Activity Cycle (BRAC) which is an Ultradian Rhythm we go through taking 90-120 minutes all day every day. When you take all the relevant elements they equal a hypnotherapy script that is about 20 minutes long.

Here is an example of a script created from scripts in this book so that you can get an idea for how the script elements fit together to create a whole full-length hypnosis session:

## (Induction Introduction) Induction introduction for clients that haven't been hypnotised before

As you...*allow your eyes to comfortably close*...I'll explain a little about what to expect as...*you enter hypnosis*...you already have all the knowledge you need to understand how to...*enter hypnosis*...you have experience of...*entering hypnosis*...many times each day...I'm sure you can recall times you have been wandering along and discovered...*your mind begins to wonder*...to thoughts, ideas and dreams...or the experience of waiting in line as...*you start to daydream...now*...as you sit there beginning to *drift comfortably into hypnosis* you can hear the sound of my voice and have awareness of different thoughts and ideas that come to mind...and while you listen to the sound of my voice I'm going to talk to you...and just like in everyday situations like when you were in school listening in class and you will have occasionally drifted off into a daydream and later realised you don't know if you remember the whole lesson...many people that...*go into hypnosis*...remember some things and forget others...and you can remember what is important to consciously remember whilst at the same time forget what is unimportant to recall after this session...so there is no need to try to...*go into hypnosis*...hypnosis can develop all by itself...and you can develop that trance in your own unique way based on your own lifetime full of experiences of entering trance states easily and effortlessly...from all those times you have discovered yourself to have been daydreaming...through to those times...*you become deeply absorbed in what you are doing...*

So, now...with your eyes closed you can enjoy a moment of quiet, while...*your (said as if to imply you're) unconscious*...prepares to enter a resourceful trance state...that is just right for the work we are doing here today...(pause for about 30 seconds)...that's it...now as people...*enter hypnosis*...they often begin to notice how the breathing changes…for some people the breathing speeds up a little before it settles on a relaxed rhythm…for others it just begins to…*comfortably relax*…and while the breathing helps to deepen and maintain hypnosis many people *become intrigued* to discover how much more youthful they look as their facial muscles smooth out…this smoothing and relaxing of the muscles in the face and throughout the body and the continued feeling of comfort that people feel when you come out of trance later (intentionally saying 'you' rather than 'when they') are some of the side effects of…*entering a hypnotic trance in this way*…so while you prepare to…*enter hypnosis*…I wonder what other positive side-effects you will receive…and while you continue into this state…your mind will wander at times and whatever happens my voice can go with you…

## (Induction) Journey through an art gallery

(Pause for about 20 seconds)…that's right…now…as you listen to me and continue to breathe in that way and notice certain sensations you can continue to *become more fully absorbed* with the sound of my voice or the spaces between my words while I talk to...*your unconscious...now*...and you can discover yourself entering an art gallery...and as you enter I wonder whether you can notice the way sound changes as you enter and the way the atmosphere seems to *become calmer and more relaxed*...and as you explore the gallery, different art work can give you different feelings and different meanings...you may look at a sculpture and understand that it started as just a lump of stone that the artist believed could be more and knew all it needed was to have some time and attention spent on removing what isn't necessary and reshaping what is left...and different pictures will convey different meanings...and as you continue to walk deeper into the art gallery you can wonder which painting you will feel a connection with and feel drawn to...and you may want to get a sense of a number of pictures before finally settling on the one that draws you in...and as *you drift deeper* with each outbreath while exploring the various paintings my voice will quieten down in the background for a minute and you can take as long as you want to explore the gallery...and when you next hear me talk you can be prepared to step inside that picture ready to search for a comfortable and familiar chair you've never seen before…(pause for about 1 minute)…

That's right…preparing now to step into that picture…and as you do I wonder what it will feel like…some people feel a sense of *deepening*…others experience a change in the feelings…and other don't notice how things have changed…and as you explore this picture I wonder where that chair will be…and when you discover that chair I wonder whether you will notice the sensations associated with approaching that comfortably familiar chair…and as you take a few moments to…relax into the chair…you can get a sense of closing your eyes and drifting off deeper into a dream…

### (Deepener) Pictures in pictures

That's right…and you can now begin to imagine a picture of a beach in front of you…and as you pay close attention to that beach you can begin to notice something different about that picture…and the more you try to see what isn't there the more you find yourself drawn into the image…and then in a blink you can find yourself in that picture searching for a path (pause for about 30 seconds)…

And as you wander around wondering where the path will be, you can notice it in another picture…and a curious thing about these pictures is that each time you drift into one you go even deeper into hypnosis…and in a blink you can find yourself on that path…searching for something new (pause for about 30 seconds)…

And I wonder what sounds each footstep makes as you walk along that path until you see that new picture…and in a blink you can find yourself in that new picture knowing that what you can learn and discover here can stay in this picture for you to use instinctively in the future like unconscious knowing (pause for about one minute)…

**(Therapeutic Script) Metaphorical 'life changer'**

That's it…and as you continue to *relax deeper and deeper* you can listen to me in the background…and as you listen to me in the background you can understand what I'm saying on an unconscious level...

Many years ago there was a prince that lived in a castle...one day he was gazing out of one of the castle windows looking out over the land that his family ruled...and from his perspective he could see people struggling...he could see people suffering...he could see people starving...while he was in this castle getting whatever he wanted with the ring of a bell...the prince ask his father why things should be this way...he was told the world is the way the world is...there's nothing you can do to change it...the prince wanted to know why not...and asked what about all of those poor people...and we are so rich...can't we help them out...his father didn't answer...the prince thought about his life...he had everything money could buy yet he felt unhappy and felt like something was missing from his life...while many of the people in the town around the castle appeared to struggle and suffer yet they would often be smiling and looking happy...

That night when everyone went to bed, the prince snuck out of the castle in disguise...he had to *discover the answer*...how can people be so happy with such miserable lives...he walked through the town and into the nearby forest...the forest was dark and eerie and the night was still...there were shards of moonlight glistening down through the leaves of the trees onto the forest floor shimmering a path for the prince to follow...the prince followed this unknown path to discovery and wonder and was curious where it would lead him...as he continued to walk, the prince could hear noises of animals and birds moving in the dark...he could feel his heart beating loudly as he continued into the unknown...

After a while the prince found a clearing and saw a frog sitting by a pond...as he approached the frog, it started to talk to him...*"you are on a journey of discovery and wonder and you can wonder what you will discover on that journey"*...the prince began to wonder as he continued to wander through the forest...he thought he could hear something behind him moving in the dark...following him...he could see the foot of a mountain and wondered how he would reach a cave he could see up in the side of the mountain.

Out of the dark some tribes people appeared...the prince couldn't understand what they were saying but could tell they were friendly...they began to cut down trees and build a ladder...the prince decided to help them...after some time they managed to complete the ladder and the prince climbed up to the cave...in the cave was a flickering fire...he sat down by the fire watching the flickering flame and noticing how the light from the fire was dancing on the walls...as he continued to watch the flickering flame he began to see things and his mind began to wonder...then everything went dark for a moment before he found himself resting beneath a tree...

And as he rested beneath that tree he began to *discover the true meaning of happiness and life*...and he knew that when you get hot you enter a pool of water to cool down...and after a while you need to warm up so you go back out in the sun...he then got an image of the Yin Yang symbol...then a coin flipping in the air...then he saw a person struggling and while the person was struggling he saw the person step outside themselves and the part of them with the problem began to change how they were dealing with the situation...then the prince saw people socialising and talking with each other...different images and ideas drifted in and out of the princes mind...and with each image the prince was learning something new about himself that was beginning to change his life in ways he didn't yet know...and the prince continued to notice what seemed like random images until they disappeared when his unconscious knew it found the answers...(pause for about a minute)...

And when the time was right he drifted back to that cave before climbing down the ladder and enjoying an adventure of learning and discovery as he headed back to the castle where he knew how the next day he was going to change his world forever...and improve the lives of those in the town...(pause for about 3 minutes)...


**(Trance Termination) Exiting hypnosis now**

That's it...and you can now just take a few moments to allow yourself to get a sense of drifting back into that chair...and I don't know whether you will take 4, 5, 6 or 8 breaths to fully re-orient back to the chair...before you then start to work your way back along the route you took into hypnosis...and as you do, your unconscious mind can ensure that all the new re-programming has been installed throughout the mind and body in every cell and neuron...your unconscious can honestly and fully integrate all your new learning into that deep and instinctive part of your mind while you continue your journey back to the here and now...and I don't know how much of what is there will be left there as you continue back and how much you will bring back with you...

And it's interesting how much you know you can be aware of while you are sat there in that seat...and you can now find yourself working all the way back away from that state to the here and now becoming more aware of sounds around you...of me, of what you will be getting on with later and other random thoughts that start to cross the mind and in a moment I'm going to count to 3 and on the count of 3 you can open your eyes and be fully back in the room...one...two...three... opening your eyes...

Hi, now you came here to see how you are able to be helped and I asked you to close your eyes earlier…so do you have any plans for later? (have a brief chat then if you are going to set any tasks etc. you can do that before they go) …

# HYPNOTIC INDUCTIONS, DEEPENERS & PRIMING

## Induction Introductions

### Induction introduction for clients that have been hypnotised before

*Prior to starting the induction, you will have asked the client about whether they have been hypnotised before or not. If they have then you will have gathered information about this previous hypnosis experience or their favourite trance experience (like experiences of being absorbed in an activity or interest or experience). Just talking with them about this will have primed the client for entering hypnosis and they are likely to have already begun to re-enter hypnosis here and now with you whilst you ask them questions and they recall that previous trance experience.*

As you think about that pleasant hypnotic trance experience you can allow your eyes to close...and as your eyes close you can begin to recall what...*going into a trance*...feels like...you can recall how you felt before you knew you were going to...*go into a trance*...and...*become absorbed in the experience*...and as you...*recall that trance experience*...you can remember what you could see and hear around you...and while you remember what you can see and hear you can begin to...*experience a little of that trance here and now...*

With each breath you take...you can...*become more absorbed in this experience*...and my voice can comfortably go with you as you drift and float deeper and more fully into this experience...preparing to absorb all that is useful and appropriate...and my words can help you to *access inner resources and strengths and skills*...as...*you hear my voice and relax*...*your unconscious*...can pick up on all the different meanings in my communication…I don't know whether…*you will drift deeper*…with each breath you take or with the sound of my voice or the spaces between my words…

## Induction introduction for clients that haven't been hypnotised before

*Prior to starting the induction, you will have asked the client whether they have been hypnotised before. If they haven't you will have explained a little about what to expect and you will have asked them what they think it will be like and what they expect. Anything they have said that they are unlikely to experience, like different hypnosis myths you will have clarified for them. Like if they say they think they will be totally unconscious and have no memory of what happened and not hear anything. You can explain it is more like when they are daydreaming. They can still hear everything and are still fully aware. It's just none of that seems so important and they are comfortable continuing to drift and dream in their mind.*

As you...*allow your eyes to comfortably close*...I'll explain a little about what to expect as...*you enter hypnosis*...you already have all the knowledge you need, to understand how to...*enter a trance*...you have experience of...*entering a trance*...many times each day...I'm sure you can recall times you have been wandering along and discovered...*your mind begins to wonder*...to thoughts, ideas and dreams...or the experience of waiting in line as...*you start to daydream...now*...as you sit there, beginning to drift into a comfortable hypnotic trance you can hear the sound of my voice and have an awareness of different thoughts and ideas that come to mind...and while you listen to the sound of my voice I'm going to talk to you...and just like in everyday situations like when you were in school listening in class and you will have occasionally drifted off into a daydream and later realised you don't know if you remember the whole lesson...many people that...*go into a trance*...remember some things and forget others...and you can remember what is important to consciously remember whilst at the same time forget what is unimportant to recall after this session...so there is no need to try to...*go into a trance*...it can develop all by itself...

And you can develop that trance in your own unique way based on your own lifetime full of experiences of entering trance states easily and effortlessly...from all those times you have discovered yourself to have been daydreaming...through to those times...*you become deeply absorbed in what you are doing*...so now...with your eyes closed you can enjoy a moments quiet while...*your unconscious*...prepares to enter a resourceful trance state...that is just right for the work we are doing here today...(pause for about 30 seconds)...

That's it...now as people...*enter trance*...they often begin to notice how the breathing changes...for some people the breathing speeds up a little before it settles on a relaxed rhythm...for others it just begins to...*comfortably relax*...and while the breathing helps to deepen and maintain hypnosis many people become intrigued to discover how much more youthful they look as their facial muscles smooth out...this smoothing and relaxing of the muscles in the face and throughout the body and the continued feeling of comfort that people feel when you come out of hypnosis later are some of the side-effects of...*entering a hypnotic trance in this way*...so while you prepare to...*enter this trance state*...I wonder what other positive side-effects you will receive...and while you continue into this state...your mind will wander at times and whatever happens my voice can go with you...

## Targeting specific types of client

### Logical analyser

And there will be times when you can focus on what I am saying and pay close attention to the words I am using and all the different meaning that I am conveying in what I am saying and how I am saying it or you could choose to focus on the stages of the process and on how your awareness changes as this experience goes on...

### Daydreamer

And you can drift and dream and allow your mind to wander...normally in everyday situations people tell you to pay attention...here you can daydream while you listen to me…and only need to follow instructions occasionally as you become more absorbed in the experience…

## Motivated & willing to follow instructions

And as you follow what I say you can continue to drift more fully and comfortably into the experience and with each step you can move closer to achievement and success…

## Passive – expects the work to be done *to* them

And as you breathe in…and out ('breathe in' said in time with the client breathing in 'and out' timed with the client breathing out)…you can wonder how *this will work for you*…you know many people experiencing hypnosis for the first time imagine that the hypnotist has to do all the work without realising that the hypnotist only does all the work while they are talking and during the session…as they *drift deeper into the experience* they…begin to discover that each session is a partnership of two minds….the hypnotist works with the unconscious mind while the client follows instructions inside and outside…the therapy session using the conscious mind…this allows the work to be completed both consciously and unconsciously…

## Polarity responder

And as you hear my voice you don't have to listen to me…or listen to the sounds around you…or pay any attention to any specific thoughts and feelings…and you don't have to *follow instructions* if you know of a better way of *getting the results you came here to achieve*…and you don't have to *believe this will work* to *get the results you want*…as you listen to me you can *respond in your own unique way* to *get the results you want* or *follow along to any instructions and suggestions*…

## *Inductions*

## Journey along a beach

(Pause for about 20 seconds)…that's right…now…as you listen to me and continue to breathe in that way and notice certain sensations you can continue to *become more fully absorbed* with the sound of my voice or the spaces between my words while I talk to you…and you know there are many different ways of experiencing the enjoyment of walking along a beach…*as you drift deeper into hypnosis*…you know some people like to walk barefoot in the sand…feeling that sand on the feet and through the toes…some people like that sand to be dry and warm…others like the sand to be cool and wet…we all have our own preferred experience of walking along a beach…you will have an idea of what you consider to be the perfect beach…what the weather conditions are like…whether it is daytime or night-time…how warm the weather is…what the temperature of the water is…whether you are barefooted…whether you are walking on stones, shingle or sand and whether the sand is find and powdery or larger grains...or a different shore line entirely...

And what sounds are in your experience......whether there are other people nearby or in the distance...or children playing...or the sounds of birds or boats out to sea...or other sounds unique to your experience...*as you drift deeper and comfortably into hypnosis*...only you know what your experience is that you can internally enjoy...and I don't know whether you will be just listening along and relaxing...or imagining your own experience whilst *you drift deeper into hypnosis*...or whether you just have a sense of strolling along a beach...(pause for about 20 seconds)...

And some people like rough water...others like calm water...others like it somewhere in between...and some people don't mind any weather as long as they are prepared for it and dressed appropriately...and as you continue to *become more fully absorbed* with each breath as the waves roll in...and out...(said in time with the clients in and out breaths) I wonder whether you can notice the small inviting hut in the distance...a hut that you don't recognise yet it seems familiar...and as you approach that hut you can *drift deeper and deeper* with each step you take...*going deeper* only at the rate and speed that is comfortable for you...and when you arrive at the hut you can be curious about what is inside it...(pause for about 20 seconds)...and when you are ready you can begin to open the door to see a chair you don't recognise yet it looks so familiar and inviting...after getting a sense of your surrounding you can make your way to the chair and relax yourself into it and get a sense of closing your eyes as you *become highly receptive to ideas and concepts that help you to achieve success...drifting deeper with each breath you take*...drifting deeper into hypnosis...

## Journey through a forest

(Pause for about 20 seconds)...that's right...now...as you listen to me and continue to breathe in that way and notice certain sensations you can continue to become more fully absorbed with the sound of my voice or the spaces between my words while I talk to you...and as you listen to the sound of my voice you can begin to get a sense of what it feels like to be wandering through a forest...some people find they recall past experiences or imagine a familiar place...others just discover *the experience unfolds* as they become more absorbed with each breath they take...and as you have a sense of wandering through that forest, there are certain sights and sounds that you can begin to become aware of...and I don't know whether you will just *develop a sense of those sights and sounds*...or whether you will *begin to dream about wandering through that forest*...or whether you will just *enjoy drifting into a focused comfortable state of mind* as you listen along to what I'm saying...

And when you wander through a forest you can feel each step you take...noticing the ground beneath your feet...the sounds associated with each step and how each step can sound different...and you can notice the different shades of greens and browns and other little flashes of colour...and sometimes you can see beams of light breaking through the leaves shimmering on the forest floor...and feel the air on your face as you hear the sounds of the forest...and it can be surprising to some people to discover just how quickly you can *become absorbed in this experience*...and you know there are some sounds everyone associates with forests, in the same way that there are certain sights everyone recognises about forests...and I'm sure you know what those experiences are...

What people often get surprised by is how the smells of the forest change as you wander...*deeper and deeper*...in the same way that you can walk through a garden and smell the different plants...and as you continue to wander in your own way *deeper and deeper* I wonder when you will notice the stream in the distance and what you will notice first about that stream...and when you discover the stream you can begin to follow it for a while, noticing sticks and leaves floating in the stream...hearing the trickling, bubbling of the water...perhaps smelling the fresh stream air...and you can take a moment to relax by that stream...maybe resting your feet into the water...closing your eyes to deepen how absorbed you are in the moment...and with your eyes closed...relaxing deeper into the experience...you can begin to have a sense of a chair you don't recognise that looks familiar and comforting...and begin to feel compelled to...*go and sit in that chair*...and as you sit down deeply into that chair you can begin to wonder what you will experience next…and you can get a sense of closing your eyes and *relaxing even deeper into hypnosis…*

## Journey through an art gallery

(Pause for about 20 seconds)…that's right…now…as you listen to me and continue to breathe in that way and notice certain sensations you can continue to *become more fully absorbed* with the sound of my voice or the spaces between my words while I talk to…*your unconscious…now…*and you can discover yourself entering an art gallery…and as you enter I wonder whether you can notice the way sound changes as you enter and the way the atmosphere seems to *become calmer and more relaxed…*and as you explore the gallery different art work can give you different feelings and different meanings…you may look at a sculpture and understand that it started as just a lump of stone that the artist believed could be more and knew all it needed was to have some time and attention spent on removing what isn't necessary and reshaping what is left...and different pictures will convey different meanings...

And as you continue to walk deeper into the art gallery you can wonder which painting you will feel a connection with and feel drawn to...and you may want to get a sense of a number of pictures before finally settling on the one that draws you in...and as *you drift deeper* with each outbreath while exploring the various paintings, my voice will quieten down in the background for a minute and you can take as long as you want to explore the gallery...and when you next hear me talk you can be prepared to step inside that picture ready to search for a comfortable and familiar chair you've never seen before...(pause for about 1 minute)...

That's right...preparing now to step into that picture...and as you do I wonder what it will feel like...some people feel a sense of *deepening*...others experience a change in the feelings...and other don't notice how things have changed...and as you explore this picture I wonder where that chair will be...and when you discover that chair I wonder whether you will notice the sensations associated with approaching that comfortably familiar chair...and as you take a few moments to...*relax into that chair*...you can get a sense of closing your eyes and drifting deeper into hypnosis...

## Journey through a country meadow

(Pause for about 20 seconds)...that's right...now...as you listen to me and continue to breathe in that way and notice certain sensations you can continue to become more fully absorbed with the sound of my voice or the spaces between my words while I talk to you...and as I talk to you certain memories, ideas and sensations can be recalled...and you can explore those re-experienced thoughts and sensations and wonder how they will assist you in going deeper into this therapeutic trance state...

And you know what it is like for someone to enjoy the pleasant experience of walking through a country meadow...being aware of the sights, the sounds, the smells and what it feels like...you have the ground beneath your feet...the sun in the sky...birds flying around and perching in trees and bushes and a sensation of movement as you wander along...and you know many people that wander through a country meadow wonder and let their mind drift and dream...they gaze around with relaxed eyes and notice the movement of grass and plants...and while wandering through the meadow you can notice certain small animals focused on living their own lives...just respectfully living in the moment...and as the wondering continues so you can continue to *drift deeper and deeper into hypnosis...deeper and deeper with each breath you take*...and in the distance is a tree...and in that tree is a tree house...and in that tree house is a door...and as you continue to wander through this meadow perhaps hearing that distant stream...you can wonder what you will discover behind that door...

And the more curious you become the faster you can walk...and the faster you walk the more absorbed you become...and the more absorbed you become the more curious you can find yourself...*now*...I don't know whether you will be imagining the experience of walking towards that tree or whether you will just have a sense of walking towards that tree or whether you will be just listening along with interest whilst your mind occasionally seems to drift off...the important thing is that while I'm talking to you...*your unconscious*...can be listening along and responding honestly and fully to all that I say of importance to helping you to create positive change...

And with each breath you take, you can find yourself getting closer and closer to that tree...(pause for about 30 seconds)...and as you now reach that tree you can enter the tree house and notice the door...and this door can be an unfamiliar door that somehow seems familiar...and as you notice that door you can prepare to open the door and step inside...but don't step inside just yet...just allow the unconscious mind to be fully prepared for a change...too often people rush in before the unconscious is prepared...(pause for about 20 seconds)...and now gently open the door and step inside to see a chair...this chair, when sat in, is the most comfortable chair imaginable...so just take some time to notice your surroundings in there before sitting comfortably in that chair and having a sense of closing your eyes and drifting deeper into hypnosis...

## Confusion – lifting and moving the arm

(Pause for about 20 seconds)…that's right…now…as you listen to me and continue to breathe in that way and notice certain sensations you can continue to become more fully absorbed in the experience…and as *you drift deeper into hypnosis*…in a minute I'm going to reach over and gently lift up that right arm…and as I move that arm you can just *let your mind wonder*…(reach over and gently hold the clients arm just above the wrist. The idea is to move the arm so gently that the client isn't fully aware of how much they are moving their arm and how much you are moving the arm. Then start by saying "and as *you go deeper into hypnosis* your arm can go up" - as you say this move the arm gently downwards – "and your arm can go down" - moving the arm gently upwards – "and your arm can go left" - moving the arm to the clients right – "and your arm can go right" - moving the arm to the clients left – "and that arm can move down…*deeper and deeper*" - moving the arm down – "and that arm can move left" - moving the arm right – "and that arm can move up" - moving the arm down – "and that arm can move down" - moving the arm upwards – "and that arm can move right" - moving the arm left – "and that arm can move down...*deeper and deeper*" - moving the arm down further than normal – "and that arm can move right" - moving the arm to the clients left – "and that arm can move left" - moving the clients arm right – "and that arm can move up" - moving the arm down – "and that arm can move down" - moving the arm up – "and that arm can move left" - moving the arm right – "and that arm can move right" - moving the arm left – "and that arm can move down...*deeper and deeper*" - move the arm down towards the leg – "and as that arm touches the leg you can begin to get a sense of noticing a familiar comfortable chair you've never seen before..." - lowering the arm the rest of the way gently to the leg)...and you can walk to that chair and as you sit down in that chair you can get a sense of closing your eyes and drifting deeper into hypnosis...

## Confusion induction

(Pause for about 20 seconds)…that's right…now…as you listen to me and continue to breathe in that way and notice certain sensations you can continue to become more fully absorbed with the sound of my voice or the spaces between my words and you can wonder whether you truly know which hand is the right hand and which hand is left and whether you would still be right about which hand is left if you had the hand you thought was left put right behind your back and wondered which hand is left in front of you…and the hand that was right becomes the one that's left while the hand you thought was left is actually right behind you…and the hand that is on the right side for me is on the left side for you and the hand that is on the left side for me is on the right side for you…and you can remember to forget what isn't important to remember whilst at the same time you can forget to remember those things that you don't need to remember being aware of thoughts that are left knowing that the right thoughts are forgotten…and you can go deeper into the right state of mind as the conscious part of you is left to think about other thoughts and sensations…and you can imagine a familiar comfortable seat in your mind you've never seen before and take some time to relax down into that chair…and as you relax down into that chair you can get a sense of closing your eyes and *going deeper into hypnosis* as you continue to listen to me…

## Early learning set induction

(Pause for about 20 seconds)…that's right…now…as you listen to me and continue to breathe in that way and notice certain sensations you can continue to become more fully absorbed with the sound of my voice or the spaces between my words while I talk to you…and as you listen to the sound of my voice you can be curious about how we learn to speak…most people have had the experience of learning languages at school and know how difficult that can be…yet without any formal lessons children learn to understand adults and to use words and phrases and learn how the way something is said and the order the words are spoken in all influences the meaning of the communication…in the same way that a child will be born not knowing that they are separate from the rest of the world...then one day the child will be trying to reach for the hand they see in front of their face with the hand in front of their face and discover that the hand they are reaching for is the same as the hand they are reaching with...and as they reach and touch different body parts and different objects they begin to learn what is them and what isn't...they begin to explore themselves as a being...touching a foot with a hand...touching the foot to the mouth...learning...discovering...

Yet even before this they had already mastered how to breathe...how to move arms and legs and the eyes and the head...they had already mastered the highly complex task of synchronising muscle tension and relaxation to move the muscles in the body...and this was done without any training or lessons they just used that part of themselves that knows more about you than you do...and over time they learn to refine their skill and make more accurate movements and actions...and the unconscious is the part of you that whilst you breathe and relax and *drift deeper into hypnosis*, can help you to achieve things...it is the part of you that *take new learning that you receive consciously and make it instinctive*...like when a child learns to walk...they first learn...then they consciously forget...anyone that has tried to walk consciously will know how uncomfortable it feels...in the same way that anyone who has tried to consciously move an arm knows how difficult this is as it happens unconsciously...

And there was a time you didn't know the difference between a b, a d or a p, thinking that they were all the same thing and not noticing the differences....and you didn't know the difference between a 3 an m or a w, was a 3 a w on its side? Was a w an upside-down m? And with practice, you learnt to recognise that each letter and number is different, and you learnt how the letters formed words and with time, you consciously stopped paying attention as this knowledge became unconscious and automatic...and as...*you now relax deeper with each breath you take*...you can begin to get a sense of a chair that appears to be familiar yet you know you've never seen it before...and you can get a sense of relaxing deeply into that chair and closing your eyes...and drifting deeply into hypnosis...

## Eyes open eyes closed induction

(Pause for about 20 seconds)...that's right...now...in a moment I'm going to ask you to open your eyes and find a spot in front of you just above eye level to gaze at whilst you keep as still as possible...and while you do this, your body can *continue to relax* in its own way...and as you look at that spot without blinking I'm going to count from 3 down to 1 and on the count of 1 the eyes can close and you can drift even deeper into that comfortable hypnotic state...and whenever I count from 1 up to 3 your eyes can open and look back at that spot and each time I count from 3 down to 1 your eyes can close and you can *drift deeper into that hypnotic state*...and each time you do you can begin to learn how you can *do this for yourself* in the future in situations that are safe and appropriate just by hearing the sound of my voice in your mind counting down from 3, 2, 1 to...*go deeply into hypnosis*...and to come back out of hypnosis you can hear the sound of my voice in your mind counting from 1, 2, 3...

So now, just allow your eyes to open and look over at a spot just above eye level...(give them a moment to do this)...that's right...really focus on that spot...focus intensely on taking in as much information as possible...making sounds crisper and clearer (start talking crisp and clearly)...making everything about that spot sharply in focus...noticing colour...texture...contrast...really paying close attention...focusing all of your attention on that spot...and on the count of one you can *relax that attention* and close the eyes...(count slowly with each count being timed with an outbreath and slow enough so that the client is beginning to strain their eyes to keep them open and really wants you to reach one and deepen your tone of voice with each number)...3...2...1...that's right closing your eyes...as *you relax deeper and deeper*...becoming more comfortable and relaxed...and with your eyes closed the muscles around the eyes can relax...the muscles in the face can relax...and you can *relax deeper and deeper*...and begin to drift off to a pleasant thought or place in your mind...(time each count to opening the eyes with the in-breaths and raise your tone of voice with each number)...(pause for about 20 seconds to allow them to begin to drift deeper internally)...that's right...and 1...2...3...opening your eyes...and really focusing all of your attention on that spot...becoming very aware of what you can see...hear...and feel...that's right and (remember to drag out the counting and time it with the outbreaths)...3...2...1...that's right closing your eyes...*deeper and deeper*...drifting inside to a pleasant thought or place in your mind...*deeper and deeper*...as the muscles *continue to relax* more fully and the muscles around the eyes can *continue to feel more comfortable* remaining in a relaxed state...as *you drift deeper and deeper* inside...(pause for about 40 seconds)...that's right...and...(remember to time counting up with in-breaths)...1...2...3...looking back at that spot...paying it all of your attention...really trying to keep those eyes open and locked on that spot...and 3...2...1...closing those eyes and *relaxing deeper and deeper* into that pleasant experience...that's right...in your own unique way... (Pause for about 1 minute)...that's right...and...1...2...3...trying to focus all of your attention back on that spot...and...3...2...1...that's right...and closing those eyes *deeper and deeper*...as *you drift even deeper* still into that experience...and whilst *you drift deeper* into that experience my voice can continue to go with you as we journey together *deeper into this experience*...and you can begin to get a sense of a chair that appears so comfortable and familiar yet you know you have never seen it before...and when you are ready you can get a sense of relaxing down into that chair and feeling so safe...comfortable and relaxed...you drift off *deeper into hypnosis*...


## Elman-style induction

(Pause for about 20 seconds)...that's right...now...in a moment I'm going to ask you to open your eyes...and when you do I'd like you to prepare to close them again...only this time when you close them I'd like you to allow those eyes to close to the point where you *know*...the muscles around those eyes will be so relaxed...*they just won't work*...and when you know...*those muscles around the eyes just won't work*...I'd like you to test those eyes to...*discover they just won't work*...that's right...and just allow those eyes to open...and now take a deep breath in and as you let that breath out and allow relaxation to occur just allow those eyes to close to the point where...*those muscles around the eyes just won't work*...where the muscles around the eyes become so relaxed...*they just won't work*...and then test to...*make sure they won't work*...(watch for attempted movement in the eyes, or a look of effort on the face. If the eyes open they weren't following along so just say 'that's right now close them again and allow them to relax even deeper to the point *they won't work* and allow yourself to *follow my instructions fully, honestly and completely*...and when you know the muscles around those eyes are so relaxed...*they just won't work*...then test to make sure *they won't work* and allow yourself to *go deeper into this relaxed state* in your own unique way as those muscles relax more fully...' if they still open their eyes again they clearly are not following along to this specific induction. At this point continue with 'that's right, and each time the eyes open you can *go deeper into hypnosis*...closing your eyes now...and open your eyes...*going deeper and deeper*...and close your eyes...(slow down what you are saying to really drag it out and say closing on the outbreath, then - for this specific option - say 'going deeper and deeper' on outbreaths as well)...and open your eyes...going deeper and deeper...(continue this getting slower and slower and hesitating occasionally until they start struggling to open their eyes) once you see they are struggling to open their eyes or starting to show effort and before they have time to succeed at opening their eyes continue)…

That's right…and now just allow those eyes to relax and allow that relaxation to spread down through your body from the top of your head right down to the tips of your toes…and as you do that, in a minute I'm going to reach over and I'm going to lift up your right arm and you don't have to do anything other than relax there…I'm going to lift up that arm and let it drop down freely in your lap…and when that arm slumps into your lap you can go twice as deep…(lean over and pick up the arm. It should be limp; the client shouldn't be helping at all and it should drop freely into the clients lap)…(drop the arm) that's right twice as deep…(repeat lifting and dropping the arm and saying 'that's right twice as deep')…and now I'm going to be quiet a moment as you drift even deeper into hypnosis…(pause for about 1 minute)…that's right…and now I'd like you to get a sense of a relaxing chair you've never seen before that looks familiar…and as you approach that chair ready to relax into it…you can be curious about what the experience will be like…and as you relax into that chair you can get a sense of closing your eyes and *drifting comfortably and deeply into hypnosis*…and my voice can go with you as your mind wonders through different thoughts and ideas and sensations as a part of you listens to the sound of my voice here while another part of you can understand the meaning of my communication…

## Four seasons induction

(Pause for about 20 seconds)…that's right…now as you listen to me I will talk to you…and as I talk to you your mind can wonder…and while your mind wonders you can begin to think about different things…and as you think about different things certain ideas and feelings can begin to come to mind…and when those ideas and feelings come to mind you can find yourself *drifting deeper and deeper* into the experience in your own unique way…and you know that spring is a time of new life…and you can be out in the countryside and notice how the air seems so fresh and clean…how the colours can appear so bright and vivid and how much variety you can notice...there are sounds you recognise in the spring...like certain sounds of birds and animals...and sights of young animals experiencing the first few months of life...and when a breeze blows it can create movement...and you can notice familiar smells that change depending on where you are and what you are doing...

And you are aware of how the state of things can change as summer approaches...and the weather changes and you know what that's like...and the wildlife changes...the sounds you can hear change...and I wonder what sounds you feel are summer sounds...as you have a sense of what makes summer, summer...and there will be certain summer smells...and you know people feel different about different seasons depending on their age and people like different things about the different seasons at different ages...and I wonder what you enjoyed about the summer when you were younger...and as you drift through the seasons certain thoughts and feelings can come to mind...as you drift into autumn...and you know how the colours change in autumn and the weather changes and the smells change...and I wonder what else changes for you in autumn...and many children enjoy crunching the fallen golden brown leaves with each step they take...and we begin to become aware of the nearing winter...and as winter falls so things change again...a scene may look different than it did before...and I wonder what you used to enjoy as a child about the winter period that isn't the same for adults...and imagine what many children feel like when crunching through snow or playing in snow...and the air is often crisp and colour often appears to have been drained out to greys...whites...and blacks...and with little wisps of colours...you can get a sense of noticing a warm and inviting log cabin...and as you approach that cabin it can seem vaguely familiar...yet unknown...and you can enter the cabin and notice what the door was like to open as you see what the inside of that cosy...*relaxing*...warm and comforting cabin looks like as you notice a chair...and you can walk to that chair getting a sense of what it will feel like to *relax* back in that chair and *drift off pleasantly into hypnosis*...as *you now relax* into that chair...close your eyes...and find yourself instinctively drifting *deeper and deeper into hypnosis*…as you continue listening to the sound of my voice…

## Staircase induction

(Pause for about 20 seconds)…that's right…now as you listen to me I will talk to you…and as I talk to you your mind can wonder…and while your mind wonders you can begin to think about different thoughts and feelings while you *begin to drift deeper inside*…and you can have a sense of noticing a grand oak tree…and you can be curious about that tree as you begin to walk toward it…and as you walk closer and closer to the tree you can notice the secret door in the base of the tree…and you can walk to the door and gently open it to reveal a grand and wonderful staircase with 20 steps…and in a moment you can begin to walk comfortably down that staircase one step at a time as I count down from 20 down to 1…and with each count you can go one twentieth of the way *deeper into hypnosis*…(make each count on the clients outbreath)…as you step onto the first step…20…that's right *deeper and deeper*…and you can notice what is around you and I wonder what you can see...and I wonder if you can hear each step you take and what it feels like to take each step *deeper and deeper into hypnosis...relaxing into the experience*...19...*deeper and deeper* in your own unique way...and I wonder whether you will take a step with each count or two steps with each count at times and at other time pause for thought or to *relax a little deeper* or just to look around or to stop a moment to *take in the experience*...or descend those steps at another rate and speed...18...*going deeper and deeper*...knowing you can take yourself down into this state anytime you please just by finding that tree...walking through the door...and walking down the steps...17...*going deeper and deeper* with each count...one twentieth of the way into hypnosis with each number...16...15...14...that's right...and I don't know whether you will *go even deeper* with the words that I say or the spaces between my words...13...12...11...*deeper and deeper*...10...9...over halfway...now into a deep and comfortable hypnotic trance...8...all the way...7...*deeper and deeper*...6...and as you approach the bottom of the stair I wonder whether you will become curious about what you will discover...5...as you shortly begin to notice a door down there...4...*all the way into hypnosis*...3...as you approach the bottom of the steps...2...and 1...*in hypnosis now*...as you push that door open and see a familiar looking room you know you've never seen before and wonder where that chair in the room will lead you...and you can...go and sit in that chair...and *drift deeply inside* getting a sense of finding that chair so comforting and relaxing your eyes relax shut and you get a sense of drifting off deeply into hypnosis...

## Conscious/unconscious separation induction

(Pause for about 20 seconds)...that's right...now...(move your head slightly left when talking in relation to 'conscious' and slightly right when you talk in relation to 'unconscious')...as you know you have a (left) conscious mind...and an (right) *unconscious* mind...and when I talk to (right) you (left) you don't have to listen...and there will be times when (right) I will be talking to you and (left) you will just hear me talking...and (right) as you hear me here and understand what I'm saying (left) you will hear me there and hear me speaking...and (right) the unconscious mind is the part of you that knows more about (left) you than you do (right) *your unconscious* is the part of you that create all of the instinctive responses...that understands patterns and contains a lifetimes worth of knowledge and experience and skills and an ability to use all that wisdom to successfully solve problems when...*the time is right*...(left) whilst the conscious part of you can just *drift and dream and relax* as (right) you do what is necessary...(left) and you can notice a chair that feels so inviting...and as *you relax* into that chair you can get a sense of your eyes closing (right) as *you drift deeply into hypnosis*...

## Body scan induction

(Pause for about 20 seconds)...that's right...(Reading slowly and timing sentences to each outbreath and leaving plenty of pauses. If the client has been showing some tension follow the script but have the client gently tense muscles first asking them to 'tense the muscles...that's right...and then let that go...that's right...' make sure they have no health problems like arthritis or joint problems etc. if you do this. You can also really take time over this induction. You can scan through the body in perhaps 5-10 minutes, or you can extend this out to maybe 45 minute of really taking time to explore as many sensations as you can think of that the client can focus on and working through the body very slowly) now…take a few moments to focus on the top of your head…notice how it feels and what sensations you have…allow that attention to focus on your ears, you can notice what temperature those ears are and any differences in the sensations of those ears…and let your attention move around to your forehead…and let the muscles in your forehead *soften and relax*…and notice the sensations on the forehead, perhaps you can notice temperature or certain feelings there and you know what it feels like to have a *calming* breeze tickling your forehead… and allow that attention to flow down your checks and jaw…*relaxing* the jaw and the muscles around your face…perhaps noticing warmth or coolness as those muscles *relax further*…as you allow that relaxation to move down to your neck…and you can notice how a little more relaxation can drift in with each breath you take…and how the muscles can soften as you allow that attention to flow through each part of your body…as you now focus on the tops of your arms…and I wonder which arm relaxation will spread down first…the right arm or the left arm…and as that relaxation continues to flow down the arms you can notice how each breath draws in something new and expels what the mind and body doesn't need…as you focus on those hands…focusing on what they are resting on…noticing which hand is the heaviest and which is the lightest…being aware of different sensations and feelings as you allow the wave of relaxation to spread down your chest towards your stomach…like a healing light cleansing your mind and body…filling your heart and lungs…helping that healing light to spread around your whole body and mind…as that relaxation flows down into your stomach…that's right…*relaxing deeper and deeper* and more fully as a body while the mind becomes comfortably focused…as you allow that attention to drift down into the legs…and I wonder which leg the relaxation will spread into fastest…and as that relaxation drifts all the way into the feet you can be curious how the mind will follow once the body is *fully relaxed*…and now as a mind begin to get a sense of entering into the mind and flowing gently around the body checking that each muscle is *comfortably relaxed*...have a sense of drifting through the head...down into the neck...and relaxing on into the shoulders...and now as I remain quiet for a few moments you can take as long as you need to drift through the body filling the body with a healing light and when I start talking again you will have finished relaxing through the body from the top of your head to the tips of your toes...and you can get a sense of being in the most wonderfully comfortable chair...as you drift through the body...*now*...(pause for about one minute)...that's right...finding yourself in that chair...*feeling so comfortable*...as you now have a sense of wanting to *drift off deeply into hypnosis*...and have a sense of closing your eyes while *you drift so deeply and comfortably into hypnosis*...

## Arm catalepsy induction

(Pause for about 20 seconds)...that's right...now...in a moment I'm going to reach over and gently lift up that right arm...and when I do I'm not going to tell you to put it down...(reach over and gently lift up the right arm. The idea is to be so gentle the client almost can't tell if you are lifting their arm or they are lifting it themselves)...that's right...(start tapping so that you begin to create a state of catalepsy in the arm. Tap near the wrist on the forearm. Tap on the bottom side of the arm, then the top side, left side then right side. Tap at a comfortable pace - not too fast or slow - take the lead from the client and how they are responding. Always tap opposing muscles so when you tap the top then tap the bottom, when you tap the left then tap the right, if you tap the bottom tap the top, if you tap the right tap the left)...and as I continue tapping I wonder whether that arm will seem like your arm but won't feel like your arm or whether that arm will feel apart from you yet you have a sense it's a part of you...that's right...*drifting deeper inside with each breath*...and you know you can notice an arm and not realise it's yours or know it's your but not feel it...that's right...*really absorbing*...that's it...and you can discover something without knowing you've discovered it or know you've discovered it without knowing what it is...that's it...and in a moment I'm not going to tell you to put that arm down any faster than *you drift deeper and comfortably into hypnosis*...

And you don't have to *be fully in a deep and comfortable hypnotic trance* until that arm lowers all the way down to your lap...that's right...(stop tapping and leave the arm 'floating' in the air. As the arm lowers just watch it. If it lowers quickly suggest 'that's right and you can just allow that lowering to comfortably slow down...that's right'. As the arm lowers, occasionally, in time with outbreaths suggest 'that's right' then as the arm finishes lowering fully, suggest 'that's it...all the way now...*deeper and deeper into a comfortable hypnotic trance*...') and with that arm resting there you can begin to get a sense of what it feels like to sit in a chair so comfortable you struggle to keep your eyes open...and as you get a sense of those eyes shutting you can drift deeper into hypnosis...

## Three things induction

(Pause for about 20 seconds)...that's right...now...in a moment I'm going to ask you to open your eyes...and when you do I'd like you to just allow those eyes to settle on looking at something in front of you just above eye level...and each time your eyes close here you can *drift deeper into hypnosis*...so just allow your eyes to open and find something in front of you just above eye level to look at...and as you look at that I'd like to have you hold your focus on that spot and begin to say slowly and out loud three things you can see...(pause as they say three things)...that's right...and now slowly say three things you can hear (pause as they say three things)...that's right...and now slowly and comfortably say three things you can feel (pause as they say three things)...that's right...and now just gently allow those eyes to close...and get a sense of that external scene inside your mind...take three deep breaths as *you drift deeper into the experience*...and then slowly say three things you can see...(pause as they say three things)...and now three things you can hear (pause as they say three things)...and now three things you can feel...(pause as they say three things)...that's right...

And now while you remain as still as you can allow the eyes to open and look back at that spot...(wait for them to look back at the spot)...that's right...and again whilst looking at that spot say three things you can see…(ideally you want them to say different things each time they do this but if they can't think of anything new they can say things they have already said but pause and let them try to come up with new things first)…and now three things you can hear…(pause while they say three things)…and three things you can feel…(pause while they say three things)…that's right…now allow the eyes to close again and drift inside getting a sense of that external scene inside your mind again…that's right…and then slowly take three breaths as you drift deeper into the experience…and then slowly say three things you can see (pause while they say three things - again ideally you want it to be three different things if they can think of three different things)…and three things you can hear…(pause while they say three things)…and three things you can feel…(pause while they say three things)…that's right…each time *going deeper and deeper into this experience*…and each time finding it harder to open those eyes…

And as you continue to relax just allow the eyes to open and look back at that spot…and as you do just begin to say three things you can see…(pause while they say three things)…and three things you can hear…(pause while they say three things)…and three things you can feel…(pause while they say three things)…that's right…and just allow the eyes to close as you drift deeper and deeper…and get a sense of that external scene inside your mind…and as you take three comfortable breaths and allow the muscles around the eyes and face to relax and allow that relaxation to spread through the body in your own unique way you may find it increasingly difficult to say three things you can see, hear and feel but try really hard to say three things you can see, hear and feel and if…*it seems too much effort*…at that point just allow yourself to *relax and drift deeper inside*…(pause for them to say three things for seeing, hearing and feeling. If they manage this repeat the process so far of having them open their eyes and saying three things, then closing their eyes and saying three things - you can repeat the wording above again up to this point until they stop saying three things because it is too much effort. If they don't seem to be responding after a few more runs through this then after the last run through of the eyes being open suggest 'that's right…and as you now allow the eyes to close and drift deeper I wonder whether you will notice just how deep into hypnosis you are going...as you listen to the sound of my voice...some people feel consciously as if nothing is different whilst unconsciously they *become more responsive* and able to respond fully to all that is helpful to creating the desired change so that they can consciously remain aware of the surroundings until they feel safe enough to...*let go*...whilst knowing they will remember everything they will remember when they come out of hypnosis at the end of the session...')...that's right...and as you drift deeper inside in your own unique way I'd like to have you begin to get a sense of a chair that looks so familiar yet you don't recall seeing it before...and as you drift deeper into the experience just get a sense of walking over to the chair and relaxing down into it as you get a sense of feeling so relaxed you just close your eyes and drift off deeply and comfortably into hypnosis...

## Self-suggestion induction (good for people that over analyse)

(Pause for about 20 seconds)…that's right…and as I talk to you I would like to have you repeat what I say to yourself…and when you do I'd like you to change each sentence I say into a sentence directed at yourself…so if I say 'and you can relax deeply to the sound of my voice'…you can say to yourself 'I can relax deeply to the sound of your voice'…so what I would like you to do is to pay close attention and repeat each sentence directing it at yourself…and as you relax there you can hear the sound of my voice (after each sentence pause long enough for the client to analyse the sentence and say it to themselves. They can say it in their head or out loud)…and you can feel sensations in the body…and as *you relax deeper* you can notice thoughts coming to mind…and you can drift deeper with the spaces between my words whilst *becoming more focused with each sentence* I say…and you can continue to enter hypnosis in your own unique way…and you know how to walk…and you know how to talk…and you know how to understand what I'm saying…and you know how to let your mind wander and daydream…and you can *drift fully into hypnosis now*...and you know how to *drift deeper with each suggestion* without knowing how you do it...you can just *drift deeper* effortlessly...and you know what a comfortable chair is like...and you can get a sense of what it feels like to discover yourself relaxing into one now...and as you relax into that chair I wonder when it will become too much effort for you to keep repeating suggestions and instead just let go and drift all the way inside a pleasant dream...all the way...deeper and deeper...and you can get a sense of being so relaxed and sleepy the eyes shut all by themselves as you drift deeper into hypnosis...

## Hand movement to face induction

(Pause for about 20 seconds)...that's it...and take a moment to gently open your eyes and look at the back of this hand (have the client look at the back of a hand on their lap)...(While the client is looking at the back of the hand gently lift the hand up and move it around softly until it is holding itself in the air. As you do this start talking about how there can be a thread between the hand and their nose and they can notice how that hand moves towards their face, like that thread is pulling that hand closer to the face. Any time you see movement in the arm or hand say 'that's it' just to encourage that movement, as the hand moves closer to their face you can say things like 'that's it, nearly there' just to continue encouraging that movement and 'deeper and deeper into hypnosis'. Sometimes the hand won't be fully on target with the client's face and they may shut their eyes, if the hand is off target you can touch on their elbow just to help move the arm into a position which lines the hand up better with the face. If the eyes aren't closed as the hand nears the face you may suggest that 'as the hand reaches your face those eyes can gently close'. After the hand reaches the face you can suggest that they can 'go deeper and deeper into hypnosis as the arm lowers slowly down to their lap'….) and as that hand rests there you can get a sense of what it feels like to discover yourself relaxing into the most comfortable chair now…and as you relax into that chair you can begin to drift all the way deeper inside into a pleasant dream…and you can get a sense of being so relaxed in that chair that you have a sense of sitting in that chair, closing your eyes and relaxing even deeper into hypnosis…

## Ambiguous arm lift induction

The ambiguous arm lift induction can be done without lifting the client's arm yourself at all. It is a great induction for quickly eliciting and testing for responsivity.

(Pause for about 20 seconds)…Start the induction by asking the client to rest the palms of their hands on their lap and to open their eyes (if their eyes are closed) and to look down at their hands. Then tell the client that in a moment you will reach over and lift up one of their arms. Once you have told the client this, reach over slowly to one of the arms. It is usually easiest to do this to the arm nearest to, or opposite the hand you are reaching with, so if you are going to lift with your right hand, it is usually easiest doing this to the client's left arm. Reach towards the client's wrist with your thumb and forefinger. What you will usually notice is that as your hand gets close to the client's wrist they automatically begin to lift up their own arm into your hand.

At this point, you can just slowly move your hand up and their arm will continue to raise up towards your grip and you will have an arm levitation without ever touching their arm. If questioned, the client will usually think that you lifted their arm. They don't realise that they lifted their own arm up. The idea of the induction is to do as little as possible. If the client's arm needs it, you can gently touch the sides of their wrist with your thumb and forefinger and gently and carefully suggest through touch that you want the arm to lift by lifting the arm very carefully using as little effort as possible so that the client does most of the lifting. This is what is ambiguous about the induction, the client can't quite tell how much you were lifting and touching and how much they were lifting their own arm.

Once you have the arm levitating about 30-50cm's above their lap they are already hypnotised, but may not realise it. They have already levitated their arm and followed the suggestions you gave behaviourally by the way you reached over and encouraged their arm to lift.

At this point you can acknowledge what they have accomplished so far by saying something like "that's right." And then suggest they close their eyes. You can then suggest they drift deeper into hypnosis as the arm lowers, or link other suggestions to the arm lowering. Or you could offer the client more freedom by saying that you are curious what will happen with that arm as they drift deeper into hypnosis. Some people may then lower their arm, or raise their arm, or it may remain levitated exactly where it is. At this point you can move on to a deepener, the deepener could be linked to the arm lowering, or you could move straight on to the therapeutic part of the session. For example:

…that's it…and as that arm lowers back down towards the lap, you can continue to *drift deeper into hypnosis*…and begin to have a sense of the most comfortable chair…and you can have a sense of relaxing in that chair…closing your eyes…and drifting off comfortably into hypnosis…

## Subject describing inner feelings induction

The only way a client can describe their inner feelings is for them to go inside themselves to explore the feelings. Ask the client to focus on what they can physically and emotionally feel and to describe their experience to you without moving. It is important that they remain still. Being still and describing their experience deepens the experience. You can ask the client to describe what their hands feel like resting on their lap, what their legs feel like touching the chair, what their back feels like touching the chair, what inhaling and exhaling feels like, what their eyelids feel like, what other sensations they can notice in their hands or arms, what relaxation feels like for them, maybe in their arms or chest, to notice warmth or coolness etc.

Sample script:

(Pause for about 20 seconds)...and as you relax there I would like you to take a moment to describe your ongoing inner experience...so without moving...just describe things like how your hands are feeling (give the client time to focus on this and describe it) what the air feels like as you breathe in...(said on an in-breath) and out (said on an outbreath)… (give time for the client to focus on this and describe this)' Let the client describe how they feel physically. (If they get stuck not seeming to be absorbed internally you can ask a few more questions to narrow their focus of attention, like talking about the chair beneath them, what does this feel like, what about the weight of their hands or sensations in their eyelids or breathing or automatic movements etc. If they aren't saying anything because (as is often the case) they have quickly become absorbed in the experience, then you can just reinforce this by saying something like 'that's it, just continuing to drift, deeper and deeper' and then transitioning into the therapy you are doing, so you might follow up with 'as I talk to you in the background' or whatever would be relevant for the work you are doing with the client. After a while, sometimes just a minute or so, the client will find it difficult to keep answering and will prefer to be able to just be quiet. At this point you can suggest they can just relax, or suggest that it may be too difficult to talk, then move into whatever you plan on doing next, like doing a deepener or moving on to mental rehearsal or another process.)

...that's it...and as you continue to *relax deeper with this experience*...you can begin to have a sense of relaxing into the most comfortable chair...closing your eyes...and *relaxing deeper* into hypnosis...

## Touching hands induction

This induction is about communicating through touch. There are very few words, but it can be a powerful experience. You put one of your hands out in front of you with the palm facing the client. You elbow will be bent about 90-degree angle so that the palm of your hand is comfortably facing the client and your hand is about 30 cm in front of you. You don't want your arm stretched out straight as this will be uncomfortable for you. You tell the client to do the same and to touch the palm of their hand against the palm of your hand. You then suggest they look at the back of their hand. While the client is looking at the back of their hand you begin to guide yourself into a deeply relaxed state, you relax your eyes, your facial muscles, your shoulders and with your breathing, you start off by breathing the same as the client, and then slow, deepen and relax your breathing and occasionally do extended slow blinks to convey the idea of relaxing and closing the eyes. All of the information about relaxing will be conveyed to the client through the palm of your hand and the non-verbal behaviours they notice out of their peripheral vision. They often don't consciously notice that their hand touching yours is picking up on the idea of relaxation but they will start to relax themselves. Their focus is being held on the back of their own hand. As you notice them relaxing you acknowledge this by saying something like "that's it", so when you see the shoulders relaxing, or outbreaths, or the eyes blink or relaxing, you acknowledge this and in a short space of time they usually have their eyes closed. Often their arm remains out in front of them, but sometimes the client's hand will gradually start to lower. If it starts to lower away from yours you can respond saying 'that's it' or 'that's right' to acknowledge that this is okay for them to do as they enter hypnosis, maybe say 'all the way' as it continues to lower down. Other times rigidity sets into the arm and it stays levitating, so once the client has their eyes shut their arm is still in the air. You can utilise this and

144

perhaps link it lowering with going deeper into hypnosis, or link doing inner therapeutic work with the arm lowering. You can use this as a deepener by suggesting that they can drift deeper as the arm begins to slowly lower down.

Sample script:

(Pause for 20 seconds)…Take a moment to gently open those eyes (assuming you have read an introduction script)…Now touch the palm of your hand to mine, look at the back of your hand, that's it…that's it…that's it…all the way…letting those eyes close as you continue to *drift deeper into the experience*…and while *you drift deeper into the experience*…you can have a sense of relaxing down into the most comfortable chair and closing your eyes…and drifting off deeper into hypnosis…

## Ideomotor energy hands induction

(Pause for 20 seconds)…Take a moment to gently open those eyes…(if their eyes are closed)…now rub your hands together like this (demonstrate to the client rubbing hands together in front of you)…and hold them apart just a little bit (demonstrate what you are talking about and have your hands in front of you about 30 centimetres apart) and just gaze between those hands…and you can perhaps notice a sensation there…almost like there is a solid object between those hands…or maybe warmth or coolness…or lightness or heaviness…or a tingling…or another sensation…and you may not notice straightaway…and you can continue to just gaze between those hands…and I don't know whether those hands will come together or move apart or stay where they are as you *go deeper and deeper into hypnosis*…and as *you go deeper into hypnosis* so your eyes can close and the hands can begin to lower to the lap…and as those hands lower to your lap you can *go deeper and deeper into hypnosis*…(the client's eyes don't need to be closed, I usually don't ask for this. You are being responsive to the client, so when you ask whether the hands will move together, apart or stay where they are, you wait and see what happens for the client and then acknowledge this with something like 'that's it' and then continue on capitalising on this, so you may decide to continue referencing what is going on for a bit longer until they are deeply absorbed in the experience and then suggesting the arms could lower)...and as the arms lower back to the lap...you can have a sense of sitting down in a comfortable chair...and as you sit down in that chair...you can *become deeper absorbed in the experience*...have a sense of closing your eyes...and drifting deeply into hypnosis...

## Ambiguous touch arm induction

(Pause for 20 seconds) (Very gently lift up one of the client's arms, likely the arm opposite or nearest to the hand you will be lifting with. As you do this, start saying something similar to what is written below. Your aim is to have the client focused on that arm. In some cases clients have their arm lose and limp so that if you let go, the arm would just fall to their lap. If this is the case with a client, then you can suggest that they can begin to stick that arm there in the air and for a little while, or if needed, tell the client directly to just hold their arm there. You may need to gently support their arm as lightly and minimally as possible with your other hand while you begin this induction. What you want to do for the induction, is while talking occasionally to suggest ideas about what the client may be able to notice about the experience, tap gently on the client's arm on the forearm, just above the wrist, tapping on the bottom of the arm, then the top, then the left side, then the right side. It doesn't matter the order of the tapping - top/bottom, left/right or bottom/top, right/left, etc, just that you are gently and slowly tapping in opposite directions, so if you tap the bottom of the arm, you will next tap the top so that you have tapped both sides, if you tap the left side, then you will tap the right side. What you are trying to do is create catalepsy with the tapping by tapping opposing points, so their arm instinctively pushes up slightly when you tap the top, it instinctively pushes down slightly when you tap the bottom, it pushes left slightly when you tap the right side and right slightly when you tap the left side, this encourages the arm to become cataleptic in place.) Just look at the back of that hand, gaze at the back of that hand. I don't know whether that arm will feel waxy, almost like a candle, or whether numbness will set in or whether something will change in that arm, perhaps starting in the shoulder or the elbow or radiating up from the hand. And as that experience continues the eyes can begin to get heavier and begin to want to close as that arm begins to lower down to your leg and as that arm does, so your eyes can close as you *go all the way into hypnosis*...and as you *relax deeply into hypnosis*...you can begin to get a sense of the most comfortable chair...you can approach that chair...sit down in that chair...close your eyes...and find yourself drifting deeply and pleasantly into hypnosis...

## Automatic finger movement induction

(Pause for 20 seconds) Take a moment to put your hands together and link your fingers...and while doing this, hold out your two forefingers and hold those forefingers apart...hold your hands in front of you and gaze between those fingers...that's it...and as you gaze between those fingers, don't *go into hypnosis* too quickly...and just watch as those fingers begin to get closer together...and don't *let the eyes close* until those fingers touch, and try to hold those fingers apart...don't *go into hypnosis* too quickly, try not to let those fingers touch too quickly…and just keep gazing between those fingers as they get closer and closer together…as those eyes begin to get heavy and begin to want to close…and really try not to *let those fingers touch* too quickly as you *drift deeper and deeper* into the experience…and as those fingers touch your eyes can close…and as your eyes close so those arms can begin to lower down towards your lap…and as those arms lower down towards your lap you can *drift deeper and deeper into hypnosis*…that's it…(it can sometimes be helpful to ask the person to really take their time, not to let this happen too quickly, like really taking time for the fingers to come together and really taking time for those arms to lower and not to enter hypnosis too quickly, or not to go deeper too quickly. The focus then is on speed of entering or deepening hypnosis and not on whether they are entering hypnosis or deepening hypnosis)…and as you continue to *relax into the experience*, you can notice yourself discovering the most comfortable chair…and as you sit down into that chair, so you can close your eyes and *drift deeply into hypnosis*…

## Look at that hand double bind induction

Just take a moment to gently open your eyes (if the client's eyes are closed) and look at the hand that you think will be the hand that will lift up as...*you go into hypnosis*...and as you look at the hand that you think will lift, I wonder whether you will be right, or whether the other hand will lift, or whether neither hand will lift, or perhaps both hands will lift, as you just continue to *drift deeper into the experience* looking at that hand...that's it...all the way...(then acknowledge whatever happens. If a hand starts to twitch or show signs of movement, then comment on this, acknowledge it with words like 'that's it' and 'as that movement begins in that hand'. Comment on the client going deeper with the experience while the induction is taking place with comments like 'that's it, continuing to drift deeper and deeper as you gaze at that hand' and as you notice they have been watching the hand for some time you can then suggest that they close their eyes and drift even deeper into the experience. If an arm (or both arms) was levitating then you can link the eye closure with this 'and as that arm continues to rise, those eyes can begin to close as you drift even deeper into hypnosis' and then you can link going even deeper with that arm lowering back down 'and as that arm begins to lower back down to your lap, I wonder how deep you can drift into hypnosis…and you can find yourself deeply absorbed in this hypnotic state as that arm reaches your lap…', if the hands remained where they were then you can just suggest 'that's it and as you continue to gaze at that hand, your eyes can close and as your eyes close, you can drift even deeper into hypnosis…')

…That's it…and as you continue to drift deeper into hypnosis, you can begin to get a sense of relaxing into the most comfortable chair…and as you relax into that chair…you can have a sense of closing your eyes…as you begin to drift deeper into hypnosis…

## Not doing induction

(Pause for 20 seconds) Just take a moment to *begin to relax*…and you don't have to pay attention to the sounds around you, you don't have to pay attention to how you are sitting, to what your back is resting against, to words that I am using or to the sound of my voice, you don't have to be aware of different thoughts and feelings that come to mind, you don't have to try to do anything at all as you *drift deeper and deeper into hypnosis*, you don't have to worry about how you are *drifting deeper* and more comfortably into hypnosis, or how *that is happening all by itself*...you don't have to think about the way your mind is *beginning to relax* or the way your body is *beginning to relax*, as you *drift into hypnosis*...you can just let it happen all by itself, not paying attention to the in-breaths or the outbreaths or to my words and the changes happening as you *drift deeper into hypnosis*, relaxation can just happen as you *drift into hypnosis*...and while you continue to *drift deeper into hypnosis* you can find yourself sitting down on the most comfortable seat...closing your eyes...and drifting deeply into hypnosis...

## In the moment induction

(Pause for 20 seconds) With your eyes closed, you can begin to notice everything about this moment in time, a part of you can hear the sound of my voice, and you can notice sounds around you, and as you pay attention to sounds around you, you can begin to differentiate between one sound and another, and you can notice how you are breathing in and breathing out and what it feels like to be breathing in and breathing out, what movement happens as you breathe in and breathe out and you can notice any feeling in the eyes, any movement of the eyes and how that movement helps you *go deeper into hypnosis*, and you can notice movements and sensations in the arms and legs and throughout your body, noticing which hand is warmest and which hand is coolest, which hand is heaviest and which hand is lightest, noticing what your shoulders feel like, what you back feels like, what your legs feel like, what thoughts are going through your mind right now as you *become deeper absorbed in hypnosis*...and while you continue to *drift deeper into hypnosis*...you can discover yourself sitting down in a comfortable chair...closing your eyes...and drifting deeply into hypnosis...

## Sensory overload induction

(Pause for 20 seconds) With your eyes closed, I would like to have you just sit there with your hands resting gently on your legs, and with those hands resting gently on your legs, notice the feelings through the fingertips, and as you notice the feelings of those fingertips on touching the legs, you can have a sense of what it feels like to be standing under a shower, what the water feels like on your head and face and running down your body, the sounds of the shower, the temperature of that water, and while you notice what those fingers feel like resting there on those legs, the sensations at the fingertips, differences in warmth and coolness between the two hands...whether those hands feel heavy or light...what sounds you can hear around you (you can direct the client's attention to sounds you can hear, like ticking clock, traffic, movement, your talking etc), and as you have awareness of those fingers, awareness of sounds around you, you can also be aware of what your feet feel like, while also being aware of the experience of standing under that shower and you can begin to be aware of walking through a country garden, what you can see in that country garden, what you can hear, what it feels like to be walking through that garden, but don't forget about what it feels like to be stood under that shower and what those fingertips feel like, the sounds you can hear around you here, the feeling of those feet and you can begin to count back in your mind from 300...299, 298, 297, 296, 295, and as you continue to count backwards and *drift deeper and deeper into hypnosis*, you can continue to be aware of the sounds around you, the feeling of those feet, the sensations at the fingertips, the experience of standing under a shower and walking through a country garden and you can *begin to let go* and *drift deeper into hypnosis*...and find yourself sitting in a comfortable chair...closing your eyes...and drifting deeply into hypnosis...

## Vague language induction

(Pause for 20 seconds) With your eyes closed you can listen to me, and as you listen to me, so you can begin to explore possibility, you can begin to wonder, you can begin to think, you can begin to feel what it is like to *enter hypnosis*, and you can have a sense of inner wellbeing, a sense of comfortable deepening, a sense of relaxation spreading, and a certain level of education and learning from *going deeper into hypnosis*, and feeling more comfortable, and you can enjoy a sense of inner discovery, enjoy a sense of personal achievement, and depth of increased knowledge and wisdom as *you enter hypnosis deeper and deeper* and more comfortably...in your own unique way...and as you continue to *drift deeper into hypnosis* in your own unique way...you can find yourself sitting in the most comfortable chair...closing your eyes...and drifting peacefully into hypnosis...

## Double binds induction

(Pause for 20 seconds) With your eyes closed I don't know whether you will *go deeper into hypnosis* with the sound of my voice or with each breath that you take, or whether you will find yourself *going deeper and more comfortably into hypnosis* because your eyes are closed, and as you *drift deeper into hypnosis* I wonder whether your left hand or right hand feels the warmest and as you notice and pay attention to which hand feels the warmest, I wonder whether you can notice which hand is the heaviest and whether the hand which is heaviest is also warmest or whether the heaviest hand is also the cooler hand, and as you listen to me and *drift into hypnosis*, you can wonder whether you are *going deeper into hypnosis* because of the relaxation spreading down through your body, or whether it is because you are paying more attention to the experience than to the sounds around you...and while you *drift into hypnosis* in your own unique way, you can notice whether that deepening is happening more with each in-breath or each outbreath...and as you continue to *drift deeper* into the experience...you can find yourself relaxing down into a comfortable chair...closing your eyes...and drifting pleasantly into hypnosis...

## Leisure induction

(Pause for 20 seconds) (Find out before the induction what the client likes to do, gather information about how they do (or did, if it is something they used to enjoy doing) that leisure activity, you can talk about the sensory experience of the activity yourself to guide the client through that, or with their eyes closed, you can ask them to begin to describe the experience slowly to you and you can draw their attention to different sensory aspects of the experience). Here is an example of what you might say if the client said they liked swimming:

With your eyes closed, you can begin to have a sense of swimming in a pool...the feeling of weightlessness as you float in the water...the temperature of that water and the feeling of the water against your skin...and the sounds of the swimming pool and how the sounds change when your head goes under the water...and how time seems to *slow right down*...and the smell of the swimming pool...and having a sense of floating on your back...relaxing in the water...gazing up at the ceiling...and the sounds and feeling of the movement of your arms and legs in the water...absorbing yourself in those sensations...and the feeling of the cool air on your face after you have been underwater...really *absorbing yourself in the experience* as you *drift deeper into hypnosis*...and as you continue to *drift deeper into hypnosis*, so you can begin to have a sense of leaving the water and finding the most comfortable seat...sitting down in that seat...closing your eyes...and drifting comfortably into hypnosis...

## Favourite place induction

(Pause for 20 seconds) (Find out before the induction a favourite place the client would like to go during hypnosis, gather information about this place so that you can describe the sensory experience of the client being in that favourite place. Usually, people say relaxing places, but sometimes they will say something a bit different, for example, I had someone say that they liked being at a waterpark going on the water rides, so I had them describe this to me, what do they see and hear there, what do they do there. I then used this for the induction, talking about them seeing the rides, all the people, the warmth of the sun (it was a hot location), the feeling of going on the different rides and the experience of that, like the experience of being in a rubber tube, rising up a ride, experiencing themselves getting higher, hearing the cranking of the conveyor belt, then floating quietly around the top of the ride, looking out over the view from up here, noticing what they can see, then reaching the drop and rapidly descending, etc. Hypnosis is about focusing attention, not specifically about relaxation, so for that individual, this induction worked great because it is what was right for them. Like with the leisure induction, you want to know enough about what the person would see, hear and feel and perhaps other senses and thoughts, so that you can feed this information back during the induction. As it is tailored to the client, it is often a very quick and effective way of hypnotising the client) Here is an example of what you might say if the client said their favourite place was relaxing in a specific park:

With your eyes closed, you can imagine yourself sat there, looking out, noticing the grass...and trees...noticing the landscape in the distance...the horizon and buildings...and I don't know whether the sun is high in the sky, setting, rising or whether it is night-time (said because of not having this information beforehand but prompting the client to think about this aspect of the experience) and you can have a sense of different times and how the view changes depending on the time of day, and you can rest there...enjoying the view...having a sense of peace...*relaxing deeper and deeper into the experience*...aware of the breeze on your face and the sounds around you as you *drift deeper into hypnosis*...and as you continue to *drift deeper* you can discover a comfortable seat...have a sense of sitting down in that seat...closing your eyes...and drifting deeper into hypnosis...

## Memory recall induction

(Pause for 20 seconds) With your eyes closed, you can begin to recall a memory (you can ask them to think of a pleasant memory or it could be that you do this induction as part of the therapy and so have them recall a time they have experienced a relevant resource in the past - like confidence, etc, or you can even have them create an imaginary memory, like asking them to think about how things can be different in the future without the problem and then have them describe this and you ask questions to get fine sensory detail to really absorb them in that experience) and as you recall that memory, you can begin to (as an example, I will continue from here as if the client has said the memory they want to recall is their roast dinner that they had on Sunday) describe that roast lamb to me (you will give time for client's to answer the questions when asked), and you can have a sense of taking your knife and fork and slicing that lamb...and the sounds that go with that...the smells that get released...and imagining lifting some of that lamb up to your mouth on the fork...perhaps noticing the salivating...noticing the smell...the texture...as you begin to eat that lamb...the experience of it being chewed...of it passing down your throat to your stomach...a sense of the roast potatoes...eating them...maybe having gravy on them...the texture and experience of eating those potatoes...absorbing yourself in enjoying that meal...and as you continue to enjoy that meal, you can continue to *drift deeper into the experience* and into hypnosis...and as you finish that meal, so you can begin to find yourself relaxing even deeper as if sitting down into the most comfortable chair and beginning to *drift deeper into hypnosis...*

## Using bodily sensations induction

(Pause for 20 seconds) With your eyes closed, you can focus on the feeling of breathing in and breathing out...aware of the feeling of your hands resting on your legs...aware of other sensations within you...aware of the feeling of your feet on the floor...the weight of the arms or the shoulders...the feeling of sitting in that chair and of the chair against your back...and the feeling of air passing in and out of your nostrils as you *continue relaxing* that breathing...and as you focus on different sensations and feelings within your body...so you can continue to *drift deeper and deeper into hypnosis*...and as you *drift deeper into hypnosis*...you can notice a comfortable chair...relax yourself down into that chair...close your eyes...and *drift deeper into hypnosis*...with each breath that you take...

## Ambiguous touch handshake induction

Introduce yourself and put your hand out (for example: 'Hi, I'm Dan') as the client's hand meets your hand, start shaking it while looking into the client's eyes and holding their gaze and continuing to talk with them, as you do, begin to non-verbally communicate relaxation and inner focus by defocusing your eyes, relaxing your facial muscles, your shoulders, your breathing, and as you continue shaking their hand, slow this down so that you are almost just holding their hand in the air, tap gently on the underside of the client's hand with your fingers, very gently, just to give the non-verbal suggestion of the hand levitating and remaining where it is, begin to loosen your grip very gently while tapping and communicating through your fingertips for the hand to stay in place, tapping lightly on the palm and back of the hand and the underside of the hand and then gradually moving your hand out from the client's hand continuing the soft touch and continuing to talk with the client in a gentle hypnotic way and as the hand pulls out from the client's hand, tapping gently on the fingers and the underside of the little finger and if you want the client's eyes to close you can then suggest they take a moment to close their eyes and begin to relax deeper into the experience (then as your hand move out from the handshake and the client closes their eyes, you can continue to tap gently on and around the hand and wrist to encourage the arm to remain in place) and as they continue to drift deeper into the experience the arm can begin to lower and they can enter hypnosis at the rate and speed that the arm lowers gently towards their lap. You can then suggest that they discover a comfortable chair, relax down into that chair, close their eyes and drift deeply into hypnosis.

## Traditional handshake induction

With this handshake induction, you are interrupting the pattern of a handshake. You reach out to shake the client's hand, the client's eyes would be open for this. As soon as your hands meet, you carry on talking to the client looking at the client and then non-verbally communicating entering hypnosis by relaxing your shoulders, defocusing your eyes, looking through the client, relaxing your facial muscles, keeping attention off of the handshake, as you gently prop up the client's hand with your opposite hand and remove your other hand (so, if you put out your right hand to do the handshake and the client put out their right hand to join the handshake, then you would gently prop up their right hand with your left hand as you move your right hand away from them). You will then continue to talk with the client and start to slow down and relax your speech. As you notice rigidity in the arm that you are gently propping up and notice the client's attention is held and perhaps their eyes are defocusing and their breathing begins to change and they appear to begin to relax, you can ask them to close their eyes and then maybe link drifting even deeper with the arm lowering to their lap. Here is a sample scrips:

Hi, I'm Dan (reaching out to shake hands and as the handshake starts and while continuing to look at the client and continuing to talk, propping up the client's hand with my opposite hand and removing my other hand)...thank you for coming in today...I hope that your journey here went well? (Communicating entering hypnosis non-verbally and beginning to slow down and relax your voice) I'm curious how things have been since we spoke on the telephone...you can take a moment to relax down...close your eyes...and begin to *drift deeper into hypnosis*...and as you do...that arm can begin to lower down to your lap...and as it lowers down to your lap…so you can continue *drifting deeper into hypnosis*…and begin to find yourself discovering the most comfortable chair…relaxing into that chair…closing your eyes…and drifting into hypnosis…

## Richard Bandler style handshake induction

Reach out to shake hands with the client, as their hand reaches your outstretched hand, take the client's arm gently by the wrist with your other hand and turn the client's hand towards their face and start gently moving it closer to their face. As the hand is parallel to their face use your forefinger on the hand not holding the client's arm to point at the centre of their palm and say 'look at that spot…and notice how it defocuses…as that hand gets closer to your face…and as that spot defocuses and the hand moves closer to your face…you can *drift deeper into hypnosis*…and notice how the eyes begin to close as that hand moves closer to the face…that's it…all the way…that's it' (As you say this you very gently begin to move the hand towards the client's face until the hand continues to move towards their face itself. The hand can continue to move towards their face and their eyes can close as they drift deeper into hypnosis. Once the hand is touching the face, you can suggest something like 'and as that hand now lowers down to your lap, you can drift even deeper into hypnosis'. If the hand moves down quickly, you can suggest they take their time going deeper into hypnosis and that they can slow the movement of the hand down.)

...And as you *drift deeper into hypnosis*, so you can begin to have a sense of sitting down in the most comfortable chair...and as you sit down in that chair...so you can have a sense of closing your eyes and drifting deeper into hypnosis...

## Imagine picking up and putting down an object induction

(Pause for 20 seconds)...(If the client's eyes are closed, you can ask them to gently open their eyes) In a moment I would like you to imagine a pen on a table in front of you...I would like you to imagine reaching for that pen, picking it up, and resting back into your current position…then reaching forward, putting the pen down…and sitting back again…and just keep imagining this and repeating this in your mind…so, you will imagine reaching forward (demonstrate the actions for real in an overly exaggerated way what it is you want the client to imagine), picking up a pen from a table, pulling your arm back and sitting back, resting your hand on your lap, then leaning forward again and reaching forward again and stretching your arm out again to put that pen back down on the table and then sitting back in the chair again with your hand resting on your lap…(you may need to remind the client that they are just imagining this, not really picking up a pen and putting it down). Imagine reaching forward, picking up that pen from the table in front of you, then sitting back, then imagine reaching forward putting that pen down on the table and sitting back, then imagine reaching forward, picking up that pen, and sitting back (repeat these instructions a few times until you see that they are absorbed in doing this), that's it, deeper and deeper…(you can say these instructions often and get far more detailed than this to absorb the client as much as possible, like talking about the feeling of the back moving, the different muscles in the arm moving, what the pen looks like and feels like, what the table looks like, etc. You are treating it all as if what you have asked them to do is real and they are really doing this, not just imagining this, some people will get so engrossed in the experience that their arm will levitate automatically, some will keep their eyes open and just be staring into space, others will close their eyes).

That's it...and you can now imagine putting that pen on the table...relaxing back in that chair...closing your eyes...and *drifting off comfortably and deeply into hypnosis*...and as you do...you can have a sense of sitting down into the world's most comfortable chair...closing your eyes...and *drifting even deeper into hypnosis*...

## Energy hand induction

(Pause for 20 seconds)...(Ask the client to place their hand palm down on your palm up hand, if they have their eyes shut currently, ask them to open their eyes) I just want you to get a sense of energy moving from my hand into yours, maybe you will notice a tingling sensation or some other kind of sensation as that energy moves from my hand to yours…maybe the sensation will be warmth or coolness…or something else entirely…and I don't know whether…*you will notice that*…in the palm of the hand or…the fingers, or somewhere else in that hand…just *picking up on that energy*, letting it pass into you, and we can call it trance energy, just *noticing that trance energy flowing*…out of me and up into your body, from my hand into you, and as *that trance energy fills your body*, so you can *go deeper and more absorbed into hypnosis*…that's it…that's it…all the way…(if needed you can suggest to the client that they close their eyes) and as you *continue to drift deeper* and *become more absorbed* in the experience you can begin to have a sense of relaxing down into a comfortable chair, closing your eyes, and *drifting deeply into hypnosis*…

## Alternative energy hand induction

(Pause for 20 seconds)…(If the client has their eyes closed, you can ask them to open their eyes. Rub your hands together and ask the client to rub their hands together at the same time, then have them place their hand palm down above your hand, very close but not touching) Take a moment to pay attention to the trance energy in that hand...and perhaps you notice a tingling, perhaps you *notice the energy* passing up from my hand into your hand...perhaps an electrical feeling...and notice the sensations in that hand and how that trance energy is passing up...jumping up from my hand into yours...that's it...that's it...all the way...as that trance energy passes up from my hand into your hand and up through your body as *you drift deeper and deeper into hypnosis*...(you can suggest they close their eyes if needed) and as you continue to *drift deeper into hypnosis*...you can discover yourself relaxing down into the most comfortable chair, closing your eyes...and drifting deeper into hypnosis...

## Imaginary arm levitation induction

(Pause for 20 seconds)...With your eyes closed...just imagine one of your arms is beginning to levitate...one of your arms is beginning to get lighter and lighter...and the other arm is beginning to get heavier and heavier...and in your mind's eye...having awareness of where that arm must be in space...and having a sense of that arm...and aware of how it lifts, whether it lifts more from the palm of the hand, or from the wrist or from the elbow, and having a sense of that arm lifting and how that arm lifts...and being aware of the sensations of the arm lifting...perhaps of the movement of the fingers on your leg as that arm gently moves...and have a sense of whether that arm is lifting quickly or slowly and notice how high that arm is lifting...and as *that arm is lifting higher and higher*...so you can go deeper into hypnosis, and as *you go deeper into hypnosis*, so that arm can lift higher and higher...and you can go all the way...and as that arm lowers down back to your leg...you can *go even deeper into hypnosis*...going *deeper and deeper* as that arm lowers all the way back down to your leg...and as that arm lowers to your leg and you go deeper into hypnosis...you can have a sense of relaxing back into the most comfortable chair...imagining closing your eyes...and drifting and relaxing deeper into hypnosis...

## The guide induction

(Pause for 20 seconds) With your eyes closed, you can imagine yourself sat in a comfortable chair...drifting off in your mind...and as you *drift off in your mind*...you can discover yourself in a special place where you meet a guide...and this guide is going to educate you...they are wise...and I don't know where you will meet that guide...whether you will be sat down with them or walking along with them...or meeting them in some other context...and when you meet that guide...you can pay attention to them...noticing what they look like...noticing what they sound like...noticing their mannerisms...perhaps noticing things about them that I would never know...noticing things about them that lets you know they are so wise...and noticing that they can guide you into hypnosis and noticing how they can guide you on other matters as well...and you can notice where it is *you are meeting that guide*...what this place looks like...what this place sounds like...as you *drift deeper into hypnosis* engaging with this guide...and I don't know whether they will guide you *deeper into hypnosis* with words that they say as you talk with them...or whether they will guide you deeper in some other way...and the role of this guide is to help you...to support you...and as you *drift even deeper into hypnosis*, you can find yourself resting down into the most comfortable chair...closing your eyes...and floating deeper into hypnosis...

## Crystal ball induction

(Pause for 20 seconds) With your eyes closed, you can place your hands palm up with one hand on each leg...and imagine a crystal ball off in the distance...and the crystal ball is floating in the air...and you can notice that crystal ball floating closer and closer and be aware of swirling colours within that crystal ball as it gets closer to you...and as that crystal ball reaches you, it can settle down into one hand or the other...and I don't know if that crystal ball is heavy or light, if it is glowing or not...and you can gaze into that crystal ball...and as you gaze into that crystal ball, you can begin to notice something wonderful...you can begin to notice something relaxing...you can begin to find yourself drawn into that crystal ball...and the more you pay attention to that crystal ball the *deeper absorbed in hypnosis* you can become...and the *deeper absorbed in hypnosis* you become, the deeper you can become absorbed into that crystal ball...and you can start to create deep change while absorbed in the crystal ball...and as you drift back out of that crystal ball you can notice that another crystal ball settles in the other hand...you can compare the balls and look deeply into the balls...seeing pleasant memories and experiences of the past...present...and future in the crystal balls...and you can become absorbed in the experiences in the crystal balls...and then you can watch as those crystal balls drift up out of those hands and as they do, so you can *drift deeper into hypnosis* and find yourself settling down in the most comfortable chair, floating and drifting deeper into hypnosis...

## Corridor of doors induction

(Pause for 20 seconds) With your eyes closed, you can imagine opening a door and finding yourself in a long corridor and you will always instinctively know your way around...you just may not always know you know it…and you can see hundreds of doors off to the left and the right of the corridor…and you can walk down the corridor…and each door can be associated with something pleasant, whether it is a pleasant feeling or image…and as you walk through a door you can feel a wave of relaxation and pleasant feeling passing through you…and find yourself in another corridor…and notice what this corridor of doors looks like…and you can choose a door…pass through it…and go *deeper and deeper into hypnosis*, feeling a deeper wave of relaxation…and finding yourself in another corridor of doors…and you can select a door in that corridor…walking into the corridor…finding yourself going *deeper into hypnosis*…walking down another corridor of doors…choosing a door…opening the door and finding yourself in another corridor walking *deeper into hypnosis*…and once you are deeply in hypnosis…you open a door in a corridor and find yourself in a pleasant location and find the most comfortable seat…you notice what this place looks like, what sounds you can hear here, what it feels like to walk to that seat…you can walk to that seat, settle down into the seat and drift comfortably deeper into hypnosis…

## Go to the north star induction

(Pause for 20 seconds) (Show a time-lapse image of stars around the north star) As you gently open your eyes (if they have their eyes closed at this point)...I would like to have you gaze at this image, look at the north star...and as you gaze at the north star, you can begin to get a sense of going to that north star...being drawn into the image...drawn into space...drawn to that north star...with all the other stars swirling around you...almost like a tunnel...like a vortex with all other stars circling around you...finding yourself drawn into space...where there is no up, no down, no left, no right, no sound, just being...as you let your eyes close and *continue drifting deeper*...drifting...floating in peace...in silence...in space...perhaps aware of colours...of the stars and nebulae...and as you continue drifting and floating comfortably and deeply into the experience...you can begin to find yourself approaching the most comfortable seat, relaxing down into that seat, closing your eyes and *drifting deeper and deeper into hypnosis*...

## That's right induction

(Pause for 20 seconds)…That's right…that's it…that's it…(said on blinks, on outbreaths, on subtle head nods, on relaxing facial muscles and other non-conscious behaviours and signs of hypnosis).

Then near the end of the induction saying things like: that's it…all the way…deeper and deeper…and as you continue to *drift deeper into hypnosis*…you can find yourself relaxing down into the most comfortable chair…closing your eyes…and *drifting deeply into hypnosis*…

## Hypnotist describing themselves entering hypnosis induction

This is a classic technique and is similar to the *My Friend John Technique*. You describe to the client how someone goes into hypnosis, but you describe it as if you are describing how you would go into hypnosis. What you are doing is a mix of describing what you see happening with the client, with ideas of what people often experience to encourage further deepening of hypnosis in the client.

For example you may say 'when I *go into hypnosis*, I *sit comfortably*, I *breathe in and out* (said in time with the client's breathing), and I normally start to *defocus the eyes* a little bit...and as I *start to drift off into hypnosis*...I find I spend more time inside my mind...I hear the odd noise outside...but it doesn't matter because my attention is drawn inward...as I *drift deeper into hypnosis*...and I may *close the eyes* as I *drift deeper into hypnosis...*'

You use various hypnotic language patterns, like linking suggestions and embedded commands and watch the client closely to see how they are responding to what you are suggesting and once you notice that they are deeply focused you can then progress on to any trance work.

Then you can follow the induction up with describing something like: and as you *continue to drift deeper into hypnosis*, you can imagine yourself relaxing into the most comfortable chair and closing your eyes...

## Pacing and leading breathing induction

There are very few words to this induction. To do this induction, sit with the client, pay them your full attention, match their breathing pattern with your breathing, initially breathe the same as the client, after a while the client will be following your breathing, so you can lead their breathing. At this point start to defocus your eyes, start to relax, relaxing your shoulders and breathing, deepening and slowing down your breathing. The client is likely to continue to follow along to this and also deepen their breathing and become increasingly internally focused. I often suggest eye closure non-verbally by matching the client's blinking at this point as well and then extending my blinks so that my eyes are shut for a little longer than a blink and doing some extended blinks that the client can see, but often is consciously unaware of, this gives the idea of eye closure. After the client closes their eyes you can move on to whatever trance work you will be doing.

When I often use this approach is while the client is talking to me. As they are talking I will defocus my eyes, smooth my facial muscles, match their breathing and begin to guide myself into hypnosis. This is a very indirect or covert way of hypnotising someone, they just continue to talk to you uninterrupted unaware that you are hypnotising them while they talk. Then when you talk with them they may drift back from hypnosis a little bit while you aren't hypnotising them in this way, then when they talk again you continue to breathe them further into hypnosis, and this works like fractionation, where you have someone go in and out of hypnosis repeatedly and each time they go into hypnosis they find it quicker and easier than before. Doing it this way, some people will just spontaneously close their eyes and stop talking, others will feel like doing this but as they haven't been given explicit permission that this is acceptable they don't, but when you get to the hypnosis and suggest 'okay, take a moment to close your eyes' they are already hypnotised and readily close their eyes and drift deeper into hypnosis.

If you are doing this induction following on from an induction introduction then you can ask the client to open their eyes a moment and talk to them a while gently as you do this induction before having them close their eyes again, or with their eyes closed you can do this induction and just add a little bit of noise to your breathing so that the client can hear the emphasis you give to your breathing, like doing pronounced out-breaths. Then at the end you can transition into saying something like: and you can imagine yourself relaxing into the most comfortable chair, closing your eyes, and *drifting deeper and deeper into hypnosis…*

## My friend John induction

The *My Friend John* induction is about describing what the client is doing and their ongoing experience using embedded suggestions within an ongoing description of a hypothetical person called John (you can obviously give the hypothetical person any name, or not mention a name of the person and perhaps refer to them as 'a client came in the other day…'. If the client has their eyes closed, you could ask them to open their eyes a moment, or just talk to them with their eyes closed.

You may say something like 'Someone asked me how…*you go into hypnosis*…and I told them that the way for…*you go into hypnosis*… is that you start to listen to me talking…and…*you breathe in that calm and comfortable way*…and you just want to…*drift off*…because you know it is *such a pleasant feeling…such a relaxing feeling…*and…you just want to…*go with that feeling…*and…*your eyes begin to blink…*and…*begin to shut…*and you just want to…*drift off into hypnosis…*'

You would do this as much or as little as is necessary for the client, following your ongoing observations of them until they appear hypnotised, perhaps with their eyes closed and showing signs of relaxation and responsivity, then you can move on to something like: and you can imagine yourself relaxing into the most comfortable chair, closing your eyes, and deeply and pleasantly into hypnosis…

## Focusing resistance induction

(Pause for 20 seconds) What I want you to do is to not respond too quickly, really do your best to go as long as you can, not responding to what I say…that's it (say that's it at times you see them responding, like on outbreaths, eye movements, twitches, etc)…and don't *go into hypnosis* too quickly…just relax and keep focused on doing your best for now to keep from going too quickly into hypnosis...and I don't know which hand has the most tension in it...and you can notice which hand that is...whether the left hand left right there has more tension than the right hand left right over there...and don't let that tension go just yet...it is helpful to keep a little tension there as you *continue to drift deeper into hypnosis*, but don't *drift deeply into hypnosis* too quickly, you can focus on that tension and on not *letting go* too quickly...as you continue to relax and *drift deeper into hypnosis*...and you can *drift all the way into hypnosis* at your own rate and speed...not at my rate and speed...entering hypnosis in your own way...and you don't have to *go deeper* too quickly with each outbreath...and after a few moments you can begin to find yourself settling down in the most comfortable chair, closing your eyes and drifting deeply and more relaxed into hypnosis...

## Non-verbal induction

There are no words for this induction and it is done starting with the client's eyes open. Reach over and pick up the client's hand gently just above the wrist (you may say that you are going to lift up their arm, just to inform them of your actions, but if the situation is appropriate to do so, you can do this without informing the client that you are about to do this, it works not saying anything, you might just ask if it is okay to hypnotise them if this is a preferred thing to state), look at the client, defocus your eyes, match the client's breathing, as the client breathes in, lift their arm, as they breathe out, lower their arm, when they blink, lower their arm in time with the blinking (like a quick jolt down of the arm), after a short period of time, begin to lead the client, deepen and slow down your breathing, defocus your eyes, relax your shoulders, when the client breathes out and you lower their arm, lower it a bit further and for a bit longer to guide their breathing to be a bit deeper and longer, when you lower their arm in time with their blinking, lower it a bit further and for a bit longer to communicate eye closure. If you want, you can also do smaller movements with the arm in time with the heart rate and can do the same with this, once matched, you can then start to slow the movement to begin to slow the heart rate, so if you do all of this, you are moving the arm in time with the breathing, blinking and heart rate and then leading these rhythms with the movement, as well as communicating through your other non-verbal behaviour, like matching and then leading breathing and blinking and doing behaviours like relaxing your body and face and defocusing your eyes. This induction can take a lot of practice to get used to the close observation of the client and to doing all of this simultaneously.

Following the induction, you can say something like: and you can find yourself approaching a comfortable chair...relaxing down in that chair...closing your eyes...and going all the way deeply and comfortably into hypnosis...

## Breathing in and out induction

(Pause for 20 seconds) And breathe in...and out...that's it, *deeper and deeper*...breathe in...and out...*going deeper and deeper*...that's it...*going deeper and deeper* (said on the outbreath)...that's it...breathing in...and out...that's it...*going deeper and deeper*...breathing in...and out...*all the way into hypnosis*...that's it...and as you continue to *go deeper into hypnosis* with each outbreath...you can begin to find yourself approaching the most comfortable chair...relaxing down in that chair...closing your eyes...and drifting deeply and relaxed into hypnosis...

## Fantasy world induction

(Pause for 20 seconds) And as you continue to *drift deeper into hypnosis* you can find yourself in a fantasy land...and you can have a sense of looking at yourself, seeing what type of armour and clothes you are wearing...what the ground looks like beneath your feet, what the sky looks like...you can be curious what sounds you can hear around you as you notice dragons off in the distance, seeing them flying, and circling in the sky...and you can go and explore this land, finding your way to the dragons...finding yourself following a path...as you get closer to the dragons flying in the sky, you can begin to hear the sound of the beating wings of the dragons...and you can mount a horse to travel quicker across the land, noticing the way the horse moves...the sounds of the horses hooves with each step it takes...the feeling of the horse beneath you...the feeling of the reigns in your hands and the breeze on your face...and I wonder whether you can notice the sounds of rustling of the trees or the way light can dance as it passes through the branches...and the open areas with views over vast vista's...and as you travel out into an open meadow...while *going deeper* into the journey...you notice the most graceful dragon circling overhead...and as it notices you, it begins to lower down and lands a short distance from you...and as it lands you can hear a thud and feel a slight rumble through the ground...and an outburst of breath...The dragon lowers its neck...and turns to look over at you...and you dismount the horse and walk over to the dragon...you climb onto the dragon's back...with a burst of energy...the dragon launches itself up into the air...you feel the wind in your face as the dragon flies you to a castle on a cliff...the dragon lands on a keep...lowers its head for you to dismount...standing at the open wooden door to the keep, you see a knight...the knight calls you over and tells you they need your help...you follow the knight into the castle, descending echoing stone steps down to a long corridor...looking in one room off the corridor you notice a nursery of baby dragons...the knight talks to you about the help they need you for and the quest they need you to go on (you can create a quest that would work as a therapeutic metaphor for the client's problem while also absorbing the client deeper into the experience, here is an example therapeutic quest)...they walk you to a room...you sit at a round table with other knights who praise you for your skills at sneaking into and out of places unseen and having patience and an ability to understand things in ways others don't...they tell you that there is a monster in the cave near the castle and that monster sounds like it is getting larger, louder and scarier...you are told that every knight so far has been too scared to fully explore the cave to find and tackle the monster...the deeper they go into the cave, the louder and scarier the monster gets and they haven't been able to find it, they flee with fear...you take on the quest...head out of the castle and trek to the cave...as you approach the cave, you can hear the monster growling...you think about what the monster could be, but unlike other knights in the past, you don't make judgement about what it is until you have evidence...to prove or disprove what you think it may be...you walk into the cave, heading *deeper and deeper* into the cave...you can hear the occasional dripping of water in the cave and see the way the flame from your torch makes shadows dance on the walls...and the sound of that flame flickering as a breeze occasionally blows into the cave, and the smell of the torch...the sound of the monster gets louder...as *you go deeper*...then you find yourself in a chamber...the growling sounds like it is in this chamber...you look around, but can't see the monster...you close your eyes as you walk around, just following your hearing to try to pinpoint where the monster is...you feel like you are close to the monster...you open your eyes and see a small hole in the floor...you look through that hole and see a dragon trapped in the cavern below...you take a heavy hammer off of your back and smash through to the cavern below...you lower down a rope, descend the rope and see that the route that this dragon took into the cavern has become blocked...and the dragon has been injured and is becoming weak...you help fix up the dragon's injuries...give the dragon something to eat and drink...and then work tirelessly to help to clear the blocked entrance...after a long time of trying to clear the entrance, you start to feel like it is too much of a task for you…that you may just give up, but then you notice a beam of light shine into the cavern through a crack in the blockage…this gives you hope and motivation to keep going…after a lot of hard work, you manage to get the blockage clear enough for the dragon to fit through, the dragon leaves the cavern…outside the cavern, the dragon rubs its head against you as if to communicate its thanks, before flying off home…you are curious about whether you will see the dragon again and are glad you could help…you head back to the castle, explain what happened before sitting down in the most comfortable seat to rest and relax…closing your eyes…and drifting deeply and comfortably into hypnosis…

## Sitting under a tree induction

(Pause for 20 seconds) Imagine yourself sat underneath a tree…and I don't know where that tree is, whether it is in a meadow or next to a stream…and as you rest back against that tree, you can feel the bark of the tree against your back…and you can look out from being sat under that tree, while hearing the sound of rustling leaves above you as the breeze blows…and noticing the silence of the leaves between the breeze…and looking up at the sky and noticing whether there are any clouds in the sky…and as you *drift deeper* and *become more absorbed* in the experience…you can notice what the ground feels like beneath you…and as you continue to rest there under that tree…you begin to read a book…slowly reading and turning the pages of that book…and hearing the sounds around you…perhaps the sounds of birds…the sounds of the rustling leaves…the feeling of the breeze on your face…maybe noticing the warmth of the sun on your face…as you continue to *drift deeper into the experience*…and as you continue to read that book…so you notice your eyes begin to want to close…and so you close the book and then close your eyes…and as you close your eyes…so you find yourself walking towards the most comfortable chair…you settle down into that chair…close your eyes…and begin to drift deeply into hypnosis…drifting deeper into hypnosis with each breath that you take…

## Secret garden induction

(Pause for 20 seconds) And as you continue to *relax and drift deeper into the experience*...you can discover that you are stood at the top of a beautiful garden...you can look out over that garden...and notice the steps down into the garden and the path weaving through the garden to the back of the garden...you can hear sounds in the garden...the sounds of birds in the trees...the rustling leaves...noticing the smells of different flowers...the movement of butterflies and bees as they fly from flower to flower...and the feeling of a slight breeze...and I wonder whether there are any clouds in the sky...and you can begin to walk down the steps as I count from 10 down to 1...and on the count of one...you can find yourself at the bottom of those steps on the path in the garden...10...9...continuing down those steps...8...7...6...walking...all the way...*deeper and deeper*...down the steps...5...4...3...that's it...and I wonder what each step sounds like...2...1...as you walk onto that path in this garden...and as you gently walk through the garden you can notice the sounds of your footsteps...notice what each step feels like...notice the flowers and walk towards the tall hedge at the back of the garden...while you walk...you can notice the different colours of the flowers...the different smells as you walk past those flowers...and when you reach the hedge at the back of the garden...you can run your hand gently along the hedge...and as you run your hand along that hedge...you can notice a small branch sticking slightly out from the hedge...and as you touch that small branch...you can notice how it opens a secret entrance through the hedge into a secret garden...and with curiosity you can step through that entrance and notice how that secret entrance closes behind you...and you discover yourself in this secret garden...the most relaxing secret garden...a garden where you can drift...dream...and wonder...and you find a bench in this garden...you relax down onto that bench...close your eyes...and *relax deeper into the experience*...and as you *relax deeper into the experience*...you get a sense of noticing the most comfortable chair...you relax down into that chair...close your eyes and *drift even deeper into hypnosis*...

## Lost world induction

(Pause for 20 seconds) As you continue to…*become more comfortable*…you can begin to get a sense of being on a canoe or a small boat…heading down a river in a jungle…and as you continue to row along this river you can hear the sounds of the rowing…pushing through the water…the sounds of birds and other animals in the jungle…the sound of the water against the boat…and you can notice what the weather is like…what the sky looks like…the jungle colours around you…as you continue your journey…and you can have a sense of curiosity and excitement about the journey you are on…in your search for a lost world…and you continue down the river…placing an oar in the water…pushing that water back…feeling the weight of the water as the oar pushes that water back…the sound of the oar entering the water…the feeling of pushing that water back…noticing the waves lapping over on the shore…and the light on the surface of the water…and after travelling down the river…you find where you are going ashore…you row up onto the shore…the sound of the boat sliding up onto the shore…getting out of the boat...dragging it the rest of the way up onto the shore...leaving the boat to continue your journey on foot...hacking through the jungle...pushing through the dense jungle...curious about what you will discover...and after a while you begin to notice that among the trees are what looks like ancient ruins...looks like the trees and plant-life have been reclaiming this land and growing over and through these ruins...as you continue to hack *deeper and deeper* through the jungle...you notice the jungle thinning out and discover a clearing...and in the clearing, you see the ruins of ancient temples and other buildings and statues...you notice that one of the temples appears to be glistening and shining and made of gold...you head to that temple...push the heavy door open...and enter the temple...and as you enter the temple, you discover something incredible...you follow the steps down deeper into and under the temple...and you notice as you pass through another door that it looks like you have just walked outside, yet you know that you are underground...you notice that there is a whole civilisation down here...and that this looks like forest and farmland and the ceiling is aglow as bright as daylight...and you begin to explore this lost world...you interact with the friendly people down here...you learn knowledge and wisdom from them...you are guided to a building where you see the most comfortable seat...you sit down in that seat...close your eyes...drift deeply relaxed...and discover yourself entering the most profound and pleasant experience of hypnosis...

## The curious rabbit hole induction

(Pause for 20 seconds) As you walk through the countryside you notice a rabbit hole...and there is something unusual about this rabbit hole...the closer you walk towards the rabbit hole the smaller you become...and the smaller you become the more curious you get...and as you get closer to that rabbit hole...you notice the grass seeming to be larger and larger around you...the plants and trees all seeming to get bigger and bigger...and as you reach that rabbit hole...you discover that you have become about the size of a rabbit...and you walk into the rabbit hole wondering why you have ended up reaching this size...what it is about this rabbit hole which has led to you shrinking down to the size of a rabbit...and as you walk into the rabbit hole you notice that it is dark in the rabbit hole...you can look back and see the light behind you...and you continue to walk *deeper and deeper* into the rabbit hole...and you can feel each footstep in the mud...and deep in the rabbit hole you discover a wooden door...you feel around the door...and you find the door handle...you slowly open the door and notice light from behind the door flood into the rabbit hole...and as your eyes adjust to the light...you discover yourself on a smooth stone floor...almost like pure white marble...you notice smooth stone walls and a smooth stone ceiling that just seems to glow...and in the middle of the room is a table and on that table is a bottle that says 'drink me' and without giving it any thought, you drink the drink and as you do...you begin to shrink...and as you shrink, smaller and smaller, you notice that there is a small door...you walk through that door and find yourself in an unusual land...and although you have shrunk...in this land, you don't notice because everything around you is in proportion to your size...and you walk through this land...walking among trees...hearing unfamiliar yet beautiful sounds of animals and birds...and then walking out into the most wonderful meadow...noticing grass and flowers...feeling a sense of wonder and curiosity about this place...interested to explore this land further...and as you walk through the meadow, you discover what looks like the most comfortable chair...you head over to that chair...relax down in the chair...close your eyes...and drift deeply and comfortably into hypnosis...

## Sitting by a stream induction

(Pause for 20 seconds) Imagine yourself sat on the edge of a stream...and I don't know whether you will be sat under a tree...or sat with your feet resting in the stream...and you can rest your feet in the water...and you can be aware of the feeling of the water around your feet...you can be aware of where you are sitting...aware of the sound of the water bubbling past...noticing the waves of the stream...noticing sticks and leaves occasionally floating past down the stream...and perhaps noticing that the air smells fresher here by the stream...and as you *continue to relax* deeper into the experience…you can *feel so comfortable* and relaxed as you hear birds and animals in the countryside…perhaps in nearby woodland…and the warmth of the sun on your face and the feeling of the breeze on your face…and I don't know whether you will decide to lie back and relax on the ground beside the stream, or just sit with your feet resting in the water…and as you relax…so your mind can begin to wander…and as your mind begins to wander…you can discover yourself approaching the most comfortable seat…and you can sit down in that seat…and as you *relax deeply* into the seat…so you can close your eyes and begin to drift and float *deeper and deeper into hypnosis*…

## Room of nothingness induction

(Pause for 20 seconds) Imagine walking towards a building…and as you walk towards this building…you see a door in front of you…and you can reach out to open the door…and as you open the door…you can *begin to relax*…and as you relax…you can step in through that door…to the first room…and in this room you can...begin to let go...of tension...of stress...and as you leave all that behind...you can walk across the room to another door across the other side of this room...and when you reach that door...you can open that door...and step through that door...and *go even deeper into hypnosis*...and the third door will be a room of nothingness...and as you *drift deeper into hypnosis*...you can walk across this room...going *deeper and deeper into hypnosis*...more relaxed into hypnosis...almost like each step is taken gently and slowly and with a level of intent as you *deepen your experience*...and as you reach that door...you can open that door...and step into the room...into this room of nothingness...this room where there is no sound...no time...no up...nor down...no left or right...nothing to see...just a peaceful sense of nothingness...just floating and drifting...*deepening your experience...drifting deeper and deeper into hypnosis*...and as you continue to *drift deeper* you can begin to get a sense of the most comfortable chair...you can relax down into that chair...close your eyes...and *drift even more comfortably into hypnosis* with each breath that you take...

## World's most comfortable chair induction

(Pause for 20 seconds) Imagine sitting in the world's most comfortable chair...imagine how your head and neck are supported by the chair...how you seem to so comfortably sink deeply into the chair...how that chair offers the perfect support for your head, neck and back...what it feels like to *relax down into that chair*...with the comfort of those legs...arms...and bum...so relaxed in that chair...with that chair supporting your body so well that you almost feel weightless resting in that chair...*deeper and deeper*...scanning through your body...noticing how each part of *your body feels so comfortable*...and as your body relaxes...noticing how that relaxation and comfort makes your mind want to drift and wonder and dream...and your eyes gently close as you become deeper absorbed in the experience...and find your mind drifting and dreaming as you *go deeper and deeper into hypnosis...*

## Another Earth induction

(Pause for 20 seconds) And with your eyes closed, just allow yourself to listen along to my voice, and as you listen along to my voice, you can continue to relax and *drift deeper into hypnosis.* and you can get a sense of lying down one night in a meadow...feeling the grass under your head...under your neck...under your hands...and maybe you can notice the temperature of that grass or the movement of the grass and how it can tickle the palms of your hands or your fingertips as you move your hands around over that grass...and perhaps you can notices sounds around you in the meadow...and as you lie there in that meadow...you can have a sense of gazing up at the nights sky...seeing the twinkling stars, seeing the milky way stretched across the sky...maybe seeing the occasional shooting star...and as you gaze up into the sky you can begin to wonder what it would be like if you were on another planet...wondering whether there could be another planet out there like Earth and what it would be like to be able to send your consciousness out into space to that other planet, so that you find yourself looking up at the night sky, at a different view of the sky, wondering whether there could be someone out there gazing up at the night sky, wondering whether there could be anyone out there lying down looking up at the night sky…and as you do this you can *drift deeper into hypnosis* as you notice what is different about this night sky…looking for a star you imagine might be the sun with a planet called Earth circling that star with someone on that planet looking up into the sky at the stars in their night sky…and you can continue to drift deeper as you begin to have a sense of being back in that you lying down in the meadow at night on Earth, standing up and slowly and relaxed…walking around and finding the most comfortable chair, relaxing down into that chair, closing your eyes and drifting comfortably and deeply into hypnosis…

## Diving induction

(Pause for 20 seconds) Have a sense of being out on a calm ocean on a nice warm sunny day…on a boat floating on the crystal clear blue water…and have a sense of putting on your scuba gear...putting the air tank on your back...pulling the goggles down over your eyes...the weight of the tank on your back...the feeling of the scuba gear...the slight movement of the boat...as you move to the side of the boat...sit on the side of the boat with your back to the water and flopping backwards into the water...feeling the splash into the water...noticing the water around your body...and once in the water, beginning that descent down under the water...noticing as your head goes underwater...the sounds of the bubbles with each outbreath...noticing the shimmering sunlight dancing through the water...the fish swimming...the changing blues...and how time seems to slow down underwater...and as you comfortably continue to descend...*deeper and deeper* underwater...you can notice a shipwreck down in the most beautiful white sand on the sea floor... continuing your descent towards that shipwreck...and the closer you get, the more you notice fish swimming among the wreck...waving seaweed...dancing light from the surface...in this clear, blue, water...you can see twinkling and sparkling coming from the ship and you notice that there is treasure in the wreck...you reach and explore the shipwreck…touching the wooden wreck…watching the fish slowly swimming through the wreck…discovering that treasure…and after your dive…you head back to the surface…and back on the boat…*you relax back*…drifting into a daydream about the experience…almost being rocked gently into that daydream by the movement of the boat on the sea…and in that daydream…you have a sense of the most comfortable chair…you relax down into that chair…close your eyes…and *drift deeper into hypnosis*…


## Sunset induction

(Pause for 20 seconds) And you can find yourself sat somewhere watching and enjoying a sunset…and I don't know where you are…whether you are on a beach…in a park…in a meadow…or somewhere completely different…and you can notice the circle of the sun…so slowly…so calmly…moving towards the horizon…and as the sun moves closer to the horizon…you can notice how the colour of the sky changes…from blues…to oranges…reds…and yellows…and you can notice that the sky opposite the sun is becoming darker blue as the sun continues to set...and you can notice the point where the sun touches the horizon...perhaps noticing the horizon seem to reach up to touch the sun...and as the sun passes down behind the horizon...you can see the stars appearing in the sky...and perhaps notice some rays from the sun illuminating distant clouds...perhaps clouds high in the sky...and you can continue to watch that sun set...becoming *deeper absorbed in hypnosis* as the light from the sun continues to fade...noticing the sky darkening and relaxing and the blanket of stars revealing itself overhead...and as the suns light fades...so you *drift deeper and more relaxed*...and your eyelids can lower...as the sun lowers...and you can find yourself *drifting in your mind*...having a sense of the most comfortable chair...approaching that chair...sitting down deeply into that chair...closing your eyes...and *drifting and floating peacefully into hypnosis*...

## Beautiful place induction

(Pause for 20 seconds) Imagine that you are walking through an awe inspiring beautiful place...and I don't know whether it will be a valley of plants and animals...perhaps with trees around it...with the sounds of birds...or whether it will be a meadow...with soft flowing grass...butterflies...the most beautiful and relaxing sounds...whether it will be a beach with the sounds of the waves...the smell of the sea air...I don't know what the weather is like for you...whether it is sunny...noticing the warmth of that sun on your face...and you can *drift deeper into the experience* of that beautiful place...and notice what you can see...what you can feel...what you can hear...as you relax in this beautiful place...and you can...enjoy relaxing in this beautiful place...and you can look around and wonder what makes this place so beautiful...and absorb yourself in this place...you can walk around...explore...hear your footsteps...touch different things in this place...noticing what they feel like...going *deeper and deeper into hypnosis* as you continue to explore...before settling down somewhere in this place...closing your eyes...while listening to the sounds...and perhaps noticing the temperature of the air on your skin...as you imagine the most comfortable chair...and relax down into that chair...closing your eyes...and *drifting peacefully and pleasantly relaxed into hypnosis...*

## Log cabin induction

(Pause for 20 seconds) Imagine yourself in a meadow...and as you explore the meadow...you can discover a log cabin...and as you begin to walk towards the log cabin...you can discover what each footstep feels like...what each footstep sounds like...what the meadow looks like...what you can notice in the meadow...what the sky looks like...and as you get closer to the log cabin you can see what the outside of it looks like...what the windows look like...the roof...the walls...and as you reach the cabin...you can open the door...hearing the sound of that door as it opens...as you step inside the cabin...feeling the warmth of the cabin...noticing a crackling, glowing log fire in the fireplace...perhaps feeling comforted by the gentle glow of the light in the cabin...and you can sit down in a comfortable seat by the fire...and as evening approaches, you can see the way shadows dance around the walls and notice that it has started to snow outside the cabin...you can see ice beginning to form on the outside of the windows...you can approach a window and rest your hand gently on the glass...feeling that coolness spreading from that glass into your hand...spreading comfort through that hand and into your body...before you sit back down into that seat...feeling like it is the most comfortable chair...relaxing deeper into the experience...closing your eyes...and drifting and floating deeply into hypnosis...

## Step into the TV induction

(Pause for 20 seconds) Take a moment to have a sense of sitting in front of a TV...and as you sit in front of that TV, you can notice where that TV is...what is around that TV...what the room looks like...what the TV looks like...what size the TV is...and you can turn that TV on and find a holiday programme on that TV which is exploring somewhere you would like to visit...and as you watch that TV and see what that place looks like on the TV...you can stand up, walk to the TV and as you touch the TV screen...you can find that your hand begins to pass through the screen...and after your hand passes through the TV you follow your hand by stepping into the TV...finding yourself in that place on the TV...discovering the sights...the sounds...what it feels like to be there...and you know you can play different things on the TV and step into different experiences in the future...and in this place you can look around you...and as you look behind you...you see the TV behind you...and you walk around and discover the most comfortable chair...you relax down into that chair...close your eyes...and drift even deeper into hypnosis...

## Sitting on a train induction

(Pause for 20 seconds) Imagine that you are stood on a railway platform waiting for a train to arrive...and you can look down the track and see a train getting closer to the platform…you notice how it starts to break and slow down as it approaches the platform…as it stops at the platform, you can board the train…feeling the way it gently starts moving again…you can find a seat and look out of the window as the scenery outside the train starts to pass you by…and as you see that scenery passing by you can hear the clickity-clack of the train on the track in a rhythmic and relaxed way…and *relax back into the seat* gazing out of the window at the fields passing by outside the train…watching birds flying in the sky…noticing what the sky looks like…trees and bushes rushing past the window…the way sun shines in the window and dances through trees and buildings the train passes…and as you follow along to the rhythmic sounds and the rhythmic feel of the train moving on the track…your eyes can begin to close as *you relax deeper*…you occasionally hear announcements on the train as you get deeper into your journey…and while you continue to *relax deeper* and become more *absorbed in the experience* with the sounds around you…with the movement…with each breath you take…you start to become aware of walking towards the most comfortable chair…you sit down deeply in that chair...close your eyes...and drift deeply and comfortably into hypnosis...

## Watching clouds induction

(Pause for 20 seconds) Begin to have a sense of lying down on the ground...perhaps under a tree...or resting against a tree...or maybe lying down...relaxing...in a meadow...or maybe even on a bench...just resting somewhere you can see clouds passing by overhead...and as you look up at the sky...watching the clouds...you can be aware of the colour of the sky...notice the texture of the clouds...the colour of the clouds...and noticing how the clouds are moving across the sky...you can be aware of any movement within the clouds...and perhaps you can notice clouds at different heights in the sky and how they look different and perhaps move different...maybe moving in different directions or different speeds...and you can see the way the sun illuminates the clouds differently depending on their height and composition...and as you watch those clouds drifting overhead...you can find yourself *drifting deeper into the experience*…and perhaps you can see rainbow colours in some of the highest clouds…while lower clouds may look soft and comfortable…and as you *drift deeper into the experience*…you can have a sense that while watching the clouds pass by…your eyes begin to shut…and as your eyes shut you have a sense of discovering the most comfortable chair…you relax down into that comfortable chair…close your eyes…and *drift even deeper into hypnosis*…

## Rocket launch into space induction

(Pause for 20 seconds) Imagine that you are sat at the top of a rocket prepared for launch…and you are looking up at the controls in front of you…you can notice all of the switches…buttons…and flashing lights around you…and you can look beside you out of the small windows…and because you are so high up off the ground at the top of this rocket, all you can see is the clear, blue sky…and you can hear ground control beginning to count down…they have done all of the checks and are now counting down for launch… 10… 9… 8… 7… 6…

5...4...the boosters ignite...you can hear a slight rumble and begin to feel that slight rumble...3...2...1...and on the count of one the rocket begins to launch...begins to lift off...and the whole rocket begins to vibrate and shake and you notice the weight of your body as that rocket starts to rise up into the air...and you can hear that rumbling...but then quickly things become quieter for you as the rocket passes the speed of sound and the sound of the exhaust can't catch up with the rocket...and can't reach your ears...and you feel yourself getting heavier and heavier...and after a short period of time...you look through the window...and can see the curvature of the Earth...as the rocket turns to circle the Earth you glimpse more of the planet below...as you reach space and everything goes quiet...and you feel a sense of weightlessness and deep relaxation set in...as you look down on the Earth below...noticing the clouds...the land...the oceans...then passing around the Earth and noticing the lights of cities and flashes of storms...and then the bright sunlight peering out from behind the Earth as you continue circling round the planet and into the daylight side...you can notice the aurora at the poles and familiar stars and the moon from a whole new perspective...and when it comes time to settle down to sleep...you strap yourself in to where you will be sleeping...and feeling weightless...you begin to drift off deeply asleep...and as you do...so you discover yourself approaching the most comfortable chair...you relax down into that chair...feeling weightless...closing your eyes...and drifting and floating...deeply into hypnosis...

## Climbing a mountain induction

(Pause for 20 seconds) And you can have a sense that you are walking towards a mountain...and you follow a path up the mountain...and sometimes the climb up the mountain is hard work...other times the climb is easier...and you continue to climb that mountain...and you can feel what each footstep feels like...hear what each footstep sounds like...and you can *drift deeper and deeper into hypnosis* with each step up the mountain...and as you continue to climb, you can occasionally stop...take a break...*relax*...and take a look back at how far you have come...and as you reach the top of the mountain...you can gaze out over where you came from...out over your whole journey...noticing perhaps how the air up here is a bit colder...maybe noticing some clouds are lower than you...or on the same level as you...what the sky looks like...perhaps noticing the warmth of the sun on your face...and maybe comparing the difference between the warmth of the sun to the coolness of the air...and you can have a sense of the success of completing this journey...and while you *take time to relax* up here...you can close your eyes...to *deeply absorb yourself in the moment...drifting deeper inside your mind*...as you begin to notice a comfortable chair in your mind...walking over to that chair...relaxing down into that chair...closing your eyes...and drifting and relaxing...peacefully...into hypnosis...

## Campfire induction

(Pause for 20 seconds) And you can have a sense of camping in a tent, out in a meadow...and the sun is setting...and as the sun sets, so you light a campfire...and as you light that campfire...you can see the way the light flickers and dances...the way the flames move...the warmth and the sound of that fire...and the comfortable glow...you can hear the sounds of night-time animals around you...while the last of the sun fades away...so you can *relax deeper* into the night...and as *you relax* and enjoy the gentle warmth of the campfire, you can notice how your mind calms and relaxes...and sitting in the entrance to the tent...you watch that campfire burn down to glowing embers...and when the time is right...you back into your tent...close up the tent...hear the sound of the sides of the tent move gently in the breeze...and *feel a deep sense of relaxation* as you close your eyes and begin to drift asleep...and as you drift asleep, you notice the most comfortable chair...you approach that chair...*relax deeper and deeper* down into that chair...*going comfortably and deeply into hypnosis*...closing your eyes...and drifting so pleasantly into hypnosis...

## Hands stuck together shock induction

Take a moment to open your eyes (if the client's eyes are closed)...put your hands out in front of you interlocking your fingers (demonstrate what you mean)…and look at those hands…push those hands *tighter and tighter* together…*stick those hands tighter and tighter together*, pushing those hands tighter and tighter…and sleep (reaching over and pushing the hands down to the client's lap at the same time a saying 'sleep')…

That's it…and as…*you drift deeper asleep*…you can get a sense of relaxing down into the most comfortable chair…*closing your eyes*…and *drifting even deeper into hypnosis*…

## Push down on my hand shock induction

(If the client's eyes are closed, ask them to open their eyes. Put your hand out, palm up, in front of you about waist-height. You can explain to the client beforehand what will be expected of them, explaining that 'in a moment I would like you to push down on my hand as hard as you can and when I say 'sleep' you can close your eyes, let your body relax and drift deeper into hypnosis'. By explaining the induction, this can help the client to follow along better and know how they are expected to respond. I often do the induction without this introduction, but it can be helpful and can increase the effectiveness of the induction)

Put your hand (choose the hand opposite the hand you have put out. So if you have put out your left hand the client will put their right hand on your hand) on my hand…palm facing down…look at the back of that hand (you look at the back of their hand as you say this)…that's right…and begin to push down on my hand…push harder and harder, keep pushing…harder and harder, keep pushing, harder and harder…that's right…(when you see that the client goes inside their mind often with confusion or to tell themselves that they can't push harder, you then say)…and close your eyes, and sleep…(As you say 'sleep' you pull your hand from under the client's hand which adds to the experience for the client of dropping deeper into hypnosis. I like to click my fingers as well for added emphasis as I say 'sleep', you also want to say 'sleep' as a command with an authoritative tone of voice. To notice someone going inside their mind their eyes will often glaze over, or they will glance off or they will defocus their eyes, they may even mouth 'I can't' or words like that when they are thinking that they can't push harder and may shake their head a little as they do or think this)...that's it...and as *you continue to drift deeper* and *relax more fully into the experience*...you can begin to have a sense of a comfortable chair...and of *relaxing* down into that chair...and having a sense of your eyes closing...and *drifting*...and *relaxing*...into hypnosis...

This induction works creating shock and confusion and then giving a clear message to follow.

## Spinning hands induction

(If the clients eyes are closed, ask them to open their eyes) What I want you to do is to spin your hands like this (have the client rotate their arms around each other - the forearms spinning around each other, demonstrate what you want the client to do and have your arms spinning either towards or away from you to start with), once they start spinning their arms around each other say something like: spinning those hands faster and faster...and the other way (reverse your spinning as you say that)...and the other way (reverse your spinning again)...faster and faster...and the other way...that's it... and the other way...faster and faster...and the other way...that's it, and sleep (keep changing the spinning and speeding up the spinning until the client shows signs of confusion and is struggling to follow the instructions. At this point continue a little bit more, asking them to go faster and keep changing direction and acknowledging when they do this and say 'sleep' as a command in an authoritative voice when you see them confused and showing signs of being ready to relax. As you say 'sleep' reach over quickly to the client's arms and gently holding their forearms, push their arms down towards their lap. If needed you can say 'close your eyes, and sleep' rather than just 'sleep')

Then continue on: and as you continue to *drift deeper* and more *comfortably asleep* I wonder whether you will continue to *go deeper* with each in-breath or each outbreath...and as *you drift deeper into hypnosis* you can begin to get a sense of seeing the most comfortable chair...and you can walk toward that chair, noticing how you can tell *that chair is just so comfortable*...and you can take a moment to sit down deeply into that chair and have a sense of closing your eyes and *drifting off into even deeper into hypnosis…*

## Arm levitation induction

(Pause for 20 seconds) (Give suggestions for arm levitation on in-breaths (when the arm naturally lifts slightly), acknowledge any movement in a hand or arm with 'that's it' or similar acknowledging phrase and deviate from the script if the client has already risen their arm well and probably no longer needs suggestions encouraging it) With your eyes closed, just rest those hands on your thighs…and take a moment to focus on which hand is warmest…and which hand is coolest…and notice which hand is heaviest…and which hand is lightest…now I don't know whether this hand right here (looking at the nearest hand to you) is heavier than that hand left right over there (looking at the hand furthest away), or whether that had left over there (looking at the hand furthest away) is heavier than this hand left right here (looking at the nearest hand)…and you can take a moment to really focus on the hand that is lightest...and as you do you can begin to turn your head to face that hand...and I don't know whether you will notice movement start in the wrist or the elbow, or perhaps the palm of that hand...or maybe movement begins in the fingertips...and as *that movement begins*...I don't know at what point you will notice it...and whether *that arm will begin to lift* before you *notice it lifting*, or whether *it will begin to lift* before I notice it lifting...and as *that hand begins to lift* you can perhaps notice how much heavier the other hand is becoming...and I don't know if that other side is becoming heavier in the hand or the arm first...at the rate and speed that this hand begins to lift...and on the lighter arm you can have a sense of helium balloons being tied to that arm near the wrist...and I wonder how many helium balloons will *lift that arm* and how many will speed up the *raising* of *that arm lifting*...as one helium balloon is tied to that arm...and then a second helium balloon...and at some point *it will become harder to keep that hand down* as those balloons *lift it up*...and a third helium balloon...and you can notice how those helium balloons are being inflated with more helium and they are getting larger and larger...lighter and lighter...and the more helium in those balloons the light and lighter they become...and you can watch as those helium balloons begin to *rise right up into the air* (if they are looking at their left hand you can say *'begin to left up into the air'*)...higher and higher...lighter and lighter...and I don't know whether *that lifting will continue* with each in-breath or each outbreath...or whether it will be with the words that I use...or the spaces between my words...(from here largely be silent, with just encouraging comments, like 'that's it' and 'lifting...lifting...' and 'all the way' when you notice any movement. The movement could be the elbow as they breathe in, or a twitch in the hand etc. If the arm doesn't lift, then you can say to the client 'in a moment, I'm going to reach over and lift up that arm and not tell you to put it down any faster than you *drift even deeper into hypnosis'*)...and now as that arm begins to lower back down to your lap...you can *drift deeper and deeper into hypnosis*...and as you do...you can discover the most comfortable chair...and take a few moments to walk over to that chair...relax down into that chair...close your eyes...and drift and float *deeper into hypnosis*...

## Ericksonian questioning arm levitation induction

(Pause for 20 seconds) Rest your hands lightly on your legs on the tips of your fingers…and I will ask you some questions and you can nod or shake your head in answer and follow those questions…have you ever been in hypnosis before?…are you willing to experience arm levitation?…and can you look at the hand that will lift?…and can you open those eyes (if they have their eyes closed) and look at the hand that will lift?…and are you willing to discover the difference between feeling hypnotised and wakeful awareness?…and those hands can feel comfortable resting there can they not?…and can you rest those hands there so lightly with just those fingertips touching the legs?…and can you notice the arms lift slightly with each in-breath?…and can you notice the movement of the hand…as it is lifting?…and can you notice the lightness of that hand?…and are you aware of other sensations as you drift into hypnosis?…and do you know what it feels like to put that hand up to answer a question in class?…or to raise that hand to get something off of a high up shelf?…or to scratch an itch?…and can you notice how that arm continues to lift all by itself with each breath that you take?…and do you notice those changes happening within you as *you are drifting deeper into hypnosis*?…and do you think that arm will have finished lifting before the eyes close and relax shut?…and as *the eyes close and relax shut* and *you drift deeper and deeper into hypnosis*…can you notice what your experience of *drifting deeper into hypnosis* feels like?…as you now begin to get a sense of the most comfortable chair…and as you walk towards that chair…those arms can rest down in your lap as you rest down into the chair…close your eyes…and drift comfortably and deeply into hypnosis…

## Look at my finger induction

(If the client's eyes are closed, ask the client to open their eyes) (Place your hand in a pointing position (with your forefinger pointing) about 60cm from the client and above eye level, about as high as they can look up when they keep their head still and facing forward) Look at my finger, keep your head facing forward but keep your eyes looking up…that's it…and notice those eyes getting heavier and heavier (very slowly lower your finger down in front of the client's face and keep lowering your finger down until it is so low that the client's eyes naturally close because it is too low to look at the finger. If the client starts to move their head down, then remind them to keep their head facing forwards, you just want the eyes to move)...all the way...that's it... (you may repeat 'all the way, that's it...' again as they drift deeper into hypnosis, perhaps timing this phrase with the client doing an outbreath) and as *you continue to drift deeper* and *relax more fully into the experience*...you can begin to have a sense of a comfortable chair...and of *relaxing* down into that chair...and having a sense of your eyes closing...and *drifting*...and *relaxing*...into a *hypnosis*...

## Look into my eyes induction

(If the client has their eyes shut, ask them to open their eyes) Ask the client to look into your eyes and as they look into your eyes you defocus your eyes, match the client's breathing and then start to slow your breathing down, you begin to relax your body, relaxing your facial muscles, head, neck, through the body and when you see the client defocus their eyes or blink and close their eyes you can say 'that's it, all the way' just to encourage them to go with that. You may need to say this a few times at times you see the client defocus their eyes or blink before their eyes remain closed. Then continue on saying: and as *you continue to drift deeper* and *relax more fully into the experience*...you can begin to have a sense of a comfortable chair...and of *relaxing* down into that chair...and having a sense of your eyes closing...and *drifting*...and *relaxing*...into hypnosis...

## Eye fixation induction

Take a moment to open your eyes (if the client has their eyes closed) and find a spot just above eye level to focus on and hold your attention on...and as you focus on that spot...keeping those eyes fixed on that spot, just allow all of your attention to be drawn into that spot...really hold your focus on that spot...and as you do...those eyes will occasionally...feel heavier...and want to...blink a little...and each time they blink...you can *drift deeper and deeper into hypnosis*...and don't let the eyes blink shut too quickly...really try to hold your attention on that spot...for as long as you can...and each time the eyes blink...they will become more difficult to open...and will want to remain shut...and I don't know whether you will *drift deeply into hypnosis* before the eyes close...or after the eyes have closed...as you continue to look at that spot...(say 'that's it' when you notice blinking and 'all the way' when you notice the client's eyes defocus or with some of the blinks and with outbreaths, if the person doesn't close their eyes, not even to blink, after a while you can suggest 'and you can take a moment to...let those eyes close...as you drift even deeper') and as you continue to *drift deeper into hypnosis* you can notice the most comfortable chair...and when you sit down in that chair...you can close your eyes...and drifting deeply and pleasantly into hypnosis...

## Swinging pocket watch induction

If the client has their eyes closed you can ask the client to open their eyes, hold a pocket watch a few feet in front of the client by the chain with the watch just above eye level and when the watch is swinging, have it swing at a comfortable pace across the field of vision of the client. Ask the client to look at the watch, keep their head still and follow the watch with their eyes. Once the client is looking at the watch, start swinging it (keeping your hand still) from side to side, occasionally give reinforcing and supportive comments like 'that's it' and 'all the way' and 'just keeping those eyes on the watch'. After a short while of the client following the swinging watch, very slowly begin to lower the swinging watch down so that it is level with the client's eyes and then as they continue to be following the watch gradually lower it down lower than eye level and gradually slow the swinging down (this begins to communicate drifting deeper and begins to encourage the eyes to close as the eyes follow the lowering pocket watch) and if after a few minutes the client's eyes haven't closed but they have been following along and the watch is perhaps in-line with their chest now and so their eyes are almost closed looking down towards the watch, then you can suggest that the eyes can get heavier and want to shut. If after another minute or so the eyes still haven't shut, you can suggest that they can now close as they drift even deeper into hypnosis. Then continue: and you can notice the most comfortable chair…and as you relax down into that chair, you can close your eyes…and *drift deeply and relaxed into hypnosis…*

## Uptime, downtime induction

(If the client's eyes are closed, ask them to open their eyes and look at a spot above eye level) Now take a moment to look at that spot, focus on it as vividly as possible, then close your eyes…and now recreate that on the inside…have a sense of that spot in your mind's eye being as vivid and real as it is out here…have a sense of the sounds from out here in your mind's eye, being clear and crisp…and each time you close your eyes and *drift deeper into the experience…*you can make that inner representation of the outer view as clear and crisp as possible…and open your eyes and look back at that spot…and close your eyes…and *drift deeper into the experience* and make that spot in your mind's eye as clear and vivid as possible…and open those eyes and look back at that spot…and then close your eyes and recreate that on the inside again...and then open your eyes...and then close your eyes...that's it...making that as realistic as you can again...finding it harder to open your eyes each time you are asked to do so...and opening those eyes...looking back at that spot...and close those eyes...*deeper and deeper*...finding it harder to open them as you *drift deeper into hypnosis*...and trying to open those eyes...and closing those eyes...seeing that spot...*drifting deeper and deeper*...and trying to open those eyes...and closing those eyes...seeing that spot in your mind's eye...drifting more relaxed into the experience...and taking time to *drift even deeper* and noticing the most comfortable chair...and as you relax down into that chair...so you can close your eyes...and find your mind *drifting and floating comfortably into hypnosis*...

## Counting backwards induction

(Pause for 20 seconds) Just take a moment to begin to count slowly backwards out loud from 600...and as you continue to count backwards you can *drift deeper into hypnosis* with each number...and as you continue to count down...it will become harder and harder to keep counting...and the numbers will become harder to grasp...and it will become more difficult to keep counting...and it will become easier and easier to just...*let them all go*...and *drift deeper* inside...and as you continue to *drift deeper and relax*...it will be more difficult to talk...and sometimes you will lose your place and skip numbers or repeat numbers...until you just want to...*let them go*...and *relax deeper into hypnosis*...going all the way...*deeper and deeper*...and as that counting gets too much effort to focus on...you can just relax...let go...and begin to have a sense of the most comfortable chair...and you can walk over to that chair...relax down into the chair...close your eyes...and *drift deeply and comfortably into hypnosis*...

## Eyes blinking induction

(If the client has their eyes closed, you can ask them to open their eyes) I'm going to count slowly up from one...and on each count I want you to close your eyes...and between each count I want you to open your eyes ready to close your eyes on the next number...so when I say one...you will close your eyes and then open your eyes before I say two...and then when I say two...you will close your eyes and open your eyes before I say three...and you can *drift deeper into hypnosis* each time you close your eyes...and it can be harder to open those eyes with each count...1...2...3...4...5...6...(count slowly and in a very relaxed way. Count slightly uneven at times, leaving occasional slightly longer pauses so that they expect you to say the number but you say it just after they expect it. When you notice them struggling to open their eyes, then you progress to suggesting they go deeper, rather than continuing to count. Between numbers you can say supportive comments like 'all the way' and 'deeper and deeper' and 'that's it' perhaps at times you see them breathe out or relax deeper etc) that's it...as you *drift deeper and deeper*...going all the way...*deeply and comfortably into hypnosis*...and as you continue to *drift deeper into hypnosis*...you can notice the most comfortable chair...and relax down into that chair...close your eyes...and discover yourself *drifting into hypnosis* in the most relaxing way...

## Bucket and balloon induction

(If the client has their eyes closed, ask them to open their eyes) Put your arms out in front of you, palms facing downward, close your eyes and imagine you have a bucket hanging on one hand and a helium-filled balloon tied to the other hand, and imagine that bucket is being filled with water and is getting heavier and heavier and the balloon is filling with more helium and is rising higher and higher and the more the balloon is filling and getting higher and higher the heavier the bucket is getting and pulling down lower and lower, and the more this is happening the deeper and deeper you can *go into hypnosis* (pause to give time for the hands to move, you can reiterate the ideas presented more times if needed. As the hands move reinforce the movement by saying things like 'that's right' and 'all the way' and commenting on the hand getting heavier and hand getting lighter, once the client is showing clear signs of responding then you can move on with the induction)…and in a moment both hands can begin to lower down to your lap as you go even *deeper into hypnosis*…that's it…all the way… and as *you continue to drift deeper* and *relax more fully into the experience*...you can begin to have a sense of a comfortable chair...and of *relaxing* down into that chair...and having a sense of your eyes closing...and *drifting*...and *relaxing*...into hypnosis...

## Hands stuck together induction

(If the client has their eyes closed, ask them to open their eyes) Put your hands out in front of you, interlocking your fingers, and look at those hands and push those hands *tighter and tighter* together keeping those *hands sticking together* and notice how the more *you stick those hands tightly together* the *deeper into hypnosis* you go and the *deeper into hypnosis* you go the tighter *those hands stick together* and notice how you can *try in vain to unstick those hands* as *they stick tighter and tighter together,* and in a moment those hands can begin to lower down to your lap and as they lower down to your lap you can *drift deeper and deeper into hypnosis* and the arms and hands can begin to relax...and as *you continue to drift deeper* and *relax more fully into the experience*...you can begin to have a sense of a comfortable chair...and of *relaxing* down into that chair...and having a sense of your eyes closing...and *drifting*...and *relaxing*...into hypnosis...

## Hand passes induction

(If the client has their eyes closed, ask them to open their eyes) Look at my hand (place your hand close to the client (about 40-50cm away from them) and above eye level so that the client is almost straining to look up at the hand) and keep your head facing forward...that's it...(very slowly move your hand down in front of the client until your hand has passed low enough for them to have closed their eyes (if they have kept their head straight) (if the client doesn't close their eyes once their eyes are looking very low, you can just say 'that's it, and close your eyes'). Then say 'that's it, *going deeper, and deeper*' as you pass your hand from above their head down passed their face in front of their closed eyes. Do this a few times, ideally in time with the client's outbreaths so that they experience a sense of deepening. From the client's experience they will notice a shadow cross their field of vision (with their eyes closed) which will give a sense of movement. If you move your hand up across their face the shadow will give them the sense they are descending, like passing floors in a lift (so you can suggest they can descend in a lift (like the lift deepener) and use this with that approach), but I have found that people respond either way, whether you move your hand up or down, they see to get the same feeling) and as *you continue to drift deeper* and *relax more fully into the experience*...you can begin to have a sense of a comfortable chair...and of *relaxing* down into that chair...and having a sense of your eyes closing...and *drifting*...and *relaxing*...into hypnosis...

## Arm lowering induction

(If the client has their eyes closed, you can either ask them to open their eyes or you can specify in the induction which arm you are going to lift up, like saying 'in a moment, I'm going to reach over and lift up your left arm...and I'm not going to tell you to put it down...') In a moment I'm going to lift this arm up and I'm not going to tell you to put it down any faster than you relax *deeper and deeper into hypnosis*. (Gently lift up one of the client's arms above head height; you can suggest they look at their hand if you want). And you can go deeper and deeper into hypnosis as that arm lowers…that's it…that's it… all the way (all said in time with the arm lowering and with the client's outbreaths, if the arm is lowering quickly you can suggest they 'really take time to enjoy entering hypnosis…letting that arm lower slowly' and make additional suggestions if needed for the arm to lower slower)…(once the arm has fully lowered to the client's lap) and as *you continue to drift deeper* and *relax more fully into the experience*…you can begin to have a sense of a comfortable chair…and of *relaxing* down into that chair…and having a sense of your eyes closing…and *drifting*…and *relaxing*…into hypnosis…

## Agreement set induction

With this induction you are stating facts that the client can't disagree with, everything you say is true and observable. If their eyes are open you may say something like: At the moment you are looking over there and you have something you can gaze off at...and every now and then your eyes are blinking...and sometimes between blinks your eyes are feeling like they want to blink...and you are breathing in...and out...that's it...and your arms are resting there, that's it...all the way...that's it...and your eyes are closed...and your breathing has deepened...and your shoulders raise...and lower...and you can hear my voice...

All you are doing in this induction is using your observations of the client to make true statements that they would agree with. So in my example, the client can be asked to gaze off somewhere, then you can say 'at the moment you are looking over there' because this is true, the same with saying 'you have something you can gaze off at' because they do, and every now and then they are blinking, so you are telling them things they can agree with when you tell them that, just like the breathing, they are breathing and you are just telling them what they are doing. The whole induction is just getting repeated agreement by stating things which are true, talking about their ongoing experience. When people repeatedly agree they are more likely to continue to agree, so it feels like a very gentle and respectful process that they are going through. You aren't leading them or telling them what to do or how to go into hypnosis, you are an observer on the client having their own experience of drifting into hypnosis, you are stating your observations and occasionally reinforcing their behaviours with statements like 'that's it' and 'all the way'.

Then you can continue: and as *you continue to drift deeper* and *relax more fully into the experience*...you can begin to have a sense of a comfortable chair...and of *relaxing* down into that chair...and having a sense of your eyes closing...and *drifting*...and *relaxing*...into hypnosis...

## Linking suggestions induction

Like with the Agreement Set Induction, this induction is one which doesn't have a script as such because you are responding to the client in front of you and to what they do and how they are responding. For example:

As you look over there you can breathe in...and breathe out...and while you breathe in...and out...your eyes can keep gazing over there, and your eyes can keep blinking, and as your eyelids blink the hands can rest on your legs...that's it...and as your hands rest on your legs, from time to time the eyes will want to shut fully...and as the eyes shut fully the breathing can slow down a little...and as the breathing slows down a little the arms can relax, and as the arms relax, so you can continue to *drift deeper into hypnosis*...that's it...and as the arms relax, so relaxation can spread within you...and warmth can perhaps spread to your cheeks...and as you sit there listening to me, you can hear sounds outside...and listening to sounds outside can help you to *drift even deeper into hypnosis*...

What you are doing with this induction is observing the client's ongoing experience and commenting on your observations, linking one thing to the next with linking words like: before, during, after, as, while, and, when. As the client follows all of your stated observations you can start to make realistic suggestions which aren't necessarily true, but because everything else has been correct they are likely to continue to follow along (like the end with drifting deeper into hypnosis, assumes they are drifting into hypnosis which is likely to be followed because of the truisms, but it may not have been true until they followed the suggestion). So if the client is gazing somewhere then you can say 'as you look over there' using 'as' to connect the breathing in and out with gazing over there, then in the above example I am linking the breathing with continuing to gaze, then with the word 'and' I link the continuing to gaze with the eyes blinking (which is likely to naturally happen), then I start linking the blinking with the hands continuing to rest on the legs, then link the hands continuing to rest on the legs with the eyes wanting to shut fully, then link the eyes wanting to shut fully with the breathing slowing down, then link the breathing slowing down with the arms relaxing, then the arms relaxing with the client drifting deeper into hypnosis, etc.

Then you can continue: and as *you continue to drift deeper* and *relax more fully into the experience*...you can begin to have a sense of a comfortable chair...and of *relaxing* down into that chair...and having a sense of your eyes closing...and *drifting*...and *relaxing*...deeper into hypnosis...

## *Deepeners*

## Staircase

That's it…as *you begin now* to imagine a secret staircase in your mind…and as you walk down that secret staircase…with each step, you can find yourself *going twice as deep into hypnosis*…and while *you go deeper with each step you take*…I will count down from 10 in the background…and on the count of one you will be at the bottom of the staircase…and I wonder whether you will go deeper without realising it or whether you will notice certain changes or sensations as *you drift deeper into hypnosis*…as you step on the first step…10…*going deeper and deeper*…stepping on the next step…9…*going twice as deep* into a comfortable hypnotic trance state…continuing down those stairs…8…*drifting deeper and deeper*…7…*becoming more absorbed*…*deeper and deeper with each breath* you take…6…*drifting deeper* honestly and fully into hypnosis…5…allowing *your unconscious now* to find its own way of helping *you go deeper and deeper into hypnosis*…4…allowing all of your attention to be absorbed into the hypnotic experience...3...almost at the bottom of the stairs now...as *you become deeper and deeper absorbed*...2...letting your mind wander and drift and dream whilst *your unconscious now*...focuses on what is important to change...and one...*now*...*into*...*hypnosis*...in your own unique way ready and prepared to make the necessary changes as you arrive at the bottom of the steps (pause for a minute)...

## Pictures in pictures

That's it...and as you now begin to imagine a picture of a beach in front of you...and as you pay close attention to that beach you can begin to notice something different about that picture...and the more you try to see what isn't there the more you find yourself drawn into the image...and then in a blink you can find yourself in that picture searching for a path (pause for about 30 seconds)...and as you wander around wondering where the path will be, you can notice it in another picture...and a curious thing about these pictures is that each time you drift into one you *go even deeper into hypnosis*...and in a blink you can find yourself on that path...searching for something new (pause for about 30 seconds)...and I wonder what sounds each foot step makes as you...walk along that path until you see that new picture...and in a blink you can find yourself in that new picture knowing that what you can learn and discover here can stay in this picture for you to use instinctively in the future like unconscious knowing (pause for about one minute)...

## Raising and lowering the arm

In a moment I'm going to lift up that right arm (you can lift either arm) and it can rest there so loose and limp...and as I let go of that arm and let it drop freely back down to the leg you can *relax deeper into hypnosis*...and I don't know whether you will go twice as deeply or four times as deeply into hypnosis...(lift up the arm (if it feels like they are helping in any way to lift the arm suggest 'that's it just allowing that arm to be loose and limp...' and then wait a moment for the arm to become loose and limp. If it doesn't go limp just continue with 'and as that arm lowers to the leg you can go deeper and deeper into hypnosis each time the arm touches the leg' and then lift it a few times letting it lower a few more times) (let the arm drop, as it hits the leg say: 'that's it *deeper and deeper into hypnosis*'. Repeat this 3 or 4 times. Notice the clients face and body language to notice signs of deeper relaxation like reddening face or slower breathing or slumping more)...that's it...and with each breath you take you can continue to increase receptivity and relaxation and continue to *drift deeper and deeper* inside...that's right...(pause for about one minute)...

## Down in a lift

That's it...and I wonder what you would imagine if you were to *imagine a trance lift*...a lift that appears to be in front of you that leads down four floors only as fast as *you drift deeper into hypnosis*...how will that lift be decorated...will there be any lift music and if there is what is playing in the background...and I wonder what that lift feels like as you go down those four floors to the basement of trance...deep into the depths of...*your unconscious*…as you step comfortably into that lift and *drift deeper and deeper* down from floor four to floor three…going only as fast as *you go deeper and deeper*…in your own unique way…down *deeper and deeper*…(pause for about 30 seconds) and you can notice what is at floor three and know it is not the floor for you…as you…*drift deeper down*…to floor two…and as the lift briefly pauses at floor two I wonder what you can discover…(pause for 30 seconds)…before continuing to *drift down deeper* to the basement…but don't reach the basement just yet…allow *your unconscious* to be fully prepared for the changes ahead in a way you may consciously not know…and the journey to that final level can be a bit further as I quieten down in the background to allow you to *complete your journey comfortably and fully*…(pause for one minute)…that's it as you reach the basement and you can now exit the lift and enter a room where change can occur…and I wonder whether you will be curious later to wonder how much change was left here with only *your unconscious* for company after you exit hypnosis…

## Gazing into space

That's it…you know as a child I used to sit down resting against trees gazing up at the clouds as they drifted gently across the sky…and I used to wonder whether there could be someone out there in space sitting beneath a tree gazing up at the sky watching those clouds wondering whether there could be someone out there in space sitting beneath a tree gazing up at the sky watching those clouds…and I used to wonder what their clouds would look like and what their space would look like from their planet…and I wonder what you think it would feel like to be sat beneath a tree…gazing up into the sky…looking at the clouds wondering whether there is someone out there in space sitting beneath a tree gazing up at the clouds…and I wonder what you think their trees would look like and what their weather would be like and what their clouds would look like…and how effortless it can be to drift across space and time to different planets in the mind as *you drift deeper into the experience* of wondering what would be different for them…what would it feel like to be them…what would be different about the way they think…as they lead a life where they have overcome great adversity and achieved enlightenment and spiritual awakenment and explored life with a sense of curiosity and wonder and excitement and achieved great change without even knowing how it happened or how it was possible...(pause for one minute)

## Using silence

That's it...and in a moment I'm going to be quiet as *you drift even deeper* still honestly and *fully into hypnosis*...and you can be curious as to how deep you will go with the spaces between my words and whether you will notice how deep you become as *you drift deeper and deeper*...and I'm going to quieten down a minute and you can take all the time you need to really honestly *become fully absorbed in hypnosis*...accessing a state of mind ideal for creating change and new discoveries...(go quiet for one minute)... (It can help to match the client's breathing and then begin to extend your outbreaths to begin to help the client become more deeply relaxed)

## *Priming*

### Priming to overcome psychological difficulties

And as you relax deeper into hypnosis...*your unconscious* can take on board all that is necessary to help you to *see things from a new perspective*...to allow for change to occur...there is an old story told about a monkey living in a forest...the monkey used to worry that one day the sky was going to fall...the monkey used to worry about having an accident and not having anyone around to help...he used to worry about what could go wrong in the future...he used to worry about what other animals thought of him...did he make too much noise...was he attractive enough...he used to worry about times in the past that made him feel guilty...this monkey would create vivid images in his mind as if he was seeing through his own eyes and really feeling all the horrible feelings and worry...then one day the monkey heard a crash through the trees behind him...he could feel his heart rush as he instinctively ran to escape the noise...'the sky is falling...the sky is falling'...the monkey shouted as he ran through the forest...the other animals heard this and started to panic...they began running around the forest shouting...'the sky is falling...the sky is falling'...before long all the animals in the forest heard this tale about the sky falling and the forest was full of panic...'the sky is falling...the sky is falling'...just then a wise old owl glided down to talk to the animals and find out what was going on...he spoke to a variety of different animals to discover where this tale came from...eventually he traced the story back to the monkey...the wise owl found the monkey shaking and hiding in the base of a tree...'what's this about the sky falling?'...the owl asked...'I heard it myself...the sky is falling the sky is falling'...replied the monkey...the wise owl decided to take the monkey back to where the sound came from...once they were back where the monkey first heard the sound they waited with anticipation...after a while they heard a crash and a thud...'was that the sound you heard?'...asked the owl...'yes...the sky is falling...the sky is falling'...the monkey replied...the wise owl asked 'how do you know the sky is falling...that sound could be anything...have you checked to see what fell?'...the owl picked up the monkey and flew above the tree tops and just glided around...from up here the monkey could look up and see the sky was still in place and he wondered what he had heard falling...he looked down and watched the trees...just then he saw a coconut fall to the floor...the monkey felt embarrassed but compelled to put things right...he knew what he had to do...he had to let the other animals know it was a mistake...the owl told the monkey he could fly him to the foot of a nearby mountain and give him directions but he had to climb the mountain himself...the monkey understood this...he knew he had a long way to climb so kept his attention on where he was going and how he was going to get there...the monkey climbed and struggled and learnt new things about himself and how much more he is capable of that previously he didn't realise...eventually after many hours of climbing and struggling he felt the satisfaction of reaching the top all by himself...he had managed to keep going even when he didn't think he would be able to...from the top of the mountain the monkey realised he could see the whole forest...the monkey shouted from the top of the mountain and the whole forest listened...as the monkey explain the whole story...and all the animals relaxed...(pause for about 1 minute)...

## Priming to overcome physical difficulties

And in hypnosis *your unconscious* can begin to make changes throughout the body...*your unconscious* can make all the changes instinctively in the same way that you can learn to walk and talk and adapt over time without any conscious effort at all...*your unconscious* knows how to make changes to muscles...changes to blood flow...changes to the immune system...changes to the digestive system...changes within any cell in the body...you know a master sailor can make sailing appear so effortless...they can tie complex knots...carry out complex tasks...they can keep the boat upright even in strong winds...they learn how to use the wind and the tide rather than fight it...yet when they began they didn't know how to do any of this...some of the skills they learnt through practice...others they developed unconsciously...like their ability to not feel the pain of working their muscles hard...and to be unaware of pain from cuts and bruises and injuries...whilst they are preoccupied with more important tasks...and it can almost feel like they have an out of body experience...their body is doing the work while their mind is observing...and you know once a sailor has learned a knot and mastered that knot they can tie the knot without paying attention...(pause for about 1 minute)

# THERAPEUTIC SCRIPTS, PROCESSES & TECHNIQUES

## *Introduction*

Before we move on to the therapeutic scripts, processes and techniques, what I have done is to share what information I could find about the evidence for using hypnosis in relation to as many of the areas these scripts cover so that you can make an informed decision about using hypnosis as part of your therapy and in what context. Unfortunately, there often very limited research that has been carried out into the use of hypnosis in many areas and often where studies have been done, they have been of a low quality. I focused on studies which were more recent and tried to look at reviews and meta-analysis where possible which evaluated multiple studies.

Where the research is lacking, doesn't mean hypnosis can't help in those areas, but it is always best to be first guided by the research as to the approach you will be taking with clients and looking at where the use of hypnosis might fit within that approach. For example, if you were helping a child to stop bedwetting, you may use an intervention, like having them set an alarm clock, then with hypnosis, you may have them mentally rehearse waking to the alarm, going to the toilet and quickly settling back down in bed to sleep. You may use hypnosis to have them mentally rehearse discovering their bed is dry and despite poor evidence of success, you may decide to use hypnotic suggestions for dry nights while the child is hypnotised, perhaps after they have carried out mental rehearsal and before awaking them from hypnosis.

## Smoking Cessation, Alcohol Reduction and other Addictions

Hypnosis can be used to help those who want to quit smoking but in studies, its effectiveness isn't in-line with what many hypnotherapists seem to claim. In a 2008 randomised trial, participants underwent either two 60-minute sessions of hypnosis or behavioural counselling (both used in conjunction with nicotine patches). At 12-month follow-up 20% of those who had the hypnosis sessions were abstinent, compared to 14% of those who had behavioural counselling (Carmody, et al., 2008) which is fairly consistent with other studies that check abstinence based on biochemical testing. In a randomised controlled trial looking at hypnotherapy, hypnotherapy and nicotine replacement therapy and nicotine replacement therapy at 26-weeks, hypnotherapy and hypnotherapy with nicotine replacement therapy were about three times more effective than nicotine replacement therapy alone, but there was no difference in effectiveness compared to those who quit themselves without hypnotherapy or nicotine replacement therapy (Hasan, et al., 2014).

In an examination of the evidence on the use of hypnosis and its effectiveness which looked at 59 studies, they concluded that "Whereas hypnotic procedures generally yield higher rates of abstinence relative to wait-list and no-treatment conditions, hypnotic interventions are generally comparable to a variety of nonhypnotic treatments." The conclusion continued that the evidence of whether hypnosis was more effective than placebo was inconclusive and that many of the positive effects of treatment could have been due to the cognitive, behavioural and educational interventions which were associated with the hypnotic treatment (Green & Lynn, 2000).

Hypnosis used in conjunction with cognitive-behavioural therapy increases the effectiveness of cognitive-behavioural therapy (Kirsch, Montgomery, & Sapirstein, 1995), so it makes sense that when used as an adjunct to therapy, it can help to increase the efficacy of that therapy. This was identified as possibly being the case in a Cochrane Systematic Review (Barnes, McRobbie, Dong, Walker, & Hartmann-Boyce, 2019) that found the available studies were generally of a low quality. This is also why the scripts here don't just do suggestion therapy and should be included within broader therapy that you are doing with your client.

There are limited randomised controlled trial on the use of hypnosis for quitting or reducing alcohol consumption. In a 2019 randomised controlled trial comparing hypnotherapy to motivational interviewing, there were slightly better reported outcomes for those who received hypnotherapy at one year follow-up, but all participants received group therapy alongside one-to-one motivational interviewing or hypnotherapy, so the findings were inconclusive about what impact the one-to-one therapies had compared to the group therapy component (Shestopal & Bramness, 2019).

In a small pilot study on treatment of opium addiction, all participants underwent psychotherapy, with half being assigned no additional sessions and half assigned 5 hypnotherapy sessions. 40% of those who had hypnotherapy relapsed, compared to 73% of those who only received the psychotherapy sessions. Many participants also reported additional benefits like reduced insomnia, restlessness, pain and autonomic disturbances (Golabadi, Taban, Yaghoubi, & Gholamrezaei, 2012).

## Weight-Loss

Hypnosis can be very helpful in supporting clients to lose weight. There is evidence that hypnosis alone can help to get initial results over a short time-span and when used in conjunction with cognitive-behavioural therapy, can increase effectiveness of cognitive-behavioural therapy over the longer term. Those who received cognitive-behavioural therapy with hypnosis lost more weight at follow-up than 79% of those who only received cognitive-behavioural therapy (Milling, Gover, & Moriarty, 2018) which matches with the research that hypnosis used as an adjunct to cognitive-behavioural therapy is generally more effective than cognitive-behavioural therapy alone (Kirsch, Montgomery, & Sapirstein, 1995).

## Depression

In a meta-analysis of hypnosis being used to help people with symptoms of depression those who received hypnosis showed more improvement than 76% of control participants and at the longest follow-up there was more improvement than 51% of control participants. These results are comparable to other psychological therapies (Milling, Valentine, McCarley, & LoStimolo, 2018) and cognitive-behavioural therapy with hypnosis being used as an adjunct to that therapy saw greater improvements than cognitive-behavioural therapy alone (Alladin & Alibhai, 2007).

## Worry

Hypnosis can be an effective in the treatment of anxiety and stress related disorders including tackling worrying (Hammond, 2010), again, it can increase effectiveness of cognitive-behavioural approaches.

## Panic Attacks

Hypnosis has been applied within the therapeutic context to address panic attacks, often as part of treatment tackling areas causing excessive stress or worry, like worrying about exams or about medical treatments. Success has been found applying hypnosis within a process of educating the client about panic attacks and exploring and addressing the reasons for the panic attacks (Reid, 2017).

## Pain

One area hypnosis has been used considerably is in pain reduction. There seem to be few high quality and large cohort studies to draw on, but the available literature frequently finds a significant decrease in pain when hypnosis is used and is often found to be more effective at pain management than non-hypnotic interventions (Elkins, Jensen, & Patterson, 2007). Hypnosis has been found to be helpful in the treatment of arthritis, both the pain management and subjective experience of arthritis and the underlying autoimmune functioning behind arthritis and the positive benefits were found to be even more significant in those who regularly used hypnosis on their arthritis (Horton-hausknecht, Mitzdorf, & Melchart, 2000). Hypnosis has also been used on areas like phantom limb pain demonstrating a reduction in pain (Bamford, 2006), but is often likely to also require additional psychological treatment, for example, of related trauma. Remember that pain should always be checked out medically first to ensure that it is safe to remove or reduce the pain. Medical advice should be followed.

## Performance Enhancement

Most of the research on the use of hypnosis on performance enhancement has focused on sports performance, like improving basketball skills (Pates, Maynard, & Westbury, An Investigation into the Effects of Hypnosis on Basketball Performance, 2001), golf performance (Pates & Maynard, Effects of Hypnosis on Flow States and Golf Performance, 2000) or cycling performance (Lindsay, Maynard, & Thomas, 2005) and on flow-state during sports performance. Hypnosis seems to have a positive effect on performance enhancement, on accessing the flow-state and improved subjective experience. It is well known that guided imagery can be used to improve performance (Abdin, 2010). This can be enhanced with the additional use of hypnosis (Liggett, 2000).

## Relaxation

There is very little specific research on using hypnosis to aid relaxation, but how hypnosis is often induced can lead to relaxation and skills can be taught during hypnosis, mental rehearsal can be carried out and relaxation techniques can be applied. What research there is, is often focused on anxiety reduction, of which there is significant research some of which is mentioned earlier in this book. There are also known relaxation techniques, which are also often used as hypnotic inductions, like the progressive body scan.

## Phobias and Post-Traumatic Stress Disorder

The approach I use to treat phobias and post-traumatic stress disorder is the Rewind Technique, I adapt the approach to suit individual clients while using the principles of the technique. It is this technique that the scripts in this book are based on. The Rewind Technique is based on the earlier Neuro-Linguistic Programming technique, the Fast Phobia Cure or V/K Dissociation Technique.

The Rewind Technique has been found to be an effective way of treating phobias and post-traumatic stress disorder, both Dr David Muss' (Muss, 1991) approach (Adams & Allan, Muss' Rewind treatment for trauma: description and multi-site pilot study, 2018) and the Human Given's variation (Adams & Allan, The effectiveness of Human Givens Rewind treatment for trauma, 2019) have shown promising results.

## Obsessive Compulsive Disorder

There is limited research that I have been able to find about the use of hypnosis in the treatment of obsessive-compulsive disorder. There are some individual case examples of the successful use of hypnosis in the treatment of obsessive-compulsive disorder often complimenting cognitive behavioural interventions (Meyerson & Konichezky, 2011).

## Sleep Problems

There are limited quality studies on the use of hypnosis in the treatment of sleep problems. In a 2018 review of the available studies which included addressing sleep problems over 58% of the studies reported benefits of using hypnosis, over 12% reported mixed results and 29% reported no benefit (Chamine, Atchley, & Oken, 2018).

## Bedwetting

In a study comparing hypnotherapy (using an audiotape for daily use) to alarm therapy for bedwetting in children aged 7-12 years, alarm therapy was significantly more successful with 55% of subjects achieving dryness, compared to 19% of hypnotherapy subjects (Seabrook,

Gorodzinsky, & Freedman, 2005). There are limited recent quality studies that I can find around the use of hypnosis to help tackle bedwetting. There are individual case studies and anecdotal evidence, including my first experience with doing therapeutic hypnosis back when I was 13. I had a self-hypnosis book due to my growing interest in hypnosis. I had a younger brother who frequently wet the bed. I read a hypnotic induction script and the stop bedwetting script and then counted him out of hypnosis and he stopped wetting the bed. I had only carried out that one impromptu session, using no skill or 'therapy', just reading scripts from a basic self-hypnosis scripts book. He didn't listen to an audiotape daily, or have multiple session.

## Childbirth

There is some evidence that hypnosis can be helpful in reducing labour pain, reducing the need for analgesia (Smith, Collins, Cyna, & Crowther, 2006). In a 2009 randomised controlled trial of HypnoBirthing, it was found to be no more effective than conventional childbirth classes (Fisher, Esplin, Stoddard, & Silver,

2009) and a 2018 study found HypnoBirthing reduced anxiety levels during delivery (Imannura & Susanti, 2018). There are reasons to think hypnosis can aid other interventions, for example, hypnosis can help with pain and anxiety. So, although there are limited quality studies of the use of hypnosis around childbirth, it may well be a helpful adjunct to childbirth therapy.

## Fibromyalgia

There are limited quality studies on the use of hypnosis to help with fibromyalgia. Some areas of fibromyalgia, like pain may well be able to be helped and it could be possible to help with any immune-functioning aspects. In a 2013 study, improvements were reported in those who received hypnosis compared to the control group who received no treatment (Picard, et al., 2013), unfortunately there wasn't a comparison with other treatments to identify how this treatment would fair in comparison to other treatments. You would expect, with most treatments, that receiving some treatment will have greater positive benefit than receiving no treatment, even if the benefit was just due to placebo.

## Skin Conditions

There are many studies of hypnosis being used with a wide range of skin conditions from acne to eczema and verrucae (Fried & Hussain, 2008). With hypnosis, people can control bodily functions and processes which are usually unconscious like blood flow and increasing the immune response. As well as this, psychological aspects of these problems can be addressed with hypnosis being used as an adjunct to other psychological therapies and relaxation to reduce stress and anxiety and reduce the client's tendency perhaps to scratch or pick at themselves.

## Irritable Bowel Syndrome (IBS) and Gastrointestinal Disorders

A review of randomised studies of gut-directed hypnotherapy for irritable bowel syndrome (IBS) found that in most of the studies there was a significant reduction in symptoms and in many of the studies efficacy was maintained long-term, there was also signs of maintained remission of ulcerative colitis (Peters,

Muir, & Gibson, 2015). Hypnosis seems like it can be a helpful adjunct to therapy in adults and children for IBS and gastrointestinal disorders in a review of the evidence hypnosis was found to be highly efficacious for IBS and indications of therapeutic potential for other gastrointestinal disorders (Palsson, 2015).

## Boosting the Immune System

Hypnosis and guided imagery (Trakhtenberg, 2008) have often been associated with being able to stimulate bodily processes which are often not controlled consciously. There have been studies which show the positive effects of hypnosis in boosting immune system response and even in boosting specific aspects of the immune response, like specific types of cells. In a study, it was found that only those who were highly hypnotisable (those responding very well to the hypnosis) had a boost in immune response (Ruzyla-Smith, Barabasz, Barabasz, & Warner, 1995). Hypnotic guided imagery was found to help increase natural killer cells and improve psychological wellbeing in patients with prior breast cancer, but found that the effects only lasted while treatment was ongoing. The effects weren't noticed at 3-month follow-up (Bakke, Purtzer, & Newton, 2002).

## Therapeutic Scripts, Processes and Techniques

### Smoking habit that currently serves a purpose (like for managing stress or boredom)

For some time now smoking has been your therapy...and now the time has come for...*your unconscious to make a change*...and as you listen to me your unconscious...can discover a new therapy for you...and you know some people smoke to relieve stress before they learn that they can breathe in to the count of 7 and out to the count of 11... and the extended outbreath releases endorphins and dopamine and other feel good chemicals into the body and brain leading to relaxation and a feel good state...and they then...*begin to replace the old habit with a new one*...breathing in to the count of 7 and out to the count of 11...other people used to smoke because it was their minds way of making them take a break or socialise or whatever the smoking was therapy for…once they realise this they…begin to find new ways…to remember to take a break or socialise or meet the need that the old smoking habit was meeting…and as they put these new habits into place the old habit disappears…some people even keep the craving just as a signal…almost like an alarm clock reminding them to take a break and they form the habit of getting the craving which goes once they fulfil it with the new habit…some people find they used smoking as a way of breaking the ice or to meet people…almost like a conversation starter…these people find a new conversation starter or ice breaker that they get in the habit of using before fully stopping the old habit…*and I wonder what it will be for you*…I wonder what your mind will find as a new habit for you…and your unconscious can pick up on ideas and possibilities within what I say and the way I say things in the same way that a sprinkle of rain on a seed bed can grow a marvellous array of flowers…and as…*you discover a new personal self-created therapy*…you can begin to…*ditch the old therapy*…and as you listen to this you can…*absorb all that is useful and relevant*…and a part of you can now drift off into the distant future looking back on this present…and as that part of you looks back it can begin to get a sense of how you developed over that time…how you evolved and created your own therapy…how you formed new habits and grew out of old habits…and…*create your own healthy therapy*…you know as a child many people suck their thumbs…many people have imaginary friends…or need to wear nappies…yet many people grow out of these old habits without really thinking about how…*that happens all by itself*…and you can now take some time to begin to create new changes in the mind and body as I quieten into the background for a few minutes to allow that reprocessing and reprogramming to occur on a deep unconscious level…(pause for about 3 minutes)…that's right…*really developing in your own unique way*…and you know sometimes it's nice to move from a smog filled congested city out into the fresh clean and relaxing air of the country with the open roads and clear views…(pause for about 1 minute)…

## *Smoking habit that no longer serves a purpose*

That's it…now…I'd like you to take a few moments to get a sense of drifting back into the past and discover a part of you that used to carry out that old smoking habit for a purpose…you know many people start smoking and continue to smoke for a reason…over time some reasons just stop existing yet the habit remains…and I would like you to take some time to honestly and genuinely thank that part of you that created the habit…many people find that smoking becomes their therapy…some people continue with the therapy long after the problem has passed…a bit like someone taking pain medication and getting so in the habit of taking that medication they don't stop even when the pain is gone…and you know you can…*stop now*…and you can…*get in the habit of doing something new*…you have a lifetime of experience changing habits without knowing quite how they changed…many children sucked their thumbs yet one day they spent a few hours where they forgot to suck their thumb…and another day they forgot entirely…and over time they forgot more and more until they suddenly look back and realise they hadn't been sucking their thumb for a while and yet they didn't miss it because it happened naturally in its own way and its own time as they no longer needed that old therapy and they grew up...and you know the country with its clean air and open roads can be a wonderful alternative to smoggy congested cities...and I don't know whether you will grow up quickly or take a few weeks to...*really settle into the new you*...and you can...*now take the time*...to...*really begin to undo all those old habits and develop new healthy habits*...and as...*you do that*...on an unconscious instinctive level...I will quieten down in the background and you can take as long as is necessary while I'm quiet to...*make the necessary changes*...(pause for about 3 minutes)...

## Scrambling

Find out from the client what the stages are of the smoking problem for that specific client. For example:

1.  Experiencing stress

2.  Getting a craving

3.  Thinking 'I need a cigarette'

4.  Grabbing cigarettes

5.  Opening the box

6.  Taking a cigarette

7.  Putting the box back down

8.  Lighting the cigarette

9.  Taking the first drag deeply and really savouring it

10. Smoking the rest of the cigarette

11. Savouring getting the last drag out of the cigarette

12. Putting it out

Then get the stages of what the client would like to instead in the same situations. For example:

1.  Experiencing stress

2.  Recognise I need to take time out of the situation

3.  Think of a way out of the situation

4.  Go and sit somewhere quiet and do a breathing technique like 7-11 breathing (breathing in to the count of 7 out to the count of 11)

5.  Repeat the breathing for about 4 or 5 breaths or until I feel relaxed

6.  Plan or write down what I need to do to overcome the stressful situation

7.  Put my plan into action

Once you have two lists. One of the problem behaviour and one of the desired behaviour you can begin the scrambling technique. To do the scrambling you want to tell the client that you will guide them through a process based on the lists you both created earlier. You then tell them to imagine 'number 1 of the old smoking habit (and say what number one was – in this case it was 'Experiencing Stress')'. Then to 'nod when they have done this'. Then to 'open their eyes and close their eyes' (as soon as their eyes open tell them to close their eyes) and imagine number 2, then nod the head once they have done this; then open their eyes and close their eyes again. Then number 3…keep repeating this until they have done this for all the stages of the problem. Once they have done that, start scrambling the numbers and do this building up speed and as you do it tell them to do each stage quicker and quicker. For example: 'Now imagine number 4 (give the description for this each number) then nod your head, (once they have nodded) open your eyes and close your eyes; now imagine number 9 (description and head nodding), open your eyes and close your eyes; now imagine number 2 (description and head nodding), open your eyes and close your eyes. Repeat this until you have randomly been through all the stages of the old problem behaviour at least four times or until they seem to really be struggling to get the stages in their mind. Then after the last eye closure suggest 'that's right and now just allow yourself to relax and imagine you are…' then read all the stages of the behaviour they would like instead. Build this up as much as possible by asking 'wondering' questions. 'I wonder what it feels like to be recognising you need to take time out of the situation and whether anyone else is noticing that' 'I wonder what others are noticing is different about you as you respond in this new way'.

You don't need to read the numbers out as you read through the preferred behaviour. You want it to flow so that the 'complete response is the preferred one whereas the incomplete 'scrambled' response is the old problem behaviour. This increases the likelihood of the client latching on to the new response as it is complete and easier to follow than the old response.

So, with the above example you would read:

'That's it...and get a sense of experiencing stress...and recognise that you need to take time out of the situation...and notice how you find a way out of that situation so that you can go and sit somewhere quiet and do 7-11 breathing...and get a sense of going somewhere quiet sitting down and breathing in counting to 7 and out counting to 11 and notice how that relaxes you...and I wonder where in your body that relaxation will begin and how it will spread...and what others could notice about you that lets them notice that you are responding in a new way...and just get a sense of planning how you will overcome that situation and how you will put that plan into action…'

Then once you have done this 'future pace' by posing questions for the client to think about like 'what will be different responding in this new way' 'who else will notice the change in you' 'what will they notice' 'what other changes may occur because you are responding in a new way'.

Then have the client imagine a variety of situations they would have smoked and to see these situations going in a new way and once they are happy with how they see these situations going then reply those situations only this time step into them to experience the situations going a new way. Noticing what they can see, hear and feel.

## *Stop smoking script for smokers that have struggled to quit before*

By remaining in hypnosis and continuing to listen to me you will be agreeing to something. You will be agreeing to follow everything I say…and that includes any suggestions for tasks or for developmental opportunities...and it is very important that you understand that by continuing to listen to me you agree honestly and fully to carry out everything I say...so by continuing to remain in hypnosis you agree to follow my instructions and suggestions and carry out any tasks...and it is no good just thinking that you are okay agreeing with this but not meaning it because if you do that you will be cheating yourself and you won't get the results that you want...the only way to get the results that you want is to follow exactly what I say...nothing I say will be immoral and everything I say will be for your benefit...but before continuing I need to know you definitely agree 100% to do everything I say...regardless of personal opinions...so you need to be sure in yourself that you agree to that now...and if you do you can keep your eyes closed and continue to *drift deeper into hypnosis*...you know people often have work colleagues they work with that really annoy them...that really irritate them...they say and do things that really wind them up...and they tolerate them but don't do anything because they think if I say something it might hurt their feelings or they might get angry or it might make it awkward at work...and people have a million and one excuses why they can't say something...and then one day they've been putting up with this for years and years and one day they just suddenly decide to say something...they don't think about how they decided to say something just for some reason or another they had that certain mind-set where the person said something to them and they just turned and responded...and they found it easy and effortless to do that...they didn't think about it...they just found it easy and effortless to...*just respond*...when the time was right...and they found the result wasn't as bad as they had imagined it would be...and this is a perfectly natural thing...in all human relationships we have situations where people irritate us and we don't say anything because we are polite and kind and eventually we feel we have to say something...and you just say it...and when it reaches that point...almost like the straw that breaks the camel's back...you hold it and hold it and hold it and then it just snaps and you say something and you don't think about the consequences...*you just do it*...and there was a parent that couldn't get their child out of bed in the morning...then there job was on the line...they were told...if you're not in work you will lose your job...and they had a million and one excuses why they couldn't get their child out of bed in the morning...most of the excuses were blaming the child and making out that they, as a parent were powerless...they would say 'I have said everything there is to say...I have tried everything there is to try...I have done all the parenting techniques in books...I have done all the parenting techniques on programmes...absolutely nothing works...I have tried everything and nothing at all works...my child still just lays in bed...I can't imagine anything ever working'...and the parent would say that over and over and over again...and now their work is saying 'if you're not in by 9am you lose your job'...this parent went up to their child's bedroom and they told their child they are getting up and getting into school because they are not losing their job just because their child is going to be lazy and not wanting to go into school...and they got their child up *easily and effortlessly*...they got their child into school *easily and effortlessly*...and they thought it was a fluke...they didn't realise they did anything different...and the next day the same thing happened...they knew the risk to their job if they didn't get their child into school...and they got their child into school...and the day after that...and the week after that...and the month after that...and it was only at this point that they realised their child had turned their behaviour around...and not only had they been putting the blame on the child for why the child wouldn't get up and go to school but they were also putting the success on the child...saying the child must have just grown up out of the blue...they must have grown up and suddenly decided to behave...yet other people could tell that that wasn't the case...that it was actually because they...*suddenly have motivation* that meant something to them...and the parent....was now using a different tone of voice...the parent had learnt to be assertive...they had always thought that they were assertive previously...but previously they were going up to their child and saying (without conviction)...'but please get up you need to be going to school'...now they were going up stairs saying (assertively)...'you need to get up, you need to go to school...you've got ten minutes'...and their tone of voice was totally different...and so the child *stop that old behaviour*...and it was because of what the parent did...and we have all had experiences like that where the motivation reaches a point where...*things become effortless and just happen*...there was a person that used to smoke...and they said...'I've tried everything, I've tried patches...I've tried gum...I've tried inhalators...I've tried changing cigarette brands before quitting...I've tried smoking more and smoking less to see if that would help'...and they said...'nothing has...*stop smoking*...yet'...and then they became pregnant and as soon as they realised they were pregnant they *never touch another cigarette*...they...*never touch another cigarette*...and that became *easy and effortless* for them...they didn't think about it at all...they just instantly...*become a non-smoker*...imagine that...you know what it's like...to be doing a behaviour for years and then...*instantly stopping*...and not even missing it or realising or paying attention to the fact that...*you've changed*...because for them when asked...what *stopped* you...you were more than happy to smoke 20 a day...what *stopped* you...they said 'what *stopped* me was...the second I knew I was pregnant I knew I wasn't going to harm my child or put my child at any unnecessary risk...so I...*stop smoking instantly*...easily and effortlessly...I didn't even have to think about it'...and they never had any therapy or anything...the change came from within them...*change just happen*...and we've all had experiences like that...where *change just happens instantly*...and you know the interesting thing about using hypnosis to help people to...*stop smoking*...is that it uses the imagination...and the imagination has tremendous power...some people say they can't imagine things visually...yet on an unconscious level that doesn't really matter because you visualise unconsciously even if you don't consciously realise it...and you know if there was a plank of wood on the floor you could walk across it...and you wouldn't need any safety gear or anything you would just comfortably walk across it...and if the same plank of wood was suspended between two hot air balloons 10,000 feet in the air and you were told without any safety gear, to walk between the balloons across the plank you would find it incredibly difficult...and most people would find it impossible...yet you know that you can walk across that plank of wood...because you did it perfectly fine when it was on the ground and it is the same plank of wood...the difference is, your imagination is thinking about how you could fall and die or fall and hurt yourself...it's thinking about all the risks...and research shows that when there is a battle between your imagination and your willpower...*your imagination wins*...so in that example no matter how much you really want to get across that plank of wood...no matter how much willpower you think you have...you still struggle to get across the plank of wood...in the same way that when you want to stay awake to watch a film late at night...no matter how much willpower you have to desperately try and stay awake you nearly always just fall asleep...and the more willpower you use...the harder you try to stay awake the more tired and sleepy you feel and the faster you just fall asleep...and likewise...when you try desperately hard to fall asleep and you try to put in all of your willpower to force yourself to fall asleep you discover that the harder you try to fall asleep the more awake you stay...many people try and quit things using willpower and wonder why willpower seems often to not work...and then they say they don't have enough willpower and they use that as an excuse...yet many people that want to give up addictions say they just don't have enough willpower and they don't realise that they could have all the willpower in the world...the difficulty is that the more willpower they use the more the opposite is being portrayed from the imagination making them even more compelled to carry out the old behaviours...and what is needed is to...*stop smoking using the imagination*...not using the willpower...because when...*you stop smoking using the imagination*...when *you quit smoking using your imagination*...then your willpower and desire is aligned with your imagination and quitting becomes so much easier...the imagination is helping...*you achieve what you want to now achieve*...when someone lives in a built up area with all the streets full of congestion...and because of all of the congestion there is often lots of smog around and noisy disgusting car engines revving up pumping out all the fumes...you would spend half your time coughing and spluttering and feeling really irritated and wanting to get away from it all...and then moving out to the country means all of a sudden the roads are open and clear the air is fresh...you can admire the blue sky...at night you can actually see all the stars and it is as if someone has opened up a whole new world of wonder and discovery and you can see things you never used to be able to see and breathe in deep fresh air...and *just enjoy life*...and walk *far more often*...and *savour each and every moment*...someone went travelling once and said they met a tribe in the Amazon rainforest and this tribe told them a story about how there used to be a path they used to all follow...almost religiously they would follow this path...and the path was the quickest route, but full of danger...and not everyone following this old path would make it...many people would die trying to make this journey or get severely injured on the trip...and then one day someone came to the tribe and said why don't you just *find a new path*...a safe path...and they said that they had used the old direct path for generations...and this person encouraged them to find a safe way through and the more they hacked through this new path, the more established it became and they eventually had a much easier and safer path to follow...and so they all just *follow this new path*...and they continued to hack away at this new path over and over again making it easier to follow each time they travelled on it...and being in a jungle it didn't take long before the old path had filled itself in and vanished and they couldn't even remember exactly where it was...and now they just had this new path which led to what they thought of as the gift of life...it was a fresh water spring...so they had fresh clean water...but they had got so in the habit before they had this new path, of following that old path that it had become tradition to just follow the old path without ever once thinking that it was even a possibility to *create a new path*...yet once they realised that *you can have a new path*...they just *follow the new path*...and as you listen to me and *respond to everything I say* on an unconscious level and respond fully and honestly I'm sure a part of you will be curious to know what I was talking about earlier about setting you a task...and at the end I will let you know...and I know that right now *you are hypnotised*...and I know that *you are learning*....on an unconscious level...how to *create new change*...you know as a child you learnt to count you learnt how to write you learnt how to read and all of these tasks you found terribly difficult to start with...and you really struggled with them...you struggled to notice the difference between a 3 and an m...between a d and a b...between a 2 and a z...there was so much confusion and it was so difficult...yet you mastered this and stopped having to give it any thought in the same way that many, many years ago you learnt how to stand up and walk and it was so difficult to start with...you would stand up...balancing your weight onto one knee and then the other knee and a hand...perhaps holding onto something and pulling yourself up a bit and as you got yourself up you would swap a knee for a foot and as you put weight on that foot you would fall over…and you would keep trying and trying until eventually you manage to get the second foot up and then you would lift a foot off the ground and you would fall over again…and you would try and try and try again until you got into that position again and this time as *you take a step* you would move your body weight and discover *you can take a step* but then when you try to *take the second step* you discover that if you try to move the same foot again you fall over again…then you keep trying until you figure out you need to move the other foot to take a step and have to shift your body weight to take a step…and it can take many months to master just taking a few simple steps yet once you have mastered it you are growing all the time so you have to keep adapting and changing because your feet are suddenly slightly larger…your legs are suddenly slightly longer…your arms are suddenly slightly longer so your centre of gravity totally shifts so you constantly have to relearn how to walk repeatedly over and over again…but within a couple of years you have mastered this and although you continue to grow and continue to change shape...continue to change size...you continue to *adapt easily and effortlessly* to all the changes that go on around you...*finding it easy and effortless to adapt to change*...now I know that you are listening to me...I know that you want to stop that old behaviour...and I know that you are *responding fully to everything I say*...and I know that at times you won't even realise that you are doing that...and with your eyes shut and your body just as it is...I'd like you to begin to *use your imagination*...and just imagine...that you go to bed one night...and imagine that you wake up in the morning...and you have amnesia for that old behaviour...you have amnesia for ever having had that old behaviour...so just imagine...*how your day will go*...what will you be doing as you get out of bed...what will the first thing be that you do...and just imagine that...and just imagine running through your day...what will be the second thing you do...how will your whole morning go...and remember as you imagine this...that *you have total 100% amnesia for ever having had that old behaviour*...so it's not a case of saying I wouldn't be doing this or I wouldn't be doing that...the question is...*what are you doing*...so what are you doing in the morning...how are you enjoying your mornings...what things are you doing...what are you having to get done...what are other people saying to you and doing around you...and then as the day progresses what are you doing throughout the day...really take time to *get absorbed deeply*...and living a day in your life...the first future day of many...look at things like...when stress occurs in your life...what do you choose to do...how do you...*deal with different stress in your life*...is it that you...*take yourself out of situations*...is it that you...*close your eyes and drift into hypnosis briefly*...is it that *you breathe in a certain way* to *relax yourself*...is it that you hear my voice in your mind...or do you do something totally different or a mixture of these depending on the type of situations...do you keep lists to help time management...are you assertive to make sure you are not overworked...what is it you do...throughout the day...especially at those times where there are extreme amounts of stress that are unavoidable and unexpected...what is it you do so well...really explore that...and take time to explore that...how the way you handle it makes *you feel so good*...make *you feel a sense of pleasure, a sense of pride, a sense of achievement*...and really explore that...(pause for about 30 seconds)...that's it...and as you explore your way through this day...just explore your way through many other days as well...and even through many different situations and the situations could just come to mind...or they could be contained within future days...in a clear structure...and just allow yourself to explore...what it is like to be in future situations...where perhaps in the past you might have thought...I'm bored...what is it you do instead of being bored...what is it you choose to do...you know the wonderful thing about boredom is it means you've got some free time...and the wonderful thing about free time is that you can do whatever you want for that period of time...because you've got nothing else more important to get on with and if you have then you should be getting on with it...and you know it is easy to become compelled to finish things once they are started...and it is easy to become compelled to start things without any commitment to necessarily finish them as long as it is all positive for your health and wellbeing...so I want you to take plenty of time now to explore many future situations...situations where...perhaps you would have struggled to manage in the past...situations where as *you manage them now*...your brain releases feel good chemicals...like endorphins and dopamine...to make you feel good for making the right decisions and the more positive decisions you make the more *you feel good* and the more feel good chemicals get released into your brain...and the more you then *enjoy making positive decisions*...and you can take as long as you like to imagine day after day after day cycling round waking up going through a day...all the way through to when you go to bed and fall asleep at night...and then waking up and going through a day all the way through to falling asleep at night...and you can imagine going day after day month after month year after year...some days can just seem to blend into others...being quite mundane with not a lot happening...other days can be full of incredibly challenging difficult events and incidents...that you can enjoy experiencing how *you can overcome those*...in a new way...and just experience year after year after year of what it is like...to live a life entirely without that old habit...because of *having amnesia of it when you wake up*...and because *you have amnesia of it when you wake up*...you can experience what this life is like...and remember...*imagination always out does willpower*...(pause for about 1 minute)...and as you continue to...*go through all those different situations in your mind*...I'm going to carry on talking to you in the background...and you don't have to pay any attention to me just pay attention to imagining more and more situations that could arise and how they can go...there was a person that used to get bullied...and they would get bullied pushed around, beaten up, be called names...they would walk around head hung low...always embarrassed, always feeling worthless...and then one day they just thought *I've had enough of this I'm quitting*...I'm not putting up with this anymore...and the bullies knocked this person to the ground...and they just stood up and the bullies knocked them to the ground again and they just stood up again...previously they used to react...previously they used to either get angry or get scared...either response fed the bully...either response meant the bully could feed off of that response and get more powerful...yet now...the bully would show their face...they would try to get a reaction out of the person...and all the person would do is stand up again...and then stand up again...they didn't show fear...they didn't show anger they showed absolutely no emotion *at all*...and within the space of a day the bully got so bored that they left them alone because suddenly they realised that it didn't matter what they did, it didn't work...and the thing about bullies is they often *give up*...if they can't manage to get a reaction whether it's an anger reaction or a fear reaction...they would *just quit*...and they would *stop*...and you know memories can seem like videos...when you play them back in your mind...they give you certain feelings...but if they are played in fast forward or rewind or with no sound or with the sound sounding like Mickey Mouse because they are fast forwarding or rewinding they don't give you those feelings or it could be the picture is too bright or too dark so you can't see what is on the video...in fact you can watch some pretty traumatic stuff on a video and not pick up on what feelings are contained within that video because of the fact that it doesn't look or sound right to give you that type of feeling and your unconscious can understand that on a deep level and apply it where necessary...now I mentioned that there was a task...and the task is this...that if you ever happen to get an old craving...you have a choice...you can either choose to ignore it...in any way that seems fit for you...you can tell yourself now 'if I get a craving, then I will ignore it' (give a few moments for the client to say this to themselves)...it could be distracting yourself it could be doing something else...it could be accepting that maybe you have been working for too long a period and the craving isn't actually a craving it is a signal telling you to take a break so you take a break as the action for the craving...or you can carry out the task...and the task is that if you get a craving and you decide that you want to act on it...you are to go outside...and run as fast as you can for five minutes...and time that five minutes exactly so that you run for exactly five minutes no longer and no shorter...but exactly five minutes...as fast as you can...and then as soon as five minutes is up, you decide whether you want a cigarette or not...and if you want one feel free to have one...and if you don't want one feel free not to...so everything is about choice...nothing is taken away from you...everything is about choice and freedom...so if on the off chance you do get any of the old cravings...you can either choose to ignore it in any way you see fit...or choose to accept that it is a signal to tell you that actually you need to take a break because you have been really busy in which case you take a break…but if on the off chance you decide you want to have a cigarette then you can feel a compulsion…*you will run*…for exactly five minutes as fast as you can…before then deciding whether to have that cigarette or not…and at that point *you can choose not to* or you can choose to have it…and you can *always keep in mind*…any time that you have made the decision that you are going to have a cigarette or that you are going to want one…*you will run for exactly five minutes* and at the end of exactly five minutes you will then decide whether you will have that cigarette or not have that cigarette and *that decision will be made at the end of you running five minutes*…(pause for a minute)…

Once the client has exited hypnosis and before they leave the session set this same task (as mentioned in the script) so that they consciously get told and have a chance to consciously agree to do the task. Tell them you look forward to hearing how they get on next session (if you aren't planning on having another session find a time where you will be calling or catching up to find out how they are getting on). It is helpful to also explain 'consciously' that they can ignore any cravings in any healthy way they like, and that they can frequently tell themselves 'if I get a craving, then I will ignore it', but if they decide that they want a cigarette then they can run for five minutes before making the final decision on whether to have the cigarette or not.

## Quit Smoking Reprogramming Technique

And as you listen to me I know you want to *quit smoking now*...this process will require your full attention and conscious involvement...what I would like to have you do now is to get a sense of that craving you have had in the past that had led to you smoking...once you have a sense of that craving and can really begin to feel it just let your head nod (wait for the head nod)...that's it...and now get a sense of where in your body that feeling is...as if it is a physical entity somewhere inside your body...get a sense of where it is inside your body...and now whilst you have got that craving there don't let it go just keep it there...and as you do, just think of the worst negative effect of giving in to that craving that could happen...so it could be something like dying because of ill health like getting lung cancer...or making a child ill because of your smoking...or it could be that you have no money because you are spending it all on smoking...whatever it is for you that you can think of...it doesn't matter if that outcome has never convinced you previously to...*stop*...because many smokers already know all of these outcomes...packets of cigarettes nowadays normally have disgusting pictures on them with the effects of smoking but it hadn't put smokers off but it is only a small part of this process...now...very assertively...say in your mind...*NO*...very assertively say in your mind...*NO*...*you don't want that*...and then when you say that see an image in your mind...almost like a movie in your mind seeing through your eyes hearing through your ears of everything playing out perfectly of having a future with the ideal outcome of saying NO...*what are the benefits of saying no to the old smoking habit* (say with curiosity)...really think about what those benefits are...because anyone that wants to...*quit smoking*...has to have an excellent reason for wanting to...*quit*...it's no good *quitting* for somebody else nobody quits unless they've got a good reason...so it could be for your health...it could be financial...it could be that *you find it very tedious* and you wish you weren't addicted...whatever it happens to be, just imagine what you will see and hear and feel having said NO and *feel incredible pleasure with yourself for saying NO*...now open your eyes and then close your eyes again and get that craving back again...try and make that craving as strong as you can...try and increase that feeling as strong as you can...and as you increase that feeling...increase the sensations of the negative side effects of giving in to that feeling...and then assertively say NO...and then see all the positive effects and feel incredible pleasure with yourself for winning for saying NO for being a success...for achieving things...and then open your eyes and then close your eyes again and try really hard to build that craving up again really try and build that craving up again and as that craving builds up really build up all those images all those negative images associated with what the outcome is if you had given in to that craving and then assertively say NO...and then see all the pleasure and experience all the pleasure of overcoming all that...experience the pleasure of success...really be aware of all the positive outcomes in the future because of having said NO...and then open your eyes and then close your eyes again...*it will be harder each time*...but really try hard to get that craving really try to increase that craving...really try to increase it...just get all those images again all the negative effects of if you had given in to that old craving...and then assertively say NO...and then get that feeling of pleasure and the positive images in your mind...images of success...images of what life is like...being fitter and healthier...more full of energy...keeping those around you fitter and healthier...what others will notice...what friends will notice...what family will notice...how it will make the home perhaps smell different...how it will make you smell different...whatever it is for you that comes to mind...then open your eyes and close your eyes and try and build that craving up whilst building up those negative images...and whilst you build up those negative images then say NO...then get all that positive feelings and positive images...then open your eyes then close your eyes...try and build up that craving again associated with those images then say NO then go to all the positive feelings again and the positive images...then open your eyes and close your eyes...and try and build up that craving again...really try hard to build up that craving again…with all those negative images and then say NO and then see all the positive feelings and positive images and experience all that positivity of having said NO…and then open your eyes and close your eyes…really try hard again to build up that old craving really try hard to build up that old craving with those images and then say NO and then see all the positive images and positive feelings and enjoy that for a moment and then open your eyes and close your eyes…try and get that craving back again…try really hard to get that craving back…with those negative feeling and negative images and then say NO…and then see the positive feelings and positive images and build all that up and let it increase and double that and double it and double it some more…*really cranking the positivity up*…and then allow yourself to *enjoy drifting into the future* to what the future holds leaving here a *new you*…explore what the future hold over the next year and in years to come…what changes will you be around to see and enjoy…what will others notice about this new you…how will you be able to enrich the lives of others because of changes you make here today…just take as long as you need to *explore that now*…(pause for about three minutes)…

## *Dissociation and reintegration quit smoking process*

Just imagine a TV in front of you…it can be a big giant TV screen so that you can see everything clearly with surround sound and you've got the remote control so you are completely in control of what is going on…and just get a sense of seeing yourself on that screen…seeing yourself sitting where you are now and I don't know whether the camera angle is from behind you or from where I'm sitting or from in front of you but just see yourself on that screen sitting there…and then just watch as that you stands up leaving something behind…*stand up as a non-smoker*…now you don't know yet how that *you become a non-smoker* that isn't important, just watch as they stand up and they *leave here as a non-smoker*…they walk through the door and just have that camera follow them as they leave…and that you goes and carries on doing what you are going to do after this and you go on into the future seeing that you doing what you will be doing later on…and maybe it is at a time you see them looking in a mirror or maybe it is whilst they are having a drink or some other situation you suddenly see a little smile come across their face and you know that although you didn't hear it you know that what just ran through their mind was that they still hadn't had a cigarette and they hadn't even thought about it...and even in situations where they would have done they still haven't thought about having one...that's it...and just imagine watching that you enjoying the rest of the day and evening and then watch that you mixing with other people...smokers and non-smokers...and see that you on that screen really be challenged...perhaps someone is constantly pestering you to have a cigarette...and see your assertive response to them...see that new response...and then watch as that you is just mixing with smokers in a new way...and watch as that you gets into a situation where they feel a little bit nervous or stressed...and see how they handle that situation differently...notice how that you can become absorbed in small things when it is the right time to do so...like being absorbed in a certain feeling or sensation or something you can see or hear...and then just move forward slightly further into the future...and watch yourself talking to someone about how pleased you are with your progress...and notice how that you quickly gets distracted to talking about other mundane things forgetting about what you were talking about...and watch that you falling asleep and then waking up the next day and going through a new day in a new way...experiencing various events and situations...watch as that you goes through a variety of different days...watching how that you takes breaks when they are needed, appropriately and in a healthy manner...enjoying socialising...eating meals...chatting with people and communicating in a variety of ways...all in a new way...and after a few months, see that you talking with someone about how they still haven't had any cigarettes since that day they were hypnotised...and you know there is a voice that you listen to on one of your shoulders that tells you all those things that are good and that are positive and I wonder which shoulder it is on...and that voice has the power to give you pleasurable experiences to remind you why you should listen to it...and you have control of that pleasurable voice and the voice on the other side...and you can turn down the volume of the voice on the other side and you can change the voice speed so that if it tries to tell you to have a cigarette it just sounds like Mickey Mouse and *you just can't take that voice seriously*...and *the more that voice talks the quieter it gets*...and the quieter it gets the stronger the other voice becomes...and just get a sense of restarting that video again on that screen in front of you and this time step inside that video into that you on the screen so that it is all in 3D so that you can see what you will see...hear what you will hear and feel what you will feel...get a sense of sitting there and getting up and leaving something behind...and then run through this experience...what you will be doing later...having that small smile as you realise you still haven't had a cigarette...and falling asleep...and waking up in a new day and enjoying it in a new way...and taking breaks...socialising...communicating with others...all in a new way...and notice that at times *when you need to relax your breathing changes and relaxes* and gets deeper and each outbreath gets slightly longer than each in-breath...that's it...and then just notice yourself in the future...a long way into the future looking back and talking to a young child and the child looks familiar but you don't know why yet...and the young child is asking about that thing that people used to do in the olden days...and that child asks did you ever used to do that smoking thing...and you explain that you did it for a while and that it was a horrible habit and *you stopped*...and like all children they can't stop asking questions and they ask why...and you explain to them why...and they ask other questions...and you tell them about the day you stopped...and you tell them that occasionally there were times where you would find situations difficult so you would *go and take time out to relax*...and as you talk to this young child you feel a sense of pride of what you have achieved as you look into this familiar child's eyes...and by *stopping smoking* you have had a lifetime to share so much love...and from that one event where *you stopped smoking* there have been many knock on events with positive changes and positive effects on the lives of others and even on the lives of people you don't yet know...and the child asks you what would life be like had you not *stopped smoking*...and as you think about this, tears come to your eyes...as you realise that the child may not be there if you hadn't stopped and that you may not have been there...and as you think about what might have been had you made a different decision...you get a thought of lying in a hospital bed with your loved ones around you seeing you lying there with the sounds of the hospital equipment and a child crying by the bed wondering what is happening to you and whether you will be coming home...and notice how that thought is the straw that breaks the camel's back...it is the thought that makes you think...*never again*...and I don't know whether this is the thought that comes to mind whenever you are offered a cigarette or think about having a cigarette...and the thought that reminds you why you are staying stopped...and that positive voice helps you and encourages you...and just take a moment to see a whole chain of events all happening almost like they are on individual slides with each one different smoking experiences from the past...just watch them all running backwards almost like they are all videos rewinding so that each and every one of those past events of smoking all at the same time running in reverse so they all start at the end and run all the way back to the beginning...each and every event all the way back to that first ever cigarette you had all run in reverse...with the images happening in reverse...the audio in reverse and the feelings happening in a new direction...and when you sleep tonight you can carry on this reprogramming...and all those videos can wear themselves out running in reverse then restarting at the end and running in reverse again...then restarting at the end again and continuing this until it just becomes too much effort...and when you exit hypnosis you can bring back a strong sense of *never again* and drift back to the you sat here with me now reintegrating fully and completely into the here and now...(pause for about one minute)...

## *Weight loss – trance-like eating, can't stop eating*

That's right...and you know there are times when you appear to be in your own world while you eat...and you can discover when to apply the brakes...and as you listen to me a part of you can begin to explore possibilities and past learning's and even one off events where you instinctively applied the brakes at the correct time without even realising you did it on a conscious level...and you know there have been times when you have eaten a healthy amount and felt full and times when you have pushed just past that healthy amount and felt bloated...and at these times you have a habit of stopping without even thinking about it...and you can learn now on an unconscious level how to apply this to all of your future eating situations…and I wonder when you are in the future looking back what the main thing was that changed an old eating habit…and at what point you noticed eating had become a conscious act and after about 5 minutes of eating it starts to become a chore…you know sometimes the things we love most when done too much become tedious…and you can take some time now to really fully and honestly integrate all that is relevant to making the necessary changes…(pause for about 1 minutes)…

## Weight loss – metaphors for putting in hard work, getting a reward, finding the inner beauty, achieving your preferred physical image

And many years ago people used to travel hundreds of miles to scoop stones out of streams…and they would work hard to remove as many of those nuggets of Gold as they could…and they knew that all they had to do was work hard…remove the stones and they would be rewarded handsomely…and the job was hard work but they kept the goal in sight...they knew that hard work was for their future...and you know a sculptor can take a piece of rock and they will look at that rock and see the inner beauty...and while they hold that inner beauty in mind they will begin chipping away...removing all the unwanted stones...and as *stones fall off*...the sculpture begins to take shape until after lots of hard work and sweat a beautiful work of art is created...and you can take some time now to really fully and honestly integrate all that is relevant to making the necessary changes...(pause for about 3 minutes)...

## Weight loss – comfort eating or emotional eating

That's it...and you can imagine a TV in your mind and on that TV you can see a version of yourself drifting back to a time before any of the emotional or comfort eating began...and you may not even consciously realise when this was...and a part of you can go through all the relevant memories from that point forward that led to that old emotional eating habit forming and as that part of you works through those old memories it can look for any hidden emotion…you know many people with emotional eating problems discover that when they think back to the events that caused the emotional eating they remember emotions like guilt or shame or sadness…and when they focus on those memories a little longer they realise that they also had a feeling of pleasure or control or anger…and your unconscious can become aware of any hidden emotions in the old memories and begin to learn to *leave the past in the past* whilst *learning what is important for you* health and wellbeing in the present and future as *you form new and exciting habits*…and while the unconscious is forming these new habits your conscious can be curious what changes it will notice first…and consciously you can get a sense of different past situations that stand out and imagine them running backwards and forwards rapidly in your mind with all the action happening rapidly…with the speech sounding all sped up and squeaky and playing backwards and forwards and just notice how the emotion can begin to drain away the faster and faster those old memories flash backwards and forwards to the point where they are just a blur or a flash of light…and after a few moments they

318

can begin to settle back down looking similar but seeming so different...and in a moment I will quieten down in the background while your unconscious makes all the necessary changes to *create new coping strategies and opportunities for achievement*...(pause for about 1 minutes)...

## *Weight loss – limited tastes; eating too much 'junk food'*

That's it...and you know when a child is born they don't know what foods they will like or dislike...and over time they get made to try one thing...then another...and another...some they like some they hate but they *try them all anyway*...and as they grow up some children get used to eating certain foods and it's as if they get stuck in a rut...and as time goes on they forget about other foods they used to like and other foods they do like and forget to *keep trying new foods* and stick to what is familiar...and some foods they really didn't like but when they grew up and tried them they found their tastes had changed...and *your tastes change automatically*...and you know, I remember this man that used to eat the same meal whenever he went out...it didn't matter what was on the menu he always ate what was familiar to him...then one day he was in an unfamiliar situation out to dinner and the meal he normally picked wasn't on the menu...he didn't want to lose face in front of the couple that had invited him out so he decided to *just pick something different and eat it anyway*...he ate the meal and was surprised to find he actually *liked it*...following that experience he began to sample other foods on different menus...he discovered he liked more than he realised...some foods he liked a lot...other foods he didn't mind but wouldn't buy them himself if he had any other option and some foods he really didn't like the taste of...and you know the beauty of a rainbow is only possible because it is made up of a full range of colours...and you can *explore new options*...and you know in a mirror everything is reversed and you can see yourself in a mirror and as you step into the mirror and look back you can notice how you appear to be changing for the better over time into the you, you are becoming...and you can take some time now to really begin to...*make all these changes*...as you *drift deeper and deeper*...and you know if you wear glasses, at first you notice them, but over time you stop feeling them on your face...in the same way that you can walk into a room and notice a smell but after a few minutes you stop being aware of it...it's as if the smell is gone...(pause for about 3 minutes)...

## *Weight loss – wanting to exercise more*

That's it...and you know people are often surprised about how much exercise they actually get in an average day...and how much exercise you can get just from walking a little faster...*taking a few more steps*...having a leg instinctively *fidget* under a table during meals...when alone...or just when it is appropriate to do so...and it is often surprising to discover just how easy it is to *exercise without even trying*...and I wonder whether *you will find yourself exercising more* throughout the whole day or just during specific times of the day...and you can be curious to discover how easy it is to form a new and healthy habit...and I don't know whether that habit will develop into making time specifically to exercise or whether you will just *find yourself being more active* throughout each day...(pause for a minute) (Recommended that you also use the weight loss metaphors)

## *Depression caused by issues in the past*

That's it and there are unresolved issues in the past...and you can drift back to a time before any of those events occurred and as you then drift forward, you can get a sense of all of those issues forming slides in your mind almost like slides of movie film...and in a moment you can begin to watch yourself watching those slides like one long continuous movie...and as you watch yourself watching that movie you can notice how it all seems to be in black and white and grainy...and you can watch yourself watching that old movie as it fast forwards and rewinds so fast it looks like a blur...and it can continue to fast forward and rewind so fast any negative emotion just seems to drain freely out of all those old memories...and as it continues to fast forward and rewind certain memories can have bits added...you know we all wish certain events went differently or that we were able to say or do things we never did...and outside of conscious awareness these things can be done or said in a way that resolves those memories *putting them firmly in the past*...and you can take as long as you need over the next 2 minutes to work through all of those memories as you watch that you watching that old movie...*now*...(pause for 2 minutes)...that's right...as you now allow the past to be left right back in the past while focusing on what you have to look forward to in the future...and you don't even have to know consciously what you have to look forward to you can just allow *your unconscious* to guide you towards *pleasure and happiness* while you focus on making sure each foot is pointing in the right direction as you take each step and make sure that you only step with one foot at a time...(pause for 2 minutes)...

## *Depression caused by issues in the present*

That's it...and you know juggling in the dark is difficult...you need someone to help by turning a light on...and as you think now about all that is going on in your life you can begin to slow things down a little and take a step back in your mind…and you can step back in your mind and see things from a new perspective…and from this new perspective you can begin to look at what you need to get done and how…*you can do it*…and you can find that place in your mind where…*you can remain calm*…work through all those issues that in your normal waking life were consuming your mind…and you can consume a new way of dealing with things…and you know it is interesting that whatever one person finds a challenge or a problem someone else in the world will find…*it won't faze you*…and you know everyone responds to things differently…almost everyone knows someone either personally or has read about someone or seen them on TV that is in a similar situation yet seems to be *coping fine with it*…and finding solutions and you can be curious about how this is possible and what is different about how they respond…and what *you can learn unconsciously from this*…and how *this knowledge can empower and enhance your future*…and you can take *time now to really begin to integrate all the necessary changes*…(pause for about 2 minutes)…

## *Depression caused by worrying about the future*

That's it...now...some people find that they spend their time focusing on what might happen rather than on what does happen or on 'what if's'...and the interesting thing about the future is that it hasn't happened yet...so unlike the past or the present the future can become whatever you make it...and sometimes this can seem unlikely until...*you begin to focus on what you want in the future*...and...*begin to focus on how you will achieve that*...and...*focus on what you need to do to overcome future difficulties*...and...*over time things improve*...and you know at the top of any hill can be a wonderful view followed by a way down the other side...and it's interesting to think that any problem any one person finds difficult to handle there will be someone else that handles that fine...and if you were going to focus on what you want in the future I wonder what it will be...many people think about a question like that and initially respond by thinking about what they hope it won't be...they think...'I wouldn't have money difficulties'...or...'I won't keep getting upset about things'...and this thinking helps to maintain problems...as they...*learn this*...they begin to think about what they actually want and what life will be like as if they were following themselves around with a video camera...they...start saying things to yourself like 'I have stepped back and sorted out my finances...I have arranged payment plans...I have sorted out my spending and now spend only what I can afford each month...I have got help that I need...I have looked at what used to upset me and worked out how to handle it...I am planning more...when I notice something that used to make me worry I am looking at what I need to do and planning how I will handle those situations...If I can't change something or have no control over something I work out what I can do so that I can handle it, remaining calm...if something difficult happens it doesn't help to also be worrying about it...I now make sure I have a clear head instead...I *smile more*...I move around more and *feel more full of energy*...my sleep has improved...people around me seem happier...I *feel more relaxed*...'...and I wonder what changes will be for you and how quickly...*you will begin to notice the changes occurring*...and as a part of...*you give some therapeutic thought to what I have said*...another part of you can begin to…*learn to relax*…and it can take all the life experience you have of relaxing from falling asleep at night to being absorbed in a good book or film or conversation…and can *apply this natural learning to the future*…there are always things we can't control or change and unexpected things, and it is how you respond to these that defines the experience and its impact on you and whether that impact will be positive and empowering or not and as you apply this learning I will quieten down in the background…(pause for about 2 minutes)…

## *Depression where the client can't work out why they feel depressed*

That's it…and some people find they can feel depressed without even knowing why…and there may be no medical physiological reason why they should be depressed…and many of these people are often surprised to discover how much emotional thinking they do…and surprised to discover that even excessive positive emotional thinking that is unresolved like really wanting to achieve something  and thinking about that thing many hours a day yet never quite managing to achieve it or find resolutions to all they are thinking about...can lead to the brain feeling overloaded with constantly firing off new patterns like constantly opening new documents on a computer...and eventually it starts to run slower and slower until it begins to crash...and all that is needed is to close many of those documents and the computer works fine again...and *your unconscious*...can understand and know what it needs to do...and while *it does that*...a part of you can begin to notice a large painting in front of you...and you can begin to get your hands in the paint and move all the colours around...mixing colours...blending...and feeling compelled to continue to move those hands around moving that paint around until it feels like the picture is done...and the picture can end up looking like something or nothing...it can be abstract or realistic...you can have a sense of its meaning or have no conscious sense of the meaning of the painting...and as you move that paint around...*your unconscious*...can begin to reorganise connections and pathways in the brain...you know learning and change can happen quickly...everybody has had experiences where they have learnt a lesson from a single event and kept that new way of responding for the rest of their life...that's it...as you now take time to continue moving that paint around until that painting is complete I will quieten down in the background for a couple of minutes and you can take as long as you need over that time to make all the necessary changes and to complete that painting...and you can wonder how life will be different and what changes you will notice in the future and who else will notice a difference and how they will react and what they will say...(pause for about 2 minutes)...

## *Worrying about events*

That's it...and you know certain thoughts about certain situations can give us feelings of anxiety nervousness or panic...and other thoughts of situations can help us to *relax* and...*feel calm*...and anxiety is a natural survival response...and in the right place at the right time it can be a useful response...and as *you continue to relax* a part of you can begin to unpick what situations anxiety is useful for and what situations should *you respond differently*...and you can...*respond differently now*...in various situations...and many people wonder how...*you stop panic attacks or anxiety*...and to...*stop them before they occur*...you can...*learn to stop worrying*...and instead...*start problem solving*...and the more you problem solve what you used to worry about the more...*anxiety stops*...and you can preoccupy your mind and become absorbed in healthy activities and relationships and conversations...and as you do...*changes will occur in your life*...and people often wonder how...*you remain calm*...and it is useful to remember that a flood of emotion only lasts a few minutes and has to keep being topped up if it is going to stay...and you can rate this emotion in your mind from 1-10 and notice how it changes over time and how quickly it subsides...and notice that any response to that emotion also passes...and during negative emotions you can...*step outside yourself*...and...*become an observer*...while that you calms down...and I don't know how...*you will integrate this learning*...and how...*you will learn more for yourself*...and I will quieten down in the background while...*you take this time to learn and update the mind and body on an unconscious level*...and you know if a car alarm is set too sensitively it keeps going off and annoying people and irritating the owner...if the alarm isn't set sensitive enough someone may steal the car...and just like Goldilocks discovered it has to *be just right*...and you can say to yourself 'if I worry then I will look at whether I can do anything about it, if I can then I will, if I can't then I will ignore the worry' and you can say that to yourself and give yourself that message, before you take this time to make the necessary changes on an unconscious level (pause for about 2 minutes)...

## *Certain situations trigger panic*

That's it...and you can now just begin to get a sense of a TV set in your mind...and on that TV set can be images of situations that in the past caused you to panic when you were in them...and as you look at those still images they can begin to change...and the changes can begin to *drain all the emotion from them*...then as you continue to watch those images you can be curious to discover what will change as all the images appear on screen like a grid of images...all very small...like thumbnail pictures...and they all begin to rapidly fast-forward and rewind to the point where each picture just looks like a blur...and you don't have to consciously know what each image is of...you can just watch that therapy being done over there on that screen with those images...and as the therapy completes itself the images can one at a time slow back down again and come to rest...and when they do you can notice how comfortable you can feel as you look at those images and...*feel comfortable with those situations*...and a deep and instinctive part of you can learn from this experience in a way that is healthy and beneficial to you...as I quieten down in the background while...*that work gets completed*...(pause for about 3 minutes)...

## Managing pain of an injury that still needs looking after

That's it...and while you remain totally stationary I'd like to have you get a sense of a healing light surrounding your body...and that light can begin to enter the body with each breath that you take and as it enters your body it can begin to work through the body to that discomfort...and as it reaches that discomfort it can begin to cushion it and wrap around it...and it can cushion and wrap around more and more with each breath that you take...and that healing light can begin to take hold of that old discomfort shrinking it down smaller and smaller...and each photon of healing light is full of energy and the more you keep breathing the more healing light wraps tighter and tighter around that discomfort...and while the unconscious mind continues to wrap that up into an ever decreasing size you can listen to me...and you know you have a lifetime of experiences of treating discomfort...and it is interesting how 70% of discomfort is *comfort*...and you have experienced playing or having fun or being absorbed in an activity to the point where you don't notice aches and pains or cuts and bruises...and you have a lifetime of experience being so deeply asleep you lose the feeling in your body...and a lifetime of experiences being distracted by something more important...and I wonder what would happen to an experience of discomfort if a hungry Lion started chasing you...and you know people...*forget about discomfort*...and people...*step outside yourself*...and people...*imagine the sensation is different*...and people *habituate to constant feelings* so they...*stop noticing it*...and that healing light really can now wrap into a smaller and smaller ball until it is so small it can fit on a pin head...and as a ball small enough to fit on a pin head just glistening with that healing light it can begin to be moved around a little before you prepare to move it outside of yourself so that you can see it in front of you...and when you see that ball of light in front of you, you can be prepared to...*let it go*...and...let it fall to the floor and roll away...and I wonder whether you will...*feel different*...in a minute or when that ball rolls away...or a few moments after the ball has rolled away...or *just before you open your eyes*...or just before you prepare to come back out of hypnosis or just after those eyes open or before you leave here today...and you can wonder when that will happen...and now over the next 2 minutes you can take as long as is necessary to achieve the comfort you desire...(pause for about 2 minutes)...

## *Managing chronic pain – like arthritis*

That's it…and as you listen to the sound of my voice you can begin to *learn how you can remove discomfort in the future*…and you know you are sitting there…and you have dis*comfort* there…and you know that dis*comfort* isn't over here…and it isn't in my chair…and it isn't in the space between this chair and that chair and it isn't on a table or at a table…or in any of the vehicles outside…and it isn't in someone else's house…and it isn't in your bed at home or any other bed…and you know all that dis*comfort* is only there in that chair where you currently sit…*now*…the other day I was getting ready to go out when someone started talking to me…I put my keys down a moment on the chair while I was listening and getting my shoes on…when I left I discovered I had forgotten my keys…and you know we all have experiences like this…and these experiences seem to just happen…we don't need to try to make them happen…*it just happens all by itself*…and when I was younger I used to wonder why adults didn't take their hair home from the hairdressers…they would go into the hairdressers and look in a mirror and know what they want removed and the hairdresser would be friendly and talkative and would cut off all the hair the customer doesn't want and then the customer would look in the mirror and be pleased and would then pay the hairdresser and would then leave...leaving an old part of themselves at the hairdressers...and I used to wonder why if it was a part of them, they didn't want to keep it...one day I asked an adult this question and they told me that...once the hairdresser has removed what you don't want...*you are pleased with the results*...and...*you don't want to take what has been removed away with you*...you want to *leave it behind*...and so that's what you do...*you have no need for it anymore*...so why would you want to keep it...I understood this and knew it was a bit like how an artist may make a sculpture out of wood or stone and they would carve or chip away all that they don't want...and this can never be reattached...and they take the finished item from the work area to put on display...and the old wood or stone that has been removed can never be put back together with the finished sculpture...and you know that dis*comfort* only exists where you sit...*it doesn't exist anywhere else*...if someone searched anywhere outside of where you are sitting they wouldn't find that discomfort...and you know you can *learn on an unconscious instinctive level*...and you can know how to *leave something behind*...and you know there is a difference between feeling and doing...and you can feel like doing something but not do it...or do something but not feel it...and I don't know whether you will feel like leaving here at the end of the session or whether you will actually decide to leave here at the end of the session...and I know you came to see me because you want to *leave something behind*...and I know that when you go you will have a feeling you want to leave...and so many people leave their coat on the chair without realising as they leave...and they come back for it...and you can *leave something on the chair you decide you can live without*...and you can learn more from this on an unconscious level than you ever thought possible on a conscious level...and you can take some time now to integrate and absorb all that is necessary to leave here having achieved what you came here to achieve...and you can learn how you can apply what you have learnt here into everyday life and you know it is OK for parts of you to remain in hypnosis with each breath you take while the rest of you enjoys getting on with life...and you can leave here, *leaving that discomfort behind* and making all the necessary changes to *reduce the pain* and replace it with comfort...and making all the necessary changes unconsciously that can address the cause of that discomfort...and you can continue to make these changes and work on this with every daydream...with every dream at night...helping *you achieve long-term comfort*...(pause for about 3 minutes)...

## Removing phantom limb pain

That's it...and I wonder whether you have thought about how by having the skill of being able to create phantom pain you also have the skill to create phantom pleasure...and many people learn unconsciously how to create phantom pain before they...*discover how to create phantom pleasure*...and this is something you don't know how to do consciously...(pause for about a minute)...and I know someone that moved into a home beside a railway line...and those first few night the person found they couldn't sleep...each time a train went by they would suddenly be aware of it...they were finding this to be such a pain...then one day they had a friend visit...this friend was complaining about the sound of the trains asking if it annoys them and how they cope...and they suddenly realised they hadn't been aware of the trains for some time...and there was a therapist that moved house and it turned out that one of his neighbours had a dog that wouldn't stop barking...and he really didn't want to have to make a complaint but he found the constant barking day and night was such a pain...then one day he realised the barking had stopped...a few days after realising the barking had stopped he was out walking when he bumped into a neighbour and he spoke about how wonderful it was that the dog's owner had either got rid of the dog or trained the dog to stop barking...this neighbour asked him what he was talking about...the barking hadn't stopped or improved...and this therapist realised that what had happened was that he had habituated to the noise so that he filtered it out and stopped being aware of it...and a number of years ago a Scientist carried out an experiment. He was curious how factory worker that work in extremely noisy conditions seem to be able to talk normally to each other without shouting or raising their voices and they seem to hear each other perfectly fine...he asked a factory owner if he could spend some time in the factory and even sleep in the factory with all that noise...the owner though this was an odd request but said he could...when the Scientist arrived he was aware of how noisy it was and how the noise hurt his ears and how he couldn't hear what anyone was saying...he spent the day in the factory and slept the night...when he woke up the next day he noticed something odd had happened...he was able to hear and understand what the factory workers were saying...his unconscious had managed to block out the old constant background noise...and there are many possibilities and experiences that your unconscious can use to help you to...*find your own answer*...and many children grow up and leave home...and often parents find their child breaking away from the family a painful experience...some parents *work through this pain quickly*...others take some time...yet parents learn that they need to *move on* and they...*let the pain go*...and you can *learn on an instinctive level what you need to do* to...*move on*...and...*create the changes you want*...and over the next few minutes you can take as long as you need to honestly and fully *create those changes*...and you can be curious about when you will be looking back and realising *the old problem has been gone for a while now*...and you notice that you have made the changes necessary for phantom comfort in place of phantom pain...it is common for the brain to re-wire sensations or to try to make sense of missing information and as it gets used to making adjustments, so your brain can recognise that there are no signals from that missing limb and the sensations can pass...and I don't know whether this will happen gradually or all of a sudden, whether you will wake one day and notice no pain where you used to know pain...and you can look at that limb and see it as a part of you...*comfortably*...in your mind's eye...and notice over time that as *that old pain passes* and *inner changes occur*...and *all the necessary changes occur*...that the limb there in your mind's eye can fade away...like working through the loss of a friend...discovering that one-day *the time is right* to...*let go*...you know you will always know them...you will always love them...and they will always be a part of you...even now when they are apart from you...and you look back on them with *feelings of pleasure*...having moved on from looking back on them with feelings of pain and loss...(pause for about 3 minutes)...

## *Performance enhancement – getting in the zone*

That's it...and you can really begin to think about those times you have naturally been *'in the zone'*...and so many people find they...*get in the zone*...without trying or without knowing...*it is going to happen*...and...*entering the zone*...is an unconscious process...and while you listen to me *your unconscious* can begin to access all the memories of times...*you naturally enter the zone when you want to*...and on a conscious level you don't have to be aware of those memories whilst the unconscious part of you begins to...*explore those memories*...and to...*look for how you naturally enter the zone*...and when...*you enter the zone*...you do so easily and effortlessly...when you put effort into...*entering the zone*...you increase the chances of not...*entering the zone*...and you can take this...*experience now*...to really delve into how...*you enter the zone*...and you know you can...*enter the zone*...with a trigger and you don't even have to know what that trigger is...or how the trigger works...*the trigger can happen automatically*...and you know you have experience of triggers happening automatically...like seeing a red light and putting on the brakes...or hearing your name and suddenly and instinctively paying your attention to where your name came from...and I wonder how *you will naturally and instinctively enter the zone*...when the time is right...and your unconscious...can *find a trigger*...many golf players...*develop a trigger*...of...*entering the zone*...when they take hold of a golf club...and many snooker players...*develop a trigger*...of...*entering the zone*...when they hold the snooker cue...and many F1 drivers...*set up a trigger*...and...*enter the zone*...when they hold the steering wheel...and I wonder how...*you will enter the zone*...and what your trigger will be...and a part of you can...*learn that instinctively*...and as...*you now learn that instinctively*...you can wonder what it will feel like...that feeling of...*focus*...that feeling that...*all of your attention narrows to the task at hand*...that all distractions disappear...that *time seems to slow down*...and you discover it's like *you're in your mind observing what your body is doing*...as Bruce Lee said 'I don't punch...it punches'…and you can now take the time to *create all the necessary changes* on an instinctive level…and you can take as long as is necessary for you over the next few minutes…to…make it possible to *enter the zone state instinctively and effortlessly* in those situations you want it to happen automatically in…(pause for about 3 minutes)…

## *Performance enhancement – improving ability*

That's it…and as you continue to relax you can take some time to create an environment in your mind where you can…*learn what you need to know*…and there was someone that needed to learn for an exam in school and they took the time to…*create a place to learn in the mind*…and they went to that place and discovered a round table with people that were the leaders in their fields sat at the table and they sat at the table with these people and enjoyed conversations about their specialist subjects as they absorbed the learning…and another person wanted to learn to sing and dance at the same time…and they knew how to sing…and they knew how to dance...they just needed to learn to sing and dance at the same time...and they created a dance studio in their mind where a top instructor guided them through months of rehearsal...*learning...and practicing*...until they mastered singing and dancing at the same time...and you can *learn what will work best for you*...and now I'd like to have you just get the sense of a large TV in your mind...and on that TV just get a sense of a slightly older version of yourself...and watch that slightly older version of yourself and you know what you want help with and what you want to improve and in a moment you can watch that slightly older version of *you perform perfectly*...everything they do will *be faultless*...and you can watch them even in challenging situations...*doing everything perfectly and effortlessly*...and I wonder how much you know about the research carried out into mental rehearsal that showed that people that used mental rehearsal with very little actual practice performed better than those that spent the same length of time practicing...in mental rehearsal they practiced *performing perfectly* over and over again...whereas in real life practice people made mistakes and learnt how not to *perform correctly* as well as how to *perform correctly*...and it is important to *carry out real life practice* and you can discover how much improvement *you achieve each time you enter hypnosis*...and you can *drift into hypnosis before you fall asleep or as you wake up or while you stand in a queue or any other situation that is appropriate and safe to do so*...and each trance you have can enhance the effectiveness of this work towards achieving what you want...and I don't know whether it will be the spaces between my words or each outbreath you take that helps you to...*improve performance*...and I wonder what will help that improvement continue...and you know it's interesting how as a child you thought differently and your thinking style allowed you to...*learn effortlessly*...and you made mistakes but they were part of the learning and they made *you learn even quicker*...and you learnt to master walking...learnt to master talking...learnt to master a whole range of complex processes, tasks and activities...and you continue to do so...and in a moment you can take all the time you need to *absorb and integrate new learning* and create and begin to *strengthen relevant neural pathways in the mind and body*...and your unconscious can draw up every single time you got a part of that correct and during this time can piece all of those parts together…in the same way someone can do this with golf and draw up that one time they made contact with the ball just right…that one time they had their feet just right…that one time they were thinking just right…the one time they got that swing just right…the one time they got the grip just right…and all these parts can be recalled unconsciously and linked together…and you can *honestly and fully carry this out…now*…that's it…as you take some time for mental rehearsal…now…(pause for about 3 minutes)…

## Learning to relax

That's it…and you can take this opportunity to…*really absorb new ideas*…and you can instinctively *begin responding in a new way*…and as you absorb new ideas and instinctively begin to respond in a new way I wonder what other benefits you will notice…now…one way to…*really learn to relax*…is to begin to master 7-11 breathing…and 7-11 breathing is a way of breathing that creates real and rapid physiological changes…and each time you breathe in counting to 7 and out counting to 11...you *begin to master the relaxation response*...and whenever your outbreath is longer than your in-breath you trigger the relaxation response...and *feel good*...chemicals and hormones release through your body...and you can learn other ways to...*discover yourself instinctively relaxing deeply*...and one way you can...*discover yourself relaxing deeply*...is to master self-hypnosis or meditation...and you know the more you enter self-hypnosis or meditation the more *relaxation becomes a part of who you are as a person*...and as...*you master relaxation*...it begins to become more instinctive and...you find *relaxation happens all by itself*...another way to...*learn to relax*...is to allow your mind to wander and to think about pleasant experiences or even think about a pleasant time you have been hypnotised or drifted off into a trance, daydream or reverie...and the more the mind faces challenges the more *the body can relax*...and there are times when relaxation isn't an appropriate response and times when it is...and you know which times are which...and I wonder what else you know that you didn't know you know yet you knew you knew it without realising...as *you master the art of relaxing* when that is the ideal response to have...and you can learn here and now how to re-enter hypnosis and really...*learn how to enter hypnosis instinctively*...and feelings occur unconsciously first and I wonder whether *your unconscious will decide to trigger relaxation when you begin to feel unconsciously stressed* or whether your unconscious will wait until you begin to think you need to relax...and you can *discover that for yourself*...and each time you enter a trance you can *learn to relax* in your own unique way...and you can take some time now to make the necessary changes on an instinctive level to...*learn to relax...now*...(pause for about 3 minutes)...

## Removing a phobia with no known origin

That's it...now as you imagine you are sitting in the world's most comfortable chair...a chair so comfortable you find all you can do in it is *relax*...as *you relax* you can (look over to where you want them to imagine the TV and do this whenever you are talking about that TV so that you are being congruent with what you are saying) begin to notice a small old fashioned black and white TV set...and at the moment the TV is switched off...and in a minute...while you continue to *relax deeper and deeper with each breath you take*...an old, old movie will appear on that black and white screen...and it will be an old movie made up from all the memories that led to the development and maintenance of the phobia...and you don't have to know what any of those memories are...you can *just relax and follow the process*...and that collection of old memories will begin from a time before that old phobia response developed...a time you were happy...calm and playful...all the way through those old memories to a time after that phobia had passed and you were calm and happy...and before that old distant movie plays I'd like you to get a sense of drifting out of your body...through space and time...drifting and relaxing to a position over beside that old TV (talk facing where you would like them to be beside the TV)...to a position where you can look over and see the you sat here (saying this looking back at where they are sitting) but can't see what is on the TV...and when you have done that allow the head to nod...(wait for the head to nod)...that's right...and in a moment I want you (talking to where they are by the TV) to watch that you over there (looking at where the client is sitting) pressing fast forward on the TV remote when I say now…and watch that you sat there watching that old distant movie rapidly all the way through from that calm point at the beginning to that calm point at the end…and then when you have done that just allow the head to nod…and do that…now…(say these parts quickly)…that's it and really, really quickly fast forwarding that old movie all the way through to the end and allowing the head to nod…(watch for the head nod)…that's right…and now drift through space and time and float into the paused end of that old distant movie (saying this facing the TV)…drift into that calm paused end of that old distant movie…seeing what you saw…hearing what you heard and feeling what you felt…and once you have done that you can allow the head to nod (wait for the head to nod)…that's right…and in a moment when I say now I'd like you to rewind all the way back to that calm point at the beginning…and I'd like you to take no more than 2 seconds to do this…then allow the head to nod…and do that…now…that's it rewinding rapidly all the way back to the beginning…everything happening backwards the speech happening backwards…the action happening backwards and all the feelings happening in a new direction...that's it...(say all of this facing the TV and wait for head nod)...and now just get a sense of drifting through space and time back into that seat (looking over at the client) and in a moment when I say now I'd like you to watch that old, old distant movie all the way through to that calm end...then allow the head to nod...and take no more than a second to do that...and do that...now...fast forwarding that old, old movie all the way to the end taking no more than a second then allowing the head to nod...that's it...and now get a sense of drifting through space and time into the end of that old distant movie (looking back at the TV)...seeing what you saw...hearing what you heard and feeling what you felt...and when I say now you can rewind all the way back to the beginning to that calm point at the beginning...and as you do everything can go in a new direction...people can speak in reverse...all the action can happen in reverse...and the feelings can go in a new direction...and you can do that taking no longer than the sound of a snap of the fingers...and then allow the head to nod...and you can do that...now (snap your fingers)...that's right...and now you can get a sense of drifting through space and time to that chair and as you relax comfortably in that chair, (said looking at the client again) when I say now you can watch that old distant movie (said while glancing over to the TV) through at a speed you are comfortable with...and when you have finished comfortably watching that old movie the head can nod...and you can do that now...that's right...and now you can get a sense of a you in the future on that screen...and the screen can become clearer and more desirable...and as it does you can watch that you in any future situations that would have led to you feeling uncomfortable in the past as that old you...and you can really begin to explore what is different when you respond in this new way...and you can *now take some time to relax and instinctively integrate and update your mind and body patterns*...(pause for 3 minutes)...

## *Removing a phobia or PTSD with a known origin*

(With phobias & PTSD it is often best to de-traumatise the worst or earliest memory first then the 2nd and 3rd worst memories if necessary. In many cases there may well only be a single memory that needs working with)

That's it...now as you imagine sitting in that comfortable chair...a chair so comfortable you find all you can do in it is *relax*...as *you relax* you can (face over to where you want them to imagine the TV and do this whenever you are talking about that TV so that you are being congruent with what you are saying) begin to notice a small old fashioned black and white TV...and at the moment the TV is off...and in a minute...while *you continue to relax deeper and deeper with each breath you take*...an old, old movie will appear on that black and white screen...and it will be an old movie of that first or the earliest remembered phobia memory...and that old memory will begin from a time before that old phobia response occurred...a time you were happy and calm...all the way through that old memory to a time after that situation had passed and you were calm and happy...and before that old distant movie plays I'd like you to get a sense of drifting out of your body...through space and time...drifting and relaxing to a position over beside that old TV...to a position where you can look over and see the you sat here but can't see what is on the TV...and when you have done that allow the head to nod...(wait for the head to nod)...that's right...and in a moment I want you to watch that you over there pressing fast forward on the TV remote when I say now...and watch that you sat there watching that old distant movie rapidly all the way through from that calm point at the beginning to that calm point at the end...and then when you have done that just allow the head to nod...and do that...now...(say these parts quickly)...that's it and really, really quickly fast forwarding that old movie all the way through to the end and allowing the head to nod...(watch for the head nod)...that's right...and now drift through space and time and float into the paused end of that old distant movie...drift into that happy paused end of that old distant movie...seeing what you saw...hearing what you heard and feeling what you felt...and once you have done that you can allow the head to nod...that's right...and in a moment when I say now I'd like you to rewind all the way back to that calm point at the beginning...and I'd like you to take no more than 2 seconds to do this...then allow the head to nod...and do that…now…that's it rewinding rapidly all the way back to the beginning…everything happening backwards the speech happening backwards…the action happening backwards and all the feelings happening in a new direction…that's it…(wait for head nod)…and now just get a sense of drifting through space and time back into that seat and in a moment when I say now I'd like you to watch that old, old distant movie all the way through to that calm end…then allow the head to nod…and take no more than a second to do that…and do that…now…fast forwarding that old, old movie all the way to the end taking no more than a second then allowing the head to nod…that's it…and now get a sense of drifting through space and time into the end of that old distant movie…seeing what you saw…hearing what you heard and feeling what you felt…and when I say now you can rewind all the way back to the beginning to that calm point at the beginning…and as you do everything can go in a new direction…people can speak in reverse…all the action can happen in reverse…and the feelings can go in a new direction…and you can do that taking no longer than the sound of a snap of the fingers…and then allow the head to nod…and you can do that...now (snapping your fingers)...that's right...and now you can get a sense of drifting through space and time to that chair and as you relax comfortably in that chair when I say now you can watch that old distant movie through at a speed you are comfortable with...and when you have finished comfortably watching that old movie the head can nod...and you can do that now...that's right...and now you can get a sense of a you in the future on that screen...and the screen can become clearer and more desirable...and as it does you can watch that you in any future situations that would have led to you feeling uncomfortable in the past as that old you...and you can really begin to explore what is different when you respond in this new way...and you can now take some time to relax and instinctively integrate and update your mind and body patterns...(pause for 3 minutes)...

## Obsessive Compulsive Disorder Relief

That's it...and you can begin to get a sense of a TV in your mind...and on that TV in your mind you can begin to notice a slightly older version of yourself...and you know there is a difference between what is appropriate and what is inappropriate and a part of you knows that difference...and as you watch that you on that TV you can begin to notice as they drift back in their mind to the initial memory that led to that OCD...and as you watch that you recall that experience you can watch as they receive all the appropriate and necessary support to help them develop a new way of handling things...and you can watch as they really recall that experience...and sometimes compulsive behaviours begin with a single event other times they have a number of events and the experience that leads to the compulsive behaviour is an event of thinking in a different way to that final event...almost like the straw the breaks the camel's back...and you can watch that slightly older version of yourself as they explain to that younger version of yourself what the future will hold if they respond in a specific way and what they need to do to prevent that response unfolding...and you can watch as they help that younger you to...*keep the problem in the past*...and you know sometimes people worry about something happening again and then develop a habit of prevention...and this habit of prevention can be set too sensitive...and while you watch that you being helped you can begin to unconsciously process what is an appropriate sensitivity that will let you know any risk is reduced to an acceptable level...and some people get really frustrated with their car alarm because it is so sensitive a leaf landing on the car triggers the alarm...and the owner has to keep going back to the car to reset the alarm...and it can be very frustrating and time consuming...and even when they don't hear the alarm going they are always on edge thinking at any time now the alarm could go again...and they feel so relieved when they have the alarm fixed or set to a lower sensitivity...and some children learn that plants need water and sunlight to live and grow...and because plants often start growing slowly some children get frustrated and think they must be doing something wrong because their plant isn't yet grown...and they will give the plant more and more water and the plant can't handle all the water and dies...other children think the plant needs more sunlight and because the plant hasn't grown enough yet they will give it more light...and then in the strong overwhelming sun the plant withers and dies...yet the child that let the plant do what the plant's got to do…and they *just relax* and have patience…and each day they check the soil is moist and only add some water if it is too dry…and they allow the plant light but not too much…and if they see signs the plant is getting too much sun they move the plant out of the sun a bit more…and they respond to the plant's needs…these children grow successful plants…and they find it more effortless because they haven't spent all their time worrying…and you can notice how that future you has been able to help that you from the past…and how they now begin to imagine future situations where that old behaviour would have happened and notice as it doesn't and notice how calm that future you looks as they watch a future you in those different situations…and at times that future you can watch some of the more challenging situations as they rapidly fast forward and rewind while they watch until they notice all the old emotion drains out of those situations completely…then they can watch the situation through at a normal speed *in a new way*…and in a minute you can begin to imagine what it would be like to *now be in that future you* watching those future situations…and *you have all the resources inside yourself* and you can instinctively

360

discover how to...*respond differently*...and what it feels like to know...*you respond differently*...and many people...*develop a new therapeutic compulsive habit*...they find that they...*feel compelled to carry out this new therapeutic habit*...and...*discover it keeps the old habit away*...and they begin to...*become compelled to enjoy life and help those around you to enjoy life*...and they often begin to notice that none of what they were concerned about actually happened...they...*become comfortable with the low level of risk*...and often report that they...*feel like a normal person again*...and that they...*gain more control in your life by stopping the old behaviour*...and often people say they behaved in a compulsive way to achieve control yet on looking back discovered that the old OCD was controlling them and they just hadn't stood up against it...and in school there was a child that was being bullied and he would walk to school late and would take different routes and would keep away from people all just to stop himself getting bullied...and the more he tried to stop it by behaving in this way the more he stood out...and the more he stood out the more he got picked on and it was a downwards spiral and the problem continued to get worse...the more he behaved differently to try to prevent the bullying the more the bullying occurred…and his life began to revolve around avoiding being bullied…and he would walk many extra miles a week and he wouldn't socialise…and he wouldn't pursue any of his hobbies and interests…and all of his free time was spent worrying about being bullied and how he could prevent it…and he just couldn't see the wood for the trees…he kept following the same over the top solution rather than *finding a new solution*…one day this child spoke to an adult about his situation because he was now beginning to get a bit older and was realising that his behaviour is controlling him and so he now feels like he can't win…if he doesn't behave that way he gets bullied and if he does he is always anxious and frustrated and unable to lead a normal life…the adult gave him some good advice…the next day the child went to school much happier and was no longer a victim he returned to being himself…he put others first which led to some people taking advantage but he learnt from each experience…and he followed his interests…and he responded differently to the old bullies…he didn't become aggressive or appear anxious…he became indifferent to them…and after they stopped getting the response they wanted they got bored of trying to bully him and left him alone...he found a whole range of new positive changes that stayed with him as he grew up...and you can *get a sense of being that future you*...feeling different and *responding in a new way to situations*...and you can take some time now for a part of you to begin to re-programme the changes into the mind and body on an instinctive level...and maintain them with each breath you take...(pause for about 3 minutes)...


## *Boosting confidence*

That's it...now you can begin to get a sense of a TV in your mind...and on that TV screen you can see yourself in situations that you feel confident in...and I don't know whether it will be six or seven or eight or more situations that go into creating that movie of confidence on that screen and each one can be like a separate scene will all of them playing one after the other and then cycling round so that at the end of the last scene you see the first scene begin again...and as you watch that a feeling of confidence can increase throughout those situations...and as you watch those situations you can begin to feel drawn into them so that you can see what you saw...feel what you felt and hear what you heard...and you can be curious about how you know you are confident as that feeling of confidence continues to cycle round and round with all the memories...and you can begin to add in brief clips of situations you used to not be confident in so that the feeling of confidence continues through all the memories and through these brief clips...and as the memories continue to cycle round the memories can begin to become brief clips while the brief clips can begin to extend whilst holding on to that confident feeling...and as you begin to continue to increase that confidence so the thumb and first finger of your right hand can begin to drift together and when they touch they can link the feeling of confidence with that action of having the thumb and first finger touching...and I don't know whether *it will happen automatically* in situations you want more confidence or whether you will consciously choose to bring that thumb and forefinger together...and as that confidence increases towards a peak the thumb and forefinger can drift apart again...and you can be curious about how *you will continue to improve your confidence* in the future…and in the future you can stand up and close your eyes as you imagine a circle on the floor in front of you…and you can imagine either yourself with that confidence or someone else that you know has that confidence standing in that circle…and you can watch them and pay attention to how you know they are confident…and turn up the volume to their internal dialogue to hear how they talk to themselves that helps them to be confident…and then you can step forwards into that person so that you become that person…and you can then experience…*being that person*…and…*make that confidence a part of you*…and then in those future situations you can open your eyes and continue to hold that confidence as a part of you or find that the *confidence is fully programmed into the mind to suddenly occur in the future when it is needed*…and you know that a little bit of nervousness helps to improve performance and ability…and you can now just take a few moments to imagine a line of events in front of you from your future with the next situation that you would have lacked confidence in at the end of that line of events…and you know true confidence comes from being confident in your abilities…many people make the mistake of lacking confidence because they can't do something…or because they aren't as good as they think they should be…you can only be confident that you will do your best…and you can imagine that line of events…and you can begin to move towards that situation and as you approach you can watch it playing out how you want it to go…and as you approach I wonder what the natural trigger will be that turns on that confidence instinctively and automatically just as you enter that situation and others like it in the future…and you can get a sense of entering that situation and notice what it feels like to…*be confident*…and you can now become more absorbed in this learning experience of *installing that confidence in your future*…and you can take as long as you need while I quieten down in the background for a moment…(pause for about 3 minutes)…

## *Enhancing motivation*

That's it…and many people think that they lack motivation without realising that they wake up in the morning...they get out of bed...they eat food...and they do many other behaviours that take motivation...and motivation consists of towards and away from motivation...there are things you are motivated towards...goals that you want...and there are things you are motivated away from...like not wanting to get in trouble...and to...*become motivated with the most efficiency*...you can have an element of towards motivation and an element of away from motivation...and you can think of something you feel motivated to do and as you...*think about that*...you can begin to get a sense of where that image is in your mind...is it in front of you...off to the left...off to the right...above you...below you...and you can think about how big that image is and whether you see yourself in the image or are viewing the image as if you are looking through your own eyes...and now you can get a sense of your mind going blank...and once your mind has gone blank you can get a sense of what it is you haven't been feeling motivated to do...and you can get a sense of where that is in your mind...whether it is above you...below you...behind you...in front of you...to the left...or to the right...and you can get a sense of whether you can see yourself in that image or whether you are viewing that image as if you are looking through your own eyes…and you can now begin to move that picture to where the motivated picture was and your unconscious mind can make the adjustments that programme that in your mind in the same way that you have the other motivational memories in your mind…and you can *fix that in place* as if each breath works like adhesive to stick that new way of representing those behaviours in place…and you can…*discover something new*…and…*respond in a new way*…and your unconscious can *make changes easily and effortlessly*…and you can begin to think about how things will be different for you when you find yourself motivated to do things that previously you felt less motivated to do…and as you listen to me you can respond more fully and when your mind wanders you can update those neural networks in the brain…to *respond in a new and improved way*…and I remember a story about a frog that was stuck in a rut on a muddy road…another frog hopped along and heard the frog asking for help…when he found the frog he tried to reach down to get him out…he couldn't reach so he asked the frog if he could jump out…the frog said it was too hard...the frog in the rut asked the other frog could you jump down let me stand on your back then I can get out...the other frog said then he would be stuck in the rut...and he didn't want that...the frog decided he would just have to leave that frog...and he continued to hop along the road...after a while the frog that was stuck in the rut hopped past him and raced off...the frog chased after him and asked I thought you were stuck in the rut...how did you get out...the frog replied...there's a truck coming...and you can *discover your inner motivation*...in a way that is unique to you...and you can take all the time you need to allow yourself to honestly and fully update your neurology...while I take a few moments to quieten down in the background...(pause for about 3 minutes)...

## *Improving self-image*

That's it...and as you continue to *relax deeper and deeper* into that instinctively responsive state of mind you can begin to wonder how you will develop the ability to...*improve your self-image*...and you can begin to...*make changes on an unconscious level*...and you don't have to know how...*these changes will occur*...and you can imagine yourself standing in front of a window...and you can be looking in through that window and see someone that you know loves you...and you might not even recognise that person all you know is that they love you...and you can be curious about how you know that that person loves you...what do they do to demonstrate they love you...how do they behave...what do they think...how do they talk to you...and as you show curiosity about this you can find yourself beginning to wonder what it would be like to...*become that person*...and you can now...*begin to get a feeling of that*...and as you begin to see the world through that person's eyes you can start to catch a glimpse of yourself and begin to see that you over there through this you's eyes...seeing what they see that makes them love you so much...and many people struggle to think of positive things about themselves when asked because all of those positive things are buried in who we are as people and for some people may not be immediately consciously available...and yet these people have friends and family that they know care about them and like them...and these people wouldn't be friends if they didn't like you...and you can think about what they would say they like about you...you know often others see the parts of us we don't pay attention to...and you can think about what others would say they like about you...and while a part of you thinks about what others like about you...you can understand and integrate what I am saying on an unconscious instinctive level...and a sculptor will take a large stone and see the beauty inside that stone...and that sculptor will keep that beauty in mind and will start chipping away...and they will sweat and work hard and struggle and at times they will want to quit...yet they will continue to...*chip away at it*...day and night...until they have removed all the unwanted stone...and they are so proud of what they have achieved and they take that work of art to a gallery to be displayed for everyone to...*admire the beauty*...and people...*admire the beauty*...and all the hard work that went in to creating that work of art...and *you really can*...now...*create your own personal work of art from the inside out*...in your own unique way...and looking at a garden you can think that the lawn looks beautiful and that all the grass looks neat and even and all the grass looks the same...yet when you get close to that grass and...*really pay attention*...you notice that each blade of grass is different...yet all of the blades together share a similarity...and all people on the planet share one similarity and that similarity is that we are all unique and different and beautiful in our own way...and you can begin to absorb the meaning in my words from the inside out...and you can take as long as you need now...to *integrate all the learning* and update psychological patterns deep within your neurology...and as you do I will quieten down into the background...and while I quieten down into the background a part of you can be wondering how all the changes will take effect and whether they will all take effect at the same time or whether some parts of the changes will occur faster than others...and you can wonder how that will happen for you and whether it will be different or the same as it is when it happens for others...(pause for about 3 minutes)...

## *Setting and achieving goals*

That's it...and as your mind continues to wander you can *integrate everything I say fully* and honestly or discover in the future that everything I said became an integral part of who you become, and you can fall asleep while you integrate what I say or you can stay awake as you listen and absorb what I am saying to you...(pause for about 15 seconds)...Now talking to you in the future as someone that has achieved what you wanted you can begin to recap to yourself what your life is now like and as you do that I will quieten down in the background...(pause for about 2 minutes)...and I understand that you got where you are today by putting in time and effort and dedication and commitment...and that it all started when you set your mind to it back in (add the month/year) and that you then began to...*make all of those changes*...and continued those changes right through to the when you achieved success...and I'm sure you had a few hurdles and I'm curious how you overcame them...and now you are here in the future...aware of the events that have passed...knowing that you can drift back to the present, to the place on that journey you know you are currently at being aware of all that has passed and aware there is more yet to come, having knowledge that the present is a gift and that the future holds many more presents for you to discover...and you can relax in the knowledge that each time you drift off into a daydream or find your mind wandering...you are taking another step closer to making your dreams reality and as you continue to take a little longer just to finish integrating all this new learning into your neurology and into the instinctive part of you I will quieten down again into the background...and you can take as long as you need over the next few minutes to fully and honestly complete that...(pause for about 3 minutes)...(As part of the therapy with the person, you will want to help them to establish the goal in sensory specific language, with the goal being something that is under their control and establishing the steps towards that goal, like sub-goals, with times when they will be likely to achieve those various sub-goals and what they will be doing from leaving therapy to start to achieve the first sub-goal. You can have them say something to themselves like 'if an opportunity arises to work towards my goal, then I will take it if it is appropriate to do so').

## Metaphorical 'life changer'

That's it...and as you continue to *relax deeper and deeper* you can listen to me in the background...and as you listen to me in the background you can understand what I'm saying on an unconscious level...many years ago there was a prince that lived in a castle...and one day he was gazing out of one of the castle windows looking out over the land that his family ruled...and from his perspective he could see people struggling...he could see people suffering...he could see people starving...while he was in this castle getting whatever he wanted with the ring of a bell...the prince ask his father why things should be this way...and was told the world is the way the world is...there's nothing you can do to *change it*...the prince wanted to know why not...and asked what about all of those poor people...and we are so rich...can't we help them out...his father didn't answer...the prince thought about his life...he had everything money can buy yet he felt unhappy and felt like something was missing from his life...while many of the people in the town around the castle appeared to struggle and suffer yet they would often be smiling and looking happy...that night when everyone went to bed the prince snuck out of the castle in disguise...he had to *discover the answer*...how can people be so happy with such miserable lives...he walked through the town and into the nearby forest...the forest was dark and eerie and the night was still...there were shards of moonlight glistening down through the leaves of the trees onto the forest floor shimmering a path for the prince to follow...the prince followed this unknown path to discovery and wonder and was curious where it would lead him...as he continued to walk the prince could hear noises of animals and birds moving in the dark...he could feel his heart beating loudly as he continued into the unknown...after a while the prince found a clearing and saw a frog sitting by a pond...as he approached the frog it started to talk to him...*'you are on a journey of discovery and wonder and you can wonder what you will discover on that journey'*...the prince began to wonder as he continued to wander through the forest...he thought he could hear something behind him moving in the dark...following him...he could see the foot of a mountain and wondered how he would reach the cave...then out of the dark some tribes people appeared...the prince couldn't understand what they were saying but could tell they were friendly...they began to cut down some trees and build a ladder...the prince decided to help them...after some time they managed to complete the ladder and the prince climbed up to the cave...in the cave was a flickering fire...he sat down by the fire watching the flickering flame and noticing how the light from the fire was dancing on the walls...as he continued to watch the flickering flame he began to see things and his mind began to wonder...then everything went dark for a moment before he found himself resting beneath a tree...and as he rested beneath that tree he began to *discover the true meaning of happiness and life*...and he knew that when you get hot you enter a pool to cool down...and after a while you need to warm up so you go back out in the sun...he then got an image of the Yin Yang symbol...then a coin flipping in the air...then he saw a person struggling and while the person was struggling he saw the person step outside themselves and the part of them with the problem began to change how they were dealing with the situation...then the prince saw people socialising and talking with each other...different images and ideas drifted in and out of the princes mind...and with each image the prince was learning something new about himself that was beginning to change his life in ways he didn't yet know...and the prince continued to notice what seemed like random images until they disappeared when his unconscious knew it found the answers...(pause for about a minute)...and when the time was right he drifted back to that cave before climbing down the ladder and enjoying an adventure of learning and discovery as he headed back to the castle where he knew how the next day he was going to change his world forever...and improve the lives of those in the town...(pause for about 3 minutes)...

## Overcoming insomnia

That's it...and you can be curious which night will be the first night...*you sleep the whole night through*...and I wonder how...*you will achieve that*...many people have found that the sleep problems they had were due to worrying too much during the day and going over things in their mind when they should have been *falling asleep*...and they found many ideas worked for them...and I'm curious which ideas will work for you...one person decided that if they weren't asleep within 20 minutes of going to bed they would get up and tidy their home...and within a week the home was tidy and they were sleeping through the night...another person decided to listen to meditation or hypnosis tracks as they were falling asleep to have something to follow that stopped their mind wandering and worrying...and I don't know what will work for you...and I wonder whether...*you will sleep through the night*...tonight...or whether...*you will sleep through the night*...tomorrow night...or whether the first night...*you sleep through the night*...will be in a weeks' time or two weeks' time or a months' time or some time sooner...many people discover the...*improved night's sleep*...develops as any day time problems or issues become resolved...and you can resolve any issues or problems in your own way...and when...*your sleep improves*...I wonder how life will be different...and a part of you can take some time now to get a sense for what that life is going to be like...who will notice that...*your sleep has improved*...what will they notice...how will it make...*you feel different*...what other life changes will occur...and how will the change be maintained...and a part of you can drift off into the future looking back and reviewing how you achieved...*sleeping better each night*...and looking at those times when you had the odd brief blip and how you overcame those few odd blips...and when your head relaxes on the pillow I wonder how quickly...*you will fall asleep*...and some people find they fall asleep as their head hits the pillow...others find they fall asleep just after their head hits the pillow...and some people find they fall asleep after they have taken a few comfortable breaths...and I wonder what will work for you...and some people tell themselves...if you go to bed and close your eyes to sleep, then you will quickly fall asleep and sleep through the night...and you can take a moment to tell yourself that...if I go to bed and close my eyes to sleep, than I will quickly fall asleep and sleep through the night...and you can now take as long as you need to reprogram your neurology...while I quieten down in the background...(pause for about 3 minutes)...

## Overcoming impotence

That's it...now a part of you can...*begin to make a difference*...and you have had experience of getting embarrassed and having your face go red and you have had experience whether you realised it or not, of blushing during intimate situations...and a part of you can learn how to stop blushing on your face when in those situations and can teach you how to send the blushing south...*well away from your face*...and that intense blushing can find a way of expressing itself and being noticed and *standing out*...because blushing is a signal that is trying to make you behave in a specific way...blushing has a message it wants you to be aware of...and you know some problems have an emotional component others have a physical component and others have both...and you can put old emotions in the past...you may as well...*forget about them*...and allow them to be totally attached to the memory they occurred in, back in the past...almost like turning over the pages of a book...you know there is writing on the previous pages but can you remember the 92nd word on the page 10 pages back...and although you know the context of the story and could give an overview of the story you can also forget lots of information that isn't helpful to remember now...and as you take my words and allow them to stimulate your thinking and your neurology they can *thrust* new ideas and understandings into your mind and body...and as those ideas *grow and develop* so you can *learn unconsciously*...and you know it is easier to forget you had a problem than you realise...and you can just get absorbed and carried away in an experience...and it can be a pleasure to experience the intense feeling of a new discovery *that stands out noticeably*...and you have experience of your head standing upright...and you do that effortlessly...and when you get tired your head flops and falls...yet when you need to...*keep it up*...*it stays up*...and many people go to watch films in the cinema and eat popcorn...and they put their hand in the popcorn and then lift it up to their mouth...and then they lower their hand down...and they repeat this...until they get excited in a moment and the hand that is rising to the mouth suddenly pauses in the air and *stays stuck their until the excitement is over*...and in a moment I'm not going to talk to you...*I'm going to talk to your penis*...and when I do *your penis can listen*...and it can *feel a compulsion to respond fully*...and after you leave here today your *penis can remain in a trance and it will always remain in a trance responding to what I say*...as I talk to your penis now...and you know how to ignore (enter clients name) and do what...*you want to have fun*...and you can *be like a rebellious teenager*...you can do things for fun...you can make yourself known a few times every day when it is appropriate to do so...so that you don't feel ignored...you can begin to crave attention and want to *be noticed*...and you can *feel compelled to come out to play* whether (enter clients name) wants you to or not...and you can always *enjoy play time* and you can crave play and *take every opportunity to come out to play when you know it is right a proper and a decent time to do so*...and sometimes you can be cheeky come out at random times when you want attention...and I wonder how you will discover you keep intensely blushing and when you do the more you try to stop blushing the more intense the blushing becomes and you can work independently to what (enter clients name) thinks and just respond independently to situations...and you know which situations you can come out and play in...(pause for about 1 minute)...that's it and now I will talk back to you...and you can take as long as you need now on an unconscious level to integrate all the necessary changes to create the future you desire...and you can take as long as you need over the next few minutes while I quieten down in the background... (pause for about 3 minutes)...

## *Overcoming enuresis (bedwetting)*

That's it...and as you listen to me, your mind can sort out that old problem in its own way...and you can begin to think about how life will be different once you have overcome that old problem...and I don't know when you will have your first *totally dry night* and whether you will have four or five nights where *you stay dry* most of the night before that first full dry night...and I don't know when you will first have two dry nights one after the other and whether this will be followed by a few wet nights before having another dry night or whether it will be followed by a few more dry nights...and I don't know when you will have a whole week of dry nights...and whether *these dry nights start next week* or the week after or maybe they start in a months' time...or sooner...and you know when children learn to write they hold a pencil in one way and as they begin to...*get used to controlling those muscles*...they get better at writing and as a child learns to colour in pictures they start by going over the lines and as they...*practice more and more*...they gradually get more and more of the colouring done inside the lines...and children learning musical instruments make many mistakes and gradually they learn how to perform all the movements correctly and link all the actions and...*learn to control the muscles*...and they improve and play better and better...and children that...*enjoy learning*...a sport have to learn how to make their body *respond correctly instinctively*...if someone learns football they have to *master muscle control* in the legs to make sure their foot is in the right place at the right time to kick the ball in the right way and with the right strength and in the right place...and someone learning baseball has to *master muscle control* in the hands and arms making sure they know where to move their hands to and when to close their fingers around a ball and how to get the strength of throws and direction correct...and you know how you would respond if you were using the toilet and someone walked in...*you stop peeing*...and *this happens by itself without thinking*…and you can now take as long as you need to learn from all that I have been saying, making it a part of who you are…and I will be quiet in the background for a few minutes to allow you to make all the changes honestly and fully…(pause for about 3 minutes)…

## Life reprocessing technique

That's it…and as you listen to the sound of my voice you can begin to *explore new possibilities* and as you explore those new possibilities you can *discover changes* occurring on an unconscious level…and as you listen to the sound of my voice you can begin to float and drift up out of yourself so that you are looking down on that memory you were currently developing and as you look over from that position you can notice that all your memories are lined-up before you stretching way back into the past…and you can begin to float back over all of those memories right back to the beginning…and in a few moments you can begin to *work through every single memory* of your life…and as you enter each memory you can save all the learning from that memory whilst *healing any memories that need resolution*...and you don't have to know how you do this...and as...*you work through each memory*...they can begin to *fill with a healing light*...and as you enter each problem memory you can notice that some memories have a pleasure or anger aspect that builds up in the memory before being cut short with another emotion that is anxiety based like embarrassment or fear or helplessness that you want to get away from...and other problem memories will have anger or pleasure that was a problem...and other memories will be anxiety based...and you have all the skills...knowledge...and resources to *resolve any issues* and...*heal every memory*...and you can take plenty of time now to *make each memory a present* and work through all those presents until you arrive back at this present here and now...and you can take as long as you need to honestly and fully...*do that now*...while I quieten down in the background...and you can be fully done when I continue talking... (pause for about 3 minutes)...

## Comfortable birth

That's it...and as you continue to relax into this state you can begin to explore the potential of your mind and body...and you know there are cultures where the man goes through the discomfort of labour while the woman just...*enjoy the sensation of birth*...and many people wonder how this can be...and in other cultures...*birth is a comfortable experience*...the mother only has the expectations of *feeling the sensations of the experience* and *enjoying the experience* yet is not accustomed to feeling any discomfort...and I don't know what changes or alterations your mind and body will make to allow you to...*enjoy the birth*...and many parents that...*experience a comfortable birth*...discover that they were paying all of their attention to the sensations of the experience and the pleasure and excitement they were feeling as they were giving birth...of bringing this new life into the world...and you know it is possible to sleep from the neck down whilst remaining awake from the head up or go into a trance as a body whilst you remain alert as a mind...as you experience the birthing process...and you can integrate and absorb all that I say here to ensure *you have a comfortable birth*...and you can...*feel so comfortable during the birth*...and...*enter a healthy state of mind*...and over the next few minutes you can take as long as you need now to really honestly and fully make all the necessary changes at an unconscious and instinctive level...to *feel comfortable during childbirth*...(pause for about 3 minutes)...

## *Overcoming fibromyalgia*

That's right...and as you continue to breathe in that way a part of you can begin to go back and review the past...and that part of you can enter every single memory and work through each memory...and as that part of you searches back through memories it can begin to *heal any memories* that...until now...had negatively impacted on the future...and some memories will contain anxiety feelings or difficult stress and others will at first appear to contain an emotion like guilt or embarrassment or fear or anxiety yet on closer inspection they will also contain anger or pleasure that until now you had forgotten all about...and this anger or pleasure feelings will have been suppressed or unable to be expressed at the time…and I knew someone that had a memory like this…and they remembered how embarrassed they were when they got caught dressing up and completely forgot the pleasure they felt before they were caught…and someone else I knew got bullied and they remembered being scared and feeling helpless but had forgotten how angry they felt and at the time they couldn't act on this anger…and on recalling these hidden or forgotten feelings both these people *recovered*…before the end of the session…and you will retain the learning made in all the memories that part of you works through…and as that part of you goes back through those memories…you can begin to discover a greater sense of comfort…and you can begin to feel like a weight is being lifted off you…and as that weight gets lifted off you so you can experience a lifting off of you of another kind…and while that part of you carries on working through those old memories another part of you can take as long as it takes between now and when you exit hypnosis to go through the whole body…through every muscle…every bone…every organ…and every cell…*applying a healing gel*…and this healing gel works by *stimulating healing* while preventing signals of discomfort...while at the same time having the properties to allow new signals unrelated to the old problem through to conscious awareness to allow you to gather further information...and making all of the changes needed to address and heal yourself of fibromyalgia...and a third part of you can begin to drift off...into the future and explore what the future holds...and explore how these changes you are making...now...impact on that future you...and how...*your life is different with these changes*...fixed in place...and you can take as long as you need to *complete all these three tasks on an unconscious level* before integrating fully back together by the time I next speak...(pause for about 3 minutes)...

## Acne removal

That's it...and as you relax in that way your unconscious can begin to work in a new way...and you can begin to alter how oily the skin is and you can begin to make all the necessary changes to...*make spots vanish*...and you can make all the necessary changes to...*keep the skin clear*…and occasionally a rogue spot may appear and I wonder if you will have a chance to notice it before it fades away again…and you know when washing up is left to pile up it can seem like such a chore…and so much hard work…and all the food is dried on…and to make the job easier you scrape off all the loose bits of food and then put the washing up in warm soapy water to soak…when you come back after a few hours and drain the water and clean the plates with fresh soapy water the plates clean easily…and you can learn on an unconscious level what you've got to do…if you feel like rubbing, scratching or picking any spots, then you will ignore that feeling…and you can always keep that in mind…if you feel like rubbing, scratching or picking any spots, then you will ignore that feeling…and I knew of this boy that wanted to…*get rid of acne*…and he had tried dozens of different medications…and none of it worked…and he was set the task of going on holiday to a log cabin in the alps with his mum and the log cabin was bare…there was minimal furniture…no pictures or mirrors on the walls…no TV…and no mobile phone signal…the boy and his mum were on holiday for a fortnight and no other intervention or therapy was carried out yet the boy came back with *clear skin*...and the boy didn't even realise that being in that log cabin was going to change his behaviour without him noticing and that this change of behaviour was going to lead to his...*face becoming clear*...and your unconscious can *make all the necessary changes now* and can understand this story on a deeper level and it can do that...Now...(pause in the background for about 3 minutes)...

## *Overcoming anger*

That's it...and as you continue to relax in that way I will begin to talk to you and what I say to you, you can understand on a deeper than conscious level...and you can really begin to explore some issues...and you can do this on an unconscious level...and as you work through those issues I will talk to you...and you know when a car alarm is set too sensitively it goes off all of the time...and a leaf lands on the car and the alarm goes off...and someone walks past the car...and the alarm goes off...and you know if you don't set the alarm the car may be at risk...and the alarm can be set to an appropriate level and it goes off only when it is genuinely at risk…and there was a story I heard many years ago about a woman that wanted to help her husband to control his anger…and she went to the village medicine man…and the medicine man told her he knows a way to help…but before receiving the answer she must pick three whiskers from a tiger…and on the first day she tried to approach the tiger but the tiger growled and lashed out at her…the second day she sat away from the tiger and didn't approach…on the third day she sat a bit closer and again spent the whole day just remaining still…after a week she had managed to get close enough to hear the tiger breathing…by the end of the ninth day she managed to get close enough to feel the tigers breath…when it approached the fourteenth day she was able to rest against the tigers belly as he slept…on the fifteenth day she gave the tiger food and did the same on the sixteenth and seventeenth days…by the eighteenth day she had managed to pick one whisker from the tiger…and the tiger flinched…on the nineteenth day she picked the second whisker and on the twentieth day she picked the third whisker…when she went back to the medicine man and told her what she had done and that she is ready for the answer now…the medicine man just told her…*you have found the answer…you no longer need my help*…and the woman went away confused and the next day her husband had changed and was…*now a much calmer person*…and there are times it is sensible to be angry, it can save your life…and times when anger can lead to unnecessary harm…and you can follow the feeling of anger back through time as if following its root back to where that pattern of responding with anger developed…and you can take time to settle on the memory or memories where that problem began…take time to explore those memories…was the anger expressed in those memories…was it right and natural that you felt that anger back then…and you can leave that anger back then…and some people find when they follow the anger back, they discover memories where anger isn't the dominant emotion…I know someone who struggled with anger, they followed the anger back into their past and discovered memories of being bullied…when they thought about these memories they had always thought about them as being anxiety memories…now they properly focused on them…they realised that although they were scared in those memories, they were also angry, but couldn't act on that anger...and now they have recalled the memories properly, putting the anger in its place and realising that it was only natural to be angry back then in those memories...the anger passed and was left back there...and you can learn from this and...*find the answer*...taking all the time you need over the next few minutes...Now...(pause for about 3 minutes)...

## Improving the nervous system

That's right...and as you continue to listen to the sound of my voice...*your unconscious*...can begin to work on a deeper level...*your unconscious*...can begin to focus on the nervous system...and as your unconscious begins to get right down to a microscopic level and work on analysing and working through the nervous system it can begin to make any necessary repairs or overcome any blocks...and...*your unconscious...now*...can also begin to work through the settings in the various aspects of the nervous system to ensure that all responses from each part of the system works harmoniously with all other parts of the system...with each part of the system ensuring it can respond to stimuli and signals just the right amount...and each neuron in the mind and body and each nerve cell can be checked and it can be a time-consuming task over the next few minutes to work through every single nerve cell in the entire mind and body...almost like carrying out an MOT or service check...and there are cells of vital importance to those neurons that outnumber the neurons and hold an important role and they can undergo a service check as well...and the neurons associated with sensory information processing...the neurons associated with motor or movement-based processing...and neurons throughout the central nervous system and any connections can all be checked to ensure they work correctly and any damage can be worked on and the pathways can be checked over to ensure clear free running and transmission of messages...and you know when you hack a path through a forest it always seems difficult the first time...after you have been through that path many times it is easy to follow and find...and you know flowing water always finds the easiest way through and water is a soft substance yet it can erode rock...and cut channels and pathways where previously there weren't any...and your unconscious can understand what I say in a new way...in a way you don't consciously understand...and you have a sympathetic nervous system that controls the fight or flight response and a parasympathetic nervous system that controls the relaxation response and...your unconscious...can ensure these systems are in balance...in the same way that Goldilocks liked things just right...and you know more about your own nervous system on an unconscious level that either I do or you do consciously...and you can now take as long as it needs to take over the next few minutes to honestly and fully work through the nervous system to ensure it is working as optimally as it can throughout... (pause for about 3 minutes)...

## Improving the endocrine system

That's it...and as you continue to relax in your own way while you listen to the sound of my voice your unconscious can begin to take a journey through your endocrine system...it can take a journey through the whole mind and body and through all related systems...organs and processes...it can work through, ensuring that chemicals and hormones are able to be released in the correct quantities at the correct times...and your unconscious...can *learn from this journey* about how...you can help yourself in ways that are unconscious and unexpected...and we all need a recharge from time to time...we all need to make sure that things are working properly and that we can respond instinctively in the correct way at the correct time...and *your unconscious now*...can honestly and fully take time to make sure your mind and body are working in harmony with you...and you can be curious on one level if you will notice any of the positive benefits straightaway...and while *your unconscious*...works on all that it needs to complete, my voice will drift off into the background...(pause for about 3 minutes)...

## Improving the digestive system

That's it...and while you listen to my voice and relax with each breath...*your unconscious*...can begin to explore an adventure through the digestive system...and it can start with the mind...and start with the thought processes and the neural pathways and neurons that control the digestive system...and *your unconscious* can *work through this process* healing where necessary as it goes...and that part of you can take as long as it needs to *complete this fully*...while I will continue to talk to you...(pause for about 1 minute)...that's it...and as that part of you continues on its healing journey it can begin to work through the whole digestive system...and I wonder what kind of a dream or mental adventure it will create for you as it carries out its work...some people find they start to imagine a journey of being in a car, travelling along motorways and down smaller roads and windy roads...and you are just enjoying the view and enjoying the journey...and other people imagine something completely different...as *your unconscious*...now...works fully and honestly outside of your conscious awareness...and that part of you can check everything necessary to ensure the experience is a smooth one and to ensure all related and relevant organs are also working fully and correctly and processing as they should...and you don't have to know how any of...*this is taking place unconsciously*...you can just wonder whether you will notice the improvements straightaway or not...and you can take as long as you need to do this fully and honestly over the next few minutes...(pause for about 3 minutes)...

## *Improving the circulatory system*

That's it...and you can make changes without even realising...and with each breath you take I'd like to have you get a sense of *breathing in a healing light*...and I don't know what colour that light is...and as you breathe out you can get a sense of breathing out problems...blocks and impurities...and as...*you breathe in that healing light*...you can get a sense of it passing down into your lungs...and as it does it can begin to *cleanse and heal*...and that cleansing and healing can continue as that healing light continues on its journey...and that light can fill the lungs and permeate each and every cell...*healing and repairing*...and that healing light can continue to follow the route into the blood and throughout the body...and be absorbed by the body...and it can take as long as it needs, to fully and honestly work all the way round the body, removing any blocks in the circulatory system and adding extra healing resources to anywhere they are needed...and you can wonder consciously whether you will notice the positive changes straightaway or whether you will notice them more over time or whether you will even attribute the positive changes to this work your unconscious is doing here for you now...and you can take as long as you need over the next few minutes to make all the necessary changes...and in the same way that a broken arm only needs to be put in plaster once to allow the healing to occur over time...so that healing light only needs to start the healing once for that *healing to continue and complete over time*...(pause for about 3 minutes)...

## *Overcoming Irritable Bowel Syndrome (IBS)*

That's it...and now as you continue to relax I would like to talk to that part of you that has been responsible for developing that old IBS response in the past...and I would like to thank that part of you that created that in the past for taking its time and energy to help to convey an important message...and you know now...*you can stop*...and think of a new more pleasant way of getting that message across...and I know you have all the skills and abilities to...*develop that new response*...in a creative manner...and I wonder what it will be...and many people remember the frustrating experience of trying to untie knots...and the harder you try to...*untie the knot*...the tighter the knot seemed to get...and many people have learnt that to...*untie the knot*...they need to...*relax and take things slow and easy*...and carefully they can...*untie that knot*...and sometimes trees grow large in a garden and need to be removed and you can think long and hard about how to remove that tree or you can worry about what will happen if you don't remove the tree or you can take action...hire someone to help you remove the tree carefully branch by branch until it is level with the ground...and then carefully dig out the roots one at a time...before planting a wonderful healthy flowerbed...and your unconscious can understand things in a way you consciously overlook...and you can wonder whether you have had IBS for the last time...or whether you may have it once...twice or even four times more...before...*you never have it again*...and you know change can be so quick when...*change happens instinctively*...and you can get splashed by a car and you know to avoid puddles when you see a car coming forever into the future...and that happens instantly without any thought...and *you can learn* and...*heal yourself*...that quickly...*here and now*...and you can discover that any discomfort, pain and bloating will disappear and be a thing of the past...each and every day your bowel habits will continue to improve...and you can be curious how you will notice this...and this will continue on into the future with each movement...continuing that improvement until there is no more room for improvement...and you can have a sense of controlling how much water passes through a dam to continue the flow of that river downstream...and you can control that flow just right...to ensure a smooth and gentle flow of water down that river...and once that river is flowing gently and relaxed and just right...you can leave that flowing at that rate and sit on the river bank...enjoying listening to that water smoothly flowing passed...feeling the warmth of the sun on your face and hands...as you rest there...relaxing...feeling so calm...as you gently rest those hands on your stomach and lie back in the warmth of the sun...feeling that warmth in those hands...the calmness and relaxation...noticing how calm the breathing is...and the warmth of those hands comforting your belly...and over the next few minutes you can take as long as you need to *make all the necessary changes* to ensure that old response and old problem remains just as a distant memory...and I don't know whether you will have all the work completed before the end of the session or just after the end of the session or tomorrow or next week but all of the necessary changes can be completed and in place over the next few minutes while my voice drifts off elsewhere allowing you to work fully and honestly on an instinctive level...(pause for about 3 minutes)...

## Boosting the immune system & fighting infections

That's it...and as you listen to me a part of your mind can begin to access your immune system on a deep level...to...begin to help it to *recognise and fight infections and illnesses* better…and it can learn from messages coming from the external world and understand that not everything that is different or alien is bad…and some things are actually on your side and there to help you to…*fight the true invaders*…and consciously, you can think about what you wants help to fight…and what you want left alone to do its job…and *fighting infections efficiently and effectively*…doesn't mean that the immune system needs to become hyper-sensitive…it can become appropriately sensitive…in the same way that many unnecessary allergies are caused by a hyper-sensitivity…and *your unconscious*…can understand this…and a part of you can now travel through the body placing a coloured substance or marker on all those bits that need eliminating…and I don't know whether that part of you will place the markers on the relevant places from the feet up or from the head down…and as that part of you responds in its own unique way…you can wonder how quickly positive change will occur…and you can begin to have a sense of the characters of the immune system patrolling your body, like organised teams of soldiers patrolling a city, keeping the streets clear of trouble, checking in on houses they pass and recognising when something doesn't seem right...and going and investigating...and if they find that they need additional support, they call in reinforcements, wait for those reinforcements to arrive, before tactically dealing with the threat and resolving the situation, before then sending the reinforcements away and continuing their patrol...and sometimes...they find that they are requiring reinforcements more frequently and so they increase the numbers on patrol and have teams of reinforcements on standby who they can call upon rapidly when needed...and you can have a sense of this playing out within your body...and some of the soldiers are specialised for infiltration...they can sneak in to dangerous situations and bring down and dismantle enemy bases and hideouts and neutralise enemy threats where those enemies have hidden in the homes of others...before they know what has hit them and before they have had time to warn others...and they can block all communication as part of their co-ordinated attack to prevent the enemies being able to communicate to others and warn others about what is happening...and they can block and monitor everything incoming and outgoing...preventing food and water and messages from passing in or out of enemy lines...and while...*change occurs on a deep instinctive level*...I will quieten down in the background...and you can take as long as you need to honestly and fully...*make all the necessary changes*...over the next few minutes...(pause for about 3 minutes)...


## *Increase fertility*

That's right...and you can...*begin to learn instinctively*...how...*it is possible*...to...*increase fertility*...and you don't have to know consciously how...*you do that now*...because the necessary changes can all take place on an unconscious level...and I don't know which changes will be physical changes and which will be psychological changes...and whether consciously you will be aware of any of the changes or whether...*all the changes will happen outside of your awareness*...and a part of you can instinctively go through all of your life history and experiences resolving negative emotions and blocks that were relevant to maintaining that old fertility response...and you don't have to know consciously what is going on unconsciously...it can just take place instinctively in its own way...and you know it is interesting...the harder you try to do something the more difficult it becomes...and the more desperately you want something the more elusive it becomes...and unconsciously you can focus energy on helping yourself to...*correct any physical or biological blocks to effective fertility*...and I don't know whether you will reach the peak of fertility in one weeks' time or in 6 days' time or in 9 days' time or sooner...and when you do you can feel uncontrollably compelled to appropriately act on this moment...and you know some seeds can fall in a desert and remain dormant for years...and any observers would assume that the dry and barren desert has no life...yet when even a single drop of rain comes the desert begins to flourish with life...as the seed soaks up the drops triggering new growth...and even if the soil isn't ideal to grow in...*that new life takes hold and grows*...and water from one place can develop into a rain shower elsewhere...and if there is significant energy exciting the rain drops it can turn into a torrential downpour or a beautiful and powerful thunderstorm...and cactus plants grow in the desert despite the lack of rain...and they can grow up big and strong...and these desert plants live in a stressful environment yet they still appear and grow and survive...and in locations with heavy rainfall and very little stress life flourishes and grows easily and effortlessly...and *your unconscious*...can *learn how to generate fertile soil* and keep the conditions just right...and you know...*life grows*...in places that seem inhospitable...and...*your unconscious*...*now*...can integrate all that is necessary...*your unconscious*...can integrate changes in the mind...in memories...in beliefs...in the way you respond to stress and in the body...in all parts of the reproductive system and the reproductive process...and in each relevant cell in the body...and as...*change happens*...taking as long as is necessary over the next few minutes...I will quieten down in the background...(pause for about 3 minutes)...

## Treating psoriasis

That's it...and as you continue to relax I will talk to you...and as I talk to you, you can listen...and while you listen *your unconscious* can begin to make changes throughout the mind and body...and *your unconscious*...can make these changes by checking to see what changes need to occur...and *your unconscious*...can start deep within the cells of the body and gradually take it's time to work from deep within the cells to how the body fights infection and whether this is happening appropriately all the way up to how you respond to stressful situations...and while your unconscious...does that I will talk to you in the background about the different causes of psoriasis...and some psoriasis has been known to have a genetic cause...and this genetic cause doesn't always lead to psoriasis...sometimes it can lie dormant until a stressful event brings it to life...and in the same way that stress can bring it to life...relaxation can turn it off...some people have overactive white blood cells that normally fight infection but because they are too active the chemicals they release make the skin cells multiply too fast...and they can *normalise themselves*...normally skin cells go through their life cycle every 30 days...yet in psoriasis that is caused in this way they can go through their life cycle in 3 to 6 days...and they can...*relax*...and often the way the person responds to stress can start or maintain psoriasis...and I don't know whether *you will respond differently to situations* as the psoriasis disappears or whether you will think you are responding the same whilst the body responds differently as the psoriasis disappears...*and your unconscious now*...can take as long as it needs over the next few minutes to...*make the change happen*...and it can be like a snowball being rolled down a hill or a stone thrown in a pond...and I don't know whether...*the skin will clear*...during the day or during the night...and whether you will notice it in the morning or in the evening...when you wake up or when you go to bed...or whether someone else will be the first to notice...and whether it happens quickly over the next day or two or whether...*the change happens*...slowly over the next few days...and you can be curious to...*discover that for yourself*...and I don't know what the experience of the psoriasis disappearing will be like for you...whether it will be like that psoriasis falls away leaving clear fresh, healthy skin, or whether it fades gradually, or seems to just wash off over a short period of time...and the skin can remain relaxed, even at times of stress...as you learn to effectively manage stress and anxiety...(pause for about 3 minutes)...

## *Self-awareness process*

That's it...and you can be curious about awareness...what does awareness really mean...what does awareness mean to you...what can you learn by...*enhancing awareness*...and you can begin to get a sense of drifting and floating up above yourself and see your life unfolding from the past to the present to the future...and you can observe how you respond to those around you...and how others respond to the way you respond to them...and sometimes we say and do things without really knowing the impact of our actions...and you can observe the impact of your actions...and you can get a sense of how you fit in with the world around you...how *you influence the world around you*...and you can discover more about yourself as a human being than you knew you knew...and you can be aware of every little action and interaction and the consequences of those actions both positive and negative...and you can really begin to know yourself on a deeper more fundamental level...and you can delve deeper in to what makes you, you...what your beliefs are...what your traits are...what your skills and abilities are...what annoys or irritates you...and you can learn something about yourself and how you can apply your discoveries to *being the person you want to be in the future*...and you can explore your role in the story of your life...what your role is...how you will be remembered at the end of your story...what character you play in the story of your life...and my voice is just going to drift off in the background for a time and when it does you can *begin a process of self-exploration and discovery*...and I don't know whether this will happen quickly or slowly and whether you will have conscious awareness of this happening or just unconscious awareness...and the longer my voice remains distant the *deeper and deeper* into the experience of self-awareness and discovery you can go...and you can do that...Now...(pause for about 5 minutes)...

## Self-acceptance process

That's it…and you can begin to explore your own natural ability to…*accept yourself*…and to…*accept yourself*…is to *be comfortable with who you are* as an individual…and you know every blade of grass in a meadow looks different on close inspection yet together a meadow can look beautiful…and you know the one thing all people have in common is that all people are unique…and I wonder what will be the trigger that makes self-acceptance possible…and you can step back and view your life…and as you view your life you can wonder how you got here…and you can look back over your decisions and wonder how they have shaped who you have become and who you will be developing into…and mistakes are unplanned lessons…and I wonder what you can learn from your mistakes…and how this learning can help to *enhance your own self-acceptance*…and *accept yourself for who you are*…and as you review the past you can learn about the future…what will it mean to you to *have self-acceptance*…how about being accepted by others…how will…*things change*…and a part of you can instinctively explore these areas…and you can learn and you can understand and you can imagine a positive role model that accepts themselves...and what is different about that person...what do they do...how do you know they accept themselves...and you can be curious about what changes will occur that lead to...*you accept yourself*...and curious to discover how this affects who you are as a person and what will be different about the way you interact with others and *develop over time*...and I wonder if you can be curious about how people accept each other and put each other's faults aside...and how they manage this...*and your unconscious now*...can take as long as it needs over the next few minutes to make *all the necessary changes on an instinctive level* to...*discover how to accept yourself*...and find that *change happens*...as I quieten down in the background...(pause for about 3 minutes)...

## Enhance intuition

That's it...and I wonder if you have ever had the experience of just knowing something but not knowing how you knew it...or just having a sense of something but not understanding where that sense came from...*and your unconscious understands*...and your unconscious understands how this happens...and have you ever looked back and thought to yourself that you saw a situation developing...*and your unconscious can learn from these types of experience*...and that instinctive part of you can now begin to draw up on all of these resources where you have...*experience a heightened state of intuition*...and you can begin to integrate this into who you are at an instinctive level...and there are times when you may not want to be so intuitive and times when you want to...*crank your intuitive abilities up to their full potential*...and to...*become instinctively intuitive*...you can begin to develop the ability to...*notice patterns*...and...*notice fine detail*...and you don't have to consciously know...*you notice these things*...it can happen unconsciously and instinctively all by itself...and you can take as long as you need over the next few minutes to really deeply integrate all that is necessary into creating the required changes to instinctively enhance your intuition and you can learn from past experiences where intuition was enhanced naturally and you just knew things...and you can be curious how much your intuition will increase and at what point it will become noticeable and whether anyone else will notice and if they do I wonder what they will notice…(pause for about 3 minutes)…

## Forgiveness process

That's it…and as you continue to drift in this journey my voice can continue with you as a comforting part of your experience…and as you just *go with this now*…you can continue to *enjoy this process of change*…and just be aware of a bench off in the distance…and you can have a sense of walking towards that bench…and allow yourself to sit down comfortably on that bench *deeper and deeper* into the experience as you sit down on that bench…and just look around and notice the view from that bench…notice what you can see…what you can hear…and notice what it feels like…sat on that bench there…and then you can have a sense of drifting up out of your body…drifting up out of your body and floating over and settling down behind some bushes off to the side of that bench so that you are looking over at that you sat on that bench…and notice how much more absorbing the experience can be...with that curiosity looking at that you wondering what is going to happen next...wondering who is going to come over and sit next to you...and as you look over at that you sat on that bench...get a sense of somebody coming over...you don't have to know exactly who that somebody is...but somebody wanting forgiveness...somebody who is wants to be forgiven...watch that you over there on that bench doing what they have to do to forgive that person who sits down with them...and as well as being aware of that you sat over there with that person they are about to forgive...you can also be aware of something odd that happens...a light seems to come up off the shoulders of that you there...up into the sky...just seems to *lift as that forgiveness is given*...and you know one of the greatest strengths is to *have the strength to be able to forgive somebody for whatever they have done*...and just get a sense of watching that you over there *forgiving that person* that has sat down with them...I don't know if they are sat a few feet away or if they are sat right beside each other...just watch what happens as that...*you forgive that person*...watch the positive outcome of it...watch how you know the moment...*they are forgiven*...and then just get a sense of how you know that you there has finished...*forgiving that person*...notice how you know they are *now happier as a person*...get a sense almost like you have got x-ray vision and you can see into them...and you can see that the way your genes are expressed are changing to calm relaxed settings...that not only has that you done something good for your mind...but also for your body...and for those people that that you interacts with...that's it...and then as this you over here watching that you over there just get a sense of thinking 'wouldn't it be nice to know what it felt like for that you over there to do what they just did'...and as you think that to yourself have a sense of drifting into that you over there before that other person had come out and joined them...and perhaps there are butterflies in the stomach from anticipation because you know someone is about to come out and join you and you know you are about to *forgive them*...and you can be nervous about what it is going to feel like...how that pleasant feeling is going to happen when *you forgive that person*...what it is going to feel like to have that light lifting off of your shoulders...what all the physical changes throughout your body will feel like...and changes in your mind...so discover a sense of that person coming out and sitting next to you and asking to be forgiven...and have a sense of forgiving that person and *letting go*...yet remembering you are not forgetting, *you are forgiving*...you are allowing them to own their own problem and live with what they did...and you can know that within yourself you are making the right decision leaving them with any guilt and leaving them holding full responsibility for their own actions...and after that light has lifted off of your shoulders and that person has got up and walked off...have a sense of leaving the bench and all that behind you as *you drift deeper into your mind to learn from this* experience preparing to exit trance with a pleasant change...(pause for about 1 minute)...

## *Finding inner peace process*

That's it...and as you continue to relax...in a moment I'm going to quieten down in the background...and when I do, you can begin to *find true and honest inner peace*...and when *you find that inner peace* you can be curious how it will translate into your everyday life...and it can have a deep influence throughout your mind and body...and the interesting thing about silence is its healing nature...not just healing physically but also its ability to heal you mentally and spiritually...and as I go quiet it can seem like you are walking through a door into a room of nothingness...into a room where the walls absorb sound preventing any echoes...and in that place of peace it can seem like you are a mind floating in space without a body...and as you drift and dream and float...with each breath...you can be aware of sounds without hearing them and be here as a body whilst you remain there as a mind...and you know when *you sleep and dream*...you *completely and comfortably separate from physical reality for a while*...and the more silence you experience the more inner peace you can discover...now...(pause for about 5 or more minutes)...

## Developing assertiveness

That's it...and I'm wondering whether you would be able to say no to me...and how you know when someone is assertive...and I wonder how you know the difference between assertiveness and aggressiveness...and I would like you to get a sense of a person in your mind that is assertive...a person you know shows no signs of aggression at all...someone that is kind and caring and supportive...someone that thinks about others and how they can be helpful to others...and as you think about them just get a sense of what they look like...get a sense of how you know they are assertive...perhaps you can be watching them in action...what is it they do that lets people know they mean what they say...how do they behave...what body language do they use...what is their tone of voice...what words do they use...how do others respond to them...if you turned up the volume to that person's internal dialogue what do they say to themselves...really explore how that person does assertiveness...now watch that person being assertive as if they are standing in for you...watch them in future situations in your life and watch how those situations go differently to how you thought they would if it was you dealing with them...that's it...now take some time to start those future memories again...only this time step into that person so that you are seeing what they see...hearing what they hear...and feeling what they feel...and experience being them in the future...and notice what it feels like to experience things in that way with those responses...what it feels like to be assertive...and as you take time to experience a wide range of future situations you can spot a mirror and see that that person is actually you and has been the whole time...and that that you has learnt from that other person how to respond assertively...and before you integrate that ability to *be comfortably assertive*, fully into your life I'd like you to take some time to look into the future at situations you don't want to be overly assertive...because there are situation where it is best to hold back or negotiate more or allow others to be assertive with you...and a whole range of different situations and circumstances...and you can take some time to explore those and how you would like to respond in those situations and then explore those situations where *you can comfortably and appropriately be assertive*...that's it...and now you can just take as long as you need to *make this assertiveness instinctive*...and you can also draw up all past successful experiences of being assertive and take as long as you need over the next few minutes to honestly and fully instinctively integrate this assertiveness...now...(pause for about 3 minutes)... (It is important to have included psychoeducation within the therapy to ensure that the client understands the difference between assertiveness and aggressiveness and the differences in behaviours and attitude and has practiced this within therapy sessions and perhaps seen assertiveness demonstrated).

## Overcoming addiction

That's it...and *you can overcome addiction*...in your own unique way...and in your own time...and you don't seem like the kind of person that likes to be bullied and pushed around...and you can *learn deeper ways of responding*...and a part of you can explore what had been keeping that addiction going...it can explore whether it is a pattern of behaviour where the cause is back in the past and no longer applies but has left behind a habit...or whether the addiction had been your own form of therapy where it was meeting a need or helping you in some way...and you know sometimes when a child gets a new toy they stop playing with their old toy...and they haven't lost the old toy...they still know where it is...they just *don't want to play with it anymore*...and I wonder what new healthy toy you will get...and all the changes that will happen will be in accord with who you are as a person and will have a positive influence on yourself and those around you...and you have experience of not having the old addiction...you have the experience of *living life differently*...and I wonder how...*that old behaviour will become redundant*...and that old addiction has been bossing you around...it has been manipulating you on a deep level...it has been controlling you and influencing your mind and decisions...and it is time to *take back control*...and you don't have to know how to do this consciously as the *changes take place on an instinctive level*...and the benefits can be achieved in new and exciting ways...and I'd like to thank that part of you that was kind enough to create that old addictive behaviour back when it was the only solution or the best solution you thought was open to you...and now would like your help to develop this new and healthy response that will *enhance your life* and the lives of others around you in ways that may not immediately be obvious...and *all the necessary changes can happen fully and honestly* from breaking old unhelpful patterns and processes to getting needs met in healthier ways...to *developing new behaviours and patterns* and *building on strengths* and *resolving issues* and *moving forwards*...and your unconscious can do that in your own unique way...now...(pause for about 3 minutes)...

## Hay fever relief

That's it...and now on an unconscious level you can begin to change the sensitivity settings to particles getting in the nose...and you can dull down the sensitivity...and your unconscious can begin to learn how to...*respond appropriately*...and your unconscious knows fully and honestly exactly what it needs to do to...*stop that old response*...and it can...*do that now*...in its own way...and it can take all the time it needs to...*make those changes*...and while...*your unconscious makes those changes*...you can begin to wonder how life will be different...what will life be like...how will...*you notice the difference*...who else will notice and what will they notice that lets them know...*you have stopped having that old hay fever problem*...and what other knock on changes will occur...what will you be able to do that you previously hadn't been able to do...and you can *fully and deeply explore these ideas*...and really honestly imagine them in the future and how life will be without that old response...what a difference it will make...and while a part of you does that another part of you can make all of those changes on an instinctive level...and you know a car alarm set too sensitively is really irritating and needs to be reset more appropriately...and as you make all the necessary changes to that instinctive and unconscious part of your mind I will quieten down in the background...and when I next talk to you, you will be just beginning to finish up making all of those necessary changes...(pause for about 3 minutes)...

## Enhance orgasms

That's it...and I don't want you to experience too much pleasure just yet...really *save it for when the time is right*...and when sexual experiences begin I don't want you to experience too much pleasure too quickly...really hold off and wait until...*the time is right*...and it is important that you don't...*overdo taking on board my suggestions*...but take them on board just right...because it is all too easy to...*overreact or be taken by surprise*...and find you didn't wait...and you know that an intimate part of your body can blush strongly and uncontrollably when certain areas are touched...and any old blocks created by old experiences can become detached from those intense blushing moments...and those blushing moments can happen at a time you want to feel pleasure or excitement or love...and you can instinctively discover those areas that get touched to trigger that intense blushing...and I want you to really try hard to wait at least a week before letting that blushing occur...and when that intense blushing occurs I wonder what feelings you will discover that go with it...and the area that experiences that intense blushing can significantly increase in sensitivity...and the mind can *feel deeply connected to those experiences*...almost like...*you enter an orgasm trance*...and with each breath you take in that special way whilst you have sexual thoughts in mind deepens and focuses that trance...and the longer...you try really hard not to let it happen too quick...*the deeper into that trance you go*…and you will discover how long you can experience that pleasure for…and your unconscious can take this time now to make all the necessary changes honestly and fully on an instinctive level while I quieten down in the background…(pause for about 3 minutes)…

## Overcome premature ejaculation

That's it…and it is possible to enjoy feeling things without acting on that feeling…and you know how to *hold back whilst having fun*…you know how to keep the punch line until the time is right…and I know you know how to *hold off ejaculating* by 1 second…and you know that would be easy and I know that would be easy…and I bet you could even *hold off ejaculating* by 3 seconds or 5 seconds…and you have been giving this compliment and you can compliment yourself on that…and you know some people struggle to ejaculate and they try and they try and they *find it really difficult to do…imagine that…going for much longer* before you can even manage to ejaculate…and *your unconscious knows how to increase the duration of pleasure*…and *you can become so absorbed in the pleasure you forget you are supposed to have ejaculated*...and you can start slow and not get too absorbed into the experience of the pleasure because you don't want to be going too long yet before ejaculating...and you can *focus all of your attention on all the ways you can please the other person and get pleasure from pleasing the other person* and really try hard not to get too drawn into the experience of pleasure and *forgetting to ejaculate*...and your unconscious can now take as long as it needs over the next few minutes to honestly and fully integrate all this information at an instinctive level while I quieten down in the background...(pause for about 3 minutes)...

## Overcoming insecurity

That's it...and as you continue to relax you can begin to create a deep and meaningful change...and that change can develop from the inside out...and with each breath you take, *that change can continue to grow*...and you can wonder what it is like to live in security to live with a sense of *feeling secure in yourself*...and living in security where previously there was insecurity can be an experience…and your unconscious can begin to make the necessary changes on an instinctive level to enhance that sense of *feeling secure in who you are as a person*…and you can learn how to feel secure in relationships and what it is like in secure relationships…and secure people in secure relationships can develop securely…and a deep part of you can develop all the necessary changes that will ensure *you are secure in yourself and in your relationships*…and that you *remain calm and clear thinking*…and you can explore what life will be like when…*you feel secure*…in yourself and in relationships and with those around you…and you can explore what you will feel like in situations that in the past would have made that old you feel insecure…and you can notice what you say to yourself and how you say that to yourself…and notice how you behave and what others will see and hear that would let them notice…*change has happened*…and what other differences does this change make to your life as you continue to…*grow up*…and…*develop*…and…*discover this new you*…and as you take some time to honestly and fully explore how *feeling secure* and *being a secure person* changes your life for the better…the instinctive part of you…that part of you that learns to respond in certain ways all by itself…that part of you can begin to take as long as it needs over the next few minutes to update fully and honestly all of your future response and make all the necessary changes to…*make those future changes reality*…(pause for about 3 minutes)…

## Heal ulcers

That's it…and you can begin to learn how to soften on the inside…and relax…and as a part of you learns how to…*manage stress in a new way*…you can wonder what changes you will notice…and a part of you can review your diet and what changes, if any, are needed…and in studies, when people have had the option of eating anything they want and they get that insight that certain foods or drinks lead to unpleasant effect they *instinctively stop consuming those foods* or consume a correct moderation of those foods…and when you experience stressful situations I wonder whether you will naturally discover yourself breathing in a new way or whether you will discover the muscles in your body *instinctively relax comfortably*…and your unconscious can *send soothing and healing to where that is required*…and that soothing and healing can take the time it needs to wrap up and protect that area and treat that area with your own internal natural healing processes…and you can begin to learn on an instinctive level how to *prevent the occurrence of ulcers in the future*…and you have a lifetime of experiences…of many examples of times when you haven't had ulcers and your unconscious can learn what is different about those times…and how it can apply all that knowledge to the present and can give you a present here and now…and your unconscious can now take as long as it needs over the next few minutes to learn and integrate into the instinctive part of you all the necessary changes to help you…*change quickly*…and help you to know how to respond in the future…(pause for about 3 minutes)…

## Enjoy everyday sensory experience

That's it…and as you wake up in the morning you can wonder how much you actually experience…imagine what the world would be like if viewed for the first time…and what those first few moments in the morning would be like as you open your eyes and perhaps notice how bright the light is…and notice the subtle shades and colours around you…and imagine how enhanced life would be if your senses were turned up…and you know it is possible to…*heighten your senses*…as if on a scale of 0-10 normal waking state of awareness is at a 5…and you can *turn your senses all the way up to 10* in pleasurable and everyday experiences…fully and honestly *enhancing your own personal daily pleasure*…and your sense of touch can increase in sensitivity and your sense of hearing and your sense of vision…and I don't know what differences you will notice…will sounds be clearer…will you hear a wider range of sounds…will you be able to notice individual notes…will you be able to recognise different smells…and appreciate finer detail in smells and tastes and colours…and I wonder what other changes you will notice as you begin to…*enjoy everyday sensory experience*…more fully…and really…*notice the difference*…as if *every day you wake up intensely happy to be alive…enjoying life*…and you can truly and honestly explore the power of your mind in ways you could only dream…and all the changes can happen with intense pleasure…and you know some people take drugs to enhance their senses…and all these drugs do is activate what is already there…and you can *activate what is already there using the power of your unconscious mind*…and really *explore new possibilities and change*…and you can be curious how much enjoyment you will get out of this…and I remember a boy that was hypnotised to increase his sense of touch and he ran his fingers over a smooth sheet of glass and thought it felt like sandpaper…and he then had his sense of smell increased and was asked what was in the hypnotists hand and he could smell the mint in the hypnotists hand from the back of the room…and there is even more…you can *achieve now*…and in a moment I'm going to quieten down and when I do your unconscious can make all the necessary changes to…*make this happen*…and it can happen fully and honestly in accordance with who you are as a person and in a way that enhances and benefits your life and the lives of those around you…and you can take as long as you need over the next few minutes to fully and honestly make all those changes on an instinctive level…now…(pause for about 3 minutes)…

## *Overcoming procrastination*

That's it...and they say the hardest part of...*doing things*...is actually to just...*get up and just do them*...and we all have something that motivates us...something that makes us think I'm just going to...*get on and do it*...and as you think now about what you feel is a *pleasure* to do...and get a sense of where that image is in your mind...and get a sense of whether you are viewing the image as if you are there...seeing what you see...hearing what you hear...and feeling what you feel...or whether you are looking at that image and can see yourself in the image...and you can get a sense of how bright or dim the image is...how much contrast and colour is in the image...whether the sound is clear and as you hold that motivational image in your mind you can begin to notice a small dot in that image and rapidly as you notice the image disappear that small image of what you find you have been procrastinating about will rapidly enlarge and come forward to fill this image...and *all that will be changing is the image*...in the same way that when you change the channels on a TV *all that changes is the image*...the setting for the sound...the colour...the brightness and all the other setting remain the same...and you want all those motivational setting to stay the same as you watch that image shrink down and disappear with the new image appearing almost instantly...and you can do that...now...flashing up that image that started as a dot while the main image shrinks...that's it...and now really take some time to look at this image and notice how it makes *you feel different*...more *motivated to take action*...and I wonder what else makes you...more *motivated to take action*...and you know how to...*start new things*...and find yourself...*compelled to carry them out*...and you have a life time of experience of...*achieving new things*...and I wonder how you did...and your unconscious can draw upon all of the resources you have used throughout your life to achieve things...and your unconscious can agree to *stop that old procrastination response*...and to signal that it has agreed it will open your eyes at the end of this session...and it has the whole session to think about whether it agrees before making that decision...and it will only make that decision if it agrees to *honestly and fully stop that old behaviour*...and it can find ways for you to step back and put things into stages and to prevent any feelings of feeling overwhelmed...and it can increase the need to *start new things and fulfil tasks*...and your unconscious knows what sort of a person you would love to be and how *you will become that person*...and you can take some time to explore in your mind what will be different in the future...who will notice you are getting on with things and achieving things...what differences will it make to your life...what positive differences will it make to the lives of others...and you can...*achieve things for yourself*...and while your unconscious takes all the time it needs over the next few minutes to fully and honestly integrate all the necessary changes into the instinctive part of your mind I will quieten down in the background...(pause for about 3 minutes)...

## Enhancing concentration

That's it...and you can discover ways to...*enhance your concentration*...and as you begin to get into a situation you want to...*concentrate fully*...in you can find yourself instinctively shutting out and ignoring distractions and gradually focusing more and more on what you are doing...and it is interesting how the more you focus on paying close attention to every little thing you do the more you shut other things out and...*enhance concentration*...and there is no need to try to...*enhance concentration at those times you need it*...because for concentration to occur fully...*it just develops by itself*...and whilst...*that concentration develops by itself*...you can just *focus your attention* on finer and finer detail about what you are doing...and if you are reading you can focus on what that voice in your mind sounds like...and how the eyes move...and what they feel like as they move...and what speed that reading is occurring at and if you are reading a book...what do the pages feel like...what do they feel like and sound like to turn...and you can focus down onto finer detail...and as you do...*your concentration will increase*...and all of this will happen unconsciously...and you can tell yourself 'if I notice distractions, then I will ignore them'...and you can say that to yourself and absorb that idea...telling yourself that if you notice distractions, then you will ignore them...and in appropriate situations you can prepare in advance to concentrate...you can get the mind-set first and set up the situation and make sure the situation has as few distractions as possible and take a few moments to really focus internally perhaps on breathing or the feeling of the air as it flows through the nose...then when you have prepared...*you can concentrate fully and effortlessly*...and I'd like to have you take a few moments just to think about those times you have entered that state of concentration...even those times it was for just a few seconds...and there are thousands of times in your life this has happened *automatically* without you being aware of it...and you can begin to gather up all of those times and learn from them how...*your unconscious knows how to concentrate fully*...and it can be instinctive...and automatic...and you can begin to get a sense of how you will know...you are *concentrating fully in the appropriate situations* in the future...if I was a fly on the wall watching you concentrating how will I know...what will I see...what behaviours...what body language...what will I hear...how does...*concentrating in those times in the future*...make thing different...what are the positives of that...how does it impact on your life and the lives of those around you...and you can now take as long as you need over the next few minutes to fully and honestly make all the necessary changes on an instinctive level to ensure you can easily and effortlessly concentrate in the necessary future situations…(pause for about 3 minutes)…

## Focus meditation

That's it…and you can now begin to prepare to *experience a focused state of meditation* and in a moment a single short word or letter or sound will come to mind and when it does you can begin to focus on it…and you can begin to focus all of your attention on that sound…and once that sound is in your mind you can begin to say that sound to yourself and you can stretch that sound out to fill your outbreath and *allow your mind to be empty on each in-breath*…and as you make that sound to yourself in your mind you can…*just observe…observe without judgement*…and just observe the full range of that sound…what colours come to mind…how the sound reverberates…how the sound is associated with certain feelings…and really just…*observe what comes up in your mind* yet focus on ignoring all distractions and associations and focus on repeating that sound with each outbreath…and *continue that*...and if your mind wanders bring it back on track and...*focus on that sound*...and with each breath out you can become...*deeper and deeper absorbed*... (pause for about 5-10 minutes)...


## Loving kindness meditation

That's it...and just begin to get a sense of the heart beating...begin to notice that it isn't just blood being pumped around the body...notice how there is a healing loving light flowing through the body and mind...and notice how this energy is pulsating with each beat of the heart and beginning to radiate out from the self...and as you observe that energy flowing out notice how that loving kindness begins to interact with the energy of others...it begins to feed in pleasure and healing and a connection with those that it touches...and get a sense of that loving kindness being transmitted into the hearts and souls of every living being...allowing you to see and connect with the inner beauty of others...and in a moment I will go silent and when I do the transmission of healing loving kindness can intensify...and you can begin to absorb the loving kindness given off by others...and you know what it feels like to be truly and unconditionally loved...and as you begin to recall that now while that heart continues to beat you can *intensify that feeling of loving kindness*...and you know what it feels like to *love truly and deeply*...and as these thoughts of all the times in your life you have felt a deep sense of love and all the times you have felt deeply loved you can take that feeling...feed it in to your heart and allow it to be pumped out into the world around you...and this loving kindness that permeates you and spreads out from you can continue indefinitely...and you can *see inner beauty*...and there is a story about a Buddhist monk...and he went to a temple and took his new expensive shoes off at the door...after he had finished praying he returned to the door only to notice his shoes were missing...the monk calmly left the temple and went home...when he arrived home he was asked where his shoes were...and the monk replied that they were taken...he was asked didn't that make him angry...no...replied the monk...I can only apologise to the thief that I have created...had I not worn such expensive shoes I never would have tempted a less fortunate person to feel the need to steal...and you can discover how every unkind act leads you to *feel a sense of compassion and understanding and loving kindness to others...and silence can intensify that*...now... (pause for about 5 minutes)...

## Overcoming nail biting

That's it...and as you continue to relax you can begin to learn new ways to respond...and up until now you had felt it was necessary to eat those nails...and you hadn't felt it was necessary to...*enjoy a new experience*...and a part of you can drift back into the past to a time before that problem began...and as it drifts slowly back forwards in time it can settle on all relevant memories and begin to...*remove all emotion from those memories*...and I don't know whether the unconscious will do this with your conscious awareness or without...and that part of you can then continue forwards until it reaches the present...which is given in the here and now...and in the future...you can begin to experience memories where in the past you would have ended up biting those nails...and you can notice how *this time things go differently*...and I wonder what will be different and new...and you can notice how calm you can be in those future situations that in the past would have led to that old nail biting behaviour...and you can mentally rehearse dozens of future situations that in the past would have led to that old nail biting behaviour...and *notice what is different*...and notice how you know...*you are responding differently*...and what you can see and hear and what it feels like to *be calm responding differently*...and what do others notice...how do they know *things are different*...and you can really learn on an instinctive level from this experience...and find that in the same way that a dropped plate that breaks doesn't suddenly jump back and fix itself neither does that old behaviour when...*it becomes this new response*...and while I quieten down in the background your unconscious can programme all the necessary changes into the instinctive part of your mind...and you can take as long as you need over the next few minutes...to do that...now...(pause for about 3 minutes)...

## *Change that problem now (generic problem resolution script)*

That's it...and as you think about what life will be like in the future...now...when that old problem has gone you can *explore what that is like*...and as you explore what that is like I wonder what will be different...and you can...*notice those differences* and *notice what life is like without that old problem*...and you can get a sense of what you do differently...what will someone else see if they are watching you...how do you feel...what does someone else hear...and how do those changes impact on other people in your life...and you can get a sense of being a long way off in the future looking back and reminiscing on how you achieved success and overcame that old problem...and whether you had any brief relapses or just remained *problem free*...and while I go silent you can take as long as you need to really fully and honestly explore how that *change* occurred...what led to you *overcoming that old problem*...how long it took you to *fully overcome that problem* and whether there were any difficulties that you had to overcome...on the road to success...and all those changes and all that is relevant can become a part of the instinctive part of you by the time I talk again and you can also drift back from that future position at the same time as…finishing all that is necessary to *overcome that problem*…(pause for about 3 minutes)…

## *Warts removal*

That's it…and you can get a sense of a vast land…and on that land are a number of invading forts…and you, as the commander of the army, have been given the task of destroying those invaders…and you can *learn from this on a deep unconscious level* and *put into practice what you learn*…and there was a case in the past where a hypnotherapist thought a boy had an extreme case of warts and the hypnotherapist *removed the warts* before discovering that it was actually a genetic disease and should have been impossible to cure…yet…*the cure happened*…and there was a case of someone being thought to have hysterical blindness…and the therapist used hypnosis to treat this…after a number of sessions the man was beginning to see again…and when he went to a neurologist it was discovered that he actually had brain damage and so should have been impossible to cure yet he was now seeing...and hypnosis has been used for centuries to *cure warts*...and sometimes the hypnotist has just suggested...*those warts will vanish...the skin there will grow back clean and clear and new...and the warts have vanished*...other hypnotists have been a bit more vague and suggested...*those warts will vanish*...and I don't know whether it will happen this week or next week or within a month...and...*the warts vanish*...and others will tell stories and the clients unconscious picks up on the patterns and understands the stories on a deep level and makes those changes to...*get rid of the warts*...and I don't know which option *you will respond* best to...and it can *happen automatically*...and you know the commander can send in an army to attack the invaders and overpower them...or the commander can stop the food supply getting to the invaders so they gradually run out of fuel and die...and I don't know what option you will choose...and how will things be different once they are gone...and I don't know whether it will be as if...*they just fall off*...or whether it will be as if...*they fade away*...and...*change happens*...all the time...it is just a matter of how and when...and I wonder how *you will behave differently*...and if there are any underlying causes behind those old warts being there then a part of you can drift back and *tackle those underlying issues*...if there are any memories associated with the creation of those warts...*your unconscious*...can remove all negative emotion from those memories whilst maintaining any important learning...and that part of you can go all the way back outside of conscious awareness to the beginning...to when the warts first appeared and what specifically caused them and how you can...*now move forward*...and you can take as long as you need over the next few minutes to make all the necessary changes on an unconscious instinctive level...and be curious how quickly *change will begin* and what you will first *notice that change happening*...(pause for about 3 minutes)...

## *Help with meeting basic emotional needs and using their innate skills correctly*

### To give and receive attention

And while you continue to relax I wonder what you are thinking...and as you think those thoughts a part of you can begin to...*create change*...and *your unconscious*...can begin to deeply consider new possibilities about how...you will find ways to honestly compliment as many people as you can each day...and I don't know whether it will be three people or five people or seven people or more or maybe even four...and each day you can look to find something you can do that will make someone else feel good without doing it to get anything out of it yourself...and it can be something as simple as smiling more or holding a door open or asking 'can I help you with that?' and helping...and there may be occasional days where opportunities don't arise...and you can relax at these times in the pleasant knowledge that you are helpful when the situations present themselves, while looking after yourself at these times as well...and you can make all the necessary changes and decisions to allow yourself to take some time to do this...(pause for about a minute)...

## Mind body connection

And as you relax, you can continue to think those thoughts and a part of you can begin to...*create change*...and *your unconscious*...can begin to deeply consider new possibilities about how...you will pay attention to the mind and body...and the mind and body are interconnected and influence each other...and when you inhibit sleep your intelligence and ability to carry out mental tasks reduces...so what is happening to your body affects the mind...and when you worry excessively and get stressed you struggle to sleep...and so your mind affects your body...and when people take drugs or alcohol or smoke the chemicals affect the body and these changes change the mind...and when people suffer depression or anxiety these create chemicals that change the body...and when you eat healthy the body stabilises...blood sugar levels stabilise...other internal chemicals and processes stabilise and work more efficiently...leading to greater alertness and clearer thinking...and when we laugh and find things funny and think about things that make us happy, that releases the body's natural opiates and feel good chemicals into the blood and creates many other positive physiological changes...*making the body healthier*...more likely to reduce sensations of discomfort...*improve sleep*...improve health and wellbeing and improve the ability to handle situations and improve the functioning of the digestive system and sex drive...and I don't know what changes you will make to make sure the mind and body develop a healthy interaction and a healthy influence on each other...and you can wonder how this will happen or just discover it happening all by itself...and a part of you knows what changes you as an individual will make to...*create change now*...(pause for about a minute)...

## Purpose and goals

And you can discover something previously unknown about a future change and whilst you are here in this state of mind you can be a key catalyst of the new change…and you can begin to plan things in the future…and I don't know whether you will plan what you will do each day or what you will achieve each week or just what you will achieve in a month or year…and you can…now…*discover what you are good at*…and you may never have previously even realised…and a part of you can *discover that now*…and I don't know whether that part of you will allow the conscious part of you to share in its discovery or if it will wait a while before sharing that discovery…and your unconscious can begin to get a sense for how…*you can start to write lists about what needs to be done each day or what you would like to achieve* each day…week…month…or year…and as…*you begin to achieve*…you can mark off all the successes and see just how much of that…*you will achieve*…and I wonder whether…*you will achieve*…50% of what you set out to achieve…or 75%…or 100%…or another amount entirely and I wonder whether…*you will begin to achieve*…and then…*discover you change your mind*…and…*set new goals and targets*…or whether you will just stick to what…*you set out to achieve*…and I don't know what types of things…*you will set to achieve*…whether it will be everyday tasks like...tidying up...planning the weekly shopping...planning what to eat at meal times...or whether it will be things like...achieving at work...like setting what needs to be done daily and ticking off each item as...*you achieve* it...or maybe setting a dream that you will achieve and how...*you will achieve* that...and when by...and setting a time scale for each achievement...and ticking off each stage as...*you achieve* it...and you can take some time to integrate this new way of thinking into the instinctive part of your mind...(pause for about a minute)...

## Belonging to the wider community

As you continue to *drift and dream* you can wonder about how you can *enjoy getting something new out of life*...and the part you play in the world around you...and for a tree to grow it needs good soil and water and nutrients and sunlight and other plants around it and animals...and without these the tree doesn't grow up big strong and healthy...and it doesn't just need any plants or any animals or any amount of sunlight or any nutrients or any type of soil...it needs to ensure that the soil is just right for the type of tree it will become...it needs to be in a location so that it will have just the right amount of water and sunlight...and it needs plants around it that work with it so that they get the right amount of support and shelter whilst offering something back to the tree in return...they will supply the tree with appropriate nutrients and protection and will work together...and the animals need to also help the tree...they need to be drawn to the tree for what the tree has to offer and in return they take on board seeds and pollen and freely and willingly carryout tasks for the tree...and together they support each other...and your unconscious can understand on a deep and meaningful level what I am saying...as you take some time now to...*integrate all that*...(pause for about a minute)...

## Stimulation and creativity

That's it...and we all need to...*feel a sense of stimulation*...and we all need to...*be creative*...and it doesn't mean we all need to become artists or musicians or to fill our lives will exciting experiences...it is more fundamental than that...we all need to find ways to...*feel a part of the world*...around us...and to feel we all...*make a contribution to the world*...around us...and creating stimulation can be as simple as taking time to read every day or to learn something new every day or to fill your day with a number of activities...if you sit in a room all day and do nothing you can get bored...if you sit in a room for a few hours a day and spend the rest of the day going out for a walk...reading a few chapters of a book...listening to music...watching a programme on TV...meeting up with a friend...playing a game for an hour or so...cooking a meal...phoning a friend or relative...planning a holiday...all of these are stimulation events...they are all small events that fill a day with stimulation...and there are many more you can think of...and it is important to *develop a variety of stimulation events* rather than just one or two and creating and thinking about stimulation events involves creative thinking and developing new ideas...and...*adapting to life*...and your unconscious can take as long as it needs over the next minute or so to develop these ideas creatively into your future and build on them…(pause for about 1 minute)…

## Understood and emotionally connected to others

And you can learn something now about how you connect with others around you…and how you *help yourself to be understood*…and there are times you are more understood and times you are less understood and times *you feel close to people* and times you feel a little more distant…and your unconscious can integrate new learning and understanding about how you connect with people in a unique way…and sometimes it can seem like you or others are speaking a different language…and that you could do with a translator…and your unconscious can act as a translator and you may not even realise…and we communicate on many levels and to be understood we have to pick up on many levels of communication…and as you listen to people you can *really focus and learn and develop* with what they are communicating to know how to put what you want to communicate into a way they will understand…and you can understand through communication and discovery and learning...and when you are around someone that spends time breathing like you and spends time using similar words to you and similar categories of words to you and spends time smiling...yet much of this is so subtle you don't consciously notice...you can find yourself *feeling deeply emotionally connected* and feeling all of your senses and emotions lighting up with pleasure...and you can *form appropriate emotional connections with those around you*...and you can learn to recognise the signs that allow you to know when to approach and when to back off...and when you approach a wild horse you know you are no threat and you know you just want to get close to them but if you approach too fast or approach looking aggressive or threatening the horse runs away...if you take time and approach at the right speed paying attention to the horse so that if the horse begins to show any signs of being uncomfortable you slow down...if they appear more comfortable you can speed up...until eventually you reach the horse...and you know if a horse approaches you for food or for petting you should feed or pet that horse and even horses can make the mistake of pushing their luck even though they have been fed or petted...and you can learn more from this than you realise on a conscious level...(pause for about one minute)...


## A sense of control and independence

That's it...and it is natural to want to have control...and sometimes people can feel too in control of what they have very little control over...and other times people can feel too out of control of what they actually have more control over...and you can begin to learn about how much control you have in different situations...and some people crave control and suffer when they can't control those things you have no control over...and others wish they had more control and feel they don't have control because they are trying to control those part of the experience that they have no control over...and if someone jumps out of a plane with a parachute on they have no control over the falling...they will continue falling...and if they want to try to control that decision they will get stressed and fail...they do have control of how they fall...where they fall...how fast or slow they fall...and when they slow the fall down...and they can pull the cord and release the parachute making the fall comfortable and controlled...and survivors in prisoner of war camps had no control over whether they were tortured or not...and the survivors all took control which helped them survive...they took control of what they could control...they took control of how long they went before screaming or what they spent their time thinking about...and they often thought about getting home to see loved ones...and too much control leads to problems forming...like obsessive problems or superstitions where people try to control things they have no control over and then the problem gets out of control and so they try to control things more...and by *letting go* and thinking...do I have real control here...and only controlling what is in your control...leads to an *improved future*...of change and discovery...and you can control how you act and behave and you can't control other people or inevitable events...and you can focus your controlling efforts on those areas you can control and control them in a way that positively benefits you and those around you in a way that enriches and enhances lives...(pause for about a minute)...

## Tolerating uncertainty

And as those eyes move in that way you can begin to explore ways you can become comfortable with a certain amount of uncertainty where it is appropriate and explore those times there has been uncertainty and pleasure and you can learn on an unconscious level how to increase comfort in situations where you don't know the outcome or how it will go or where you are only in control of yourself and how you react in that situation…and you don't want to react in uncertain way that makes it appear you have lost control and you can react in a way that displays true honest unconscious control…and you can programme that into your neurology now…(pause for about 2 minutes)…

## Helping the client challenge their emotional thinking

And as you continue to listen to me you can begin to learn how you can…*step back in your mind*…and how you can…learn to *step back in your mind* in future situations…and how this…*stepping back in your mind*…can allow you to *get a new perspective on a problem*...and in situations in the future you can...*step back in your mind*...and see the wood for the trees...and you know it is easy for a football fan watch football on a TV and shout at the TV and know the player should have passed the ball...yet the player who is the expert didn't notice the opportunity because they were in the game and too busy focusing on not losing the ball...and you can learn from this how you can...*change your mind*...and *develop in new ways*...(pause for about 2 minutes)...

## Transferring natural resources, skills and strengths

That's it...and you have all the resources and skills you need at an unconscious level based on all of your life experiences and as you *relax here and...now*...you can begin to...*learn unconsciously*...how to link skills...resources...and abilities from one area of your life to other areas of your life...and you don't have to know how...*you do this*...it can happen automatically...as you take time to *drift deeper and deeper into this state*...(pause for about 2 minutes)...

## Managing attention

*Drifting deeper and deeper*...that's it...and you know some things make us *become absorbed* while other things we just find we can't concentrate on...and as you listen to me talking you have been learning how to...*manage attention*...on an unconscious level...and you know if there was an emergency your attention would be fully on that emergency...and you know on an instinctive level how to...*manage your attention*...and can really master...*managing your attention*...and you can discover that changes to how...*you manage your attention*...occur automatically over time without any effort on your part...and you can take time now to *let that integration take place fully and honestly*...(pause for about 2 minutes)...

## Using creative thinking and thinking of alternative viewpoints

And you know there is often more than one meaning to an event or situation and *your unconscious can instinctively begin to offer you different meanings to situations* that could in the past have caused distress...I remember the story about the driver that was driving along the motorway when someone cut them up...they were fuming but then they started laughing....and another person was driving down a motorway and they got cut up and were fuming...and then they behaved differently...and on a quiet country road a Porsche and a Ferrari crashed into each other causing lots of damage to the vehicles...yet the owners started laughing...and why did people respond in such odd ways...well the first person to be cut up saw the driver of the car in front wave and recognised her as a good friend...the second driver that was cut up noticed what looked like a distressed pregnant woman in the back seat of the car and was now more concerned that the person gets to the hospital quickly and the two expensive cars that crashed turned out to be a brother and sister and the brother had bought the sister the Ferrari as a present and they saw the funny side of the incident as no-one was hurt and it was at a slow speed...and you can now take time to learn on an unconscious level how to *hold multiple view points and understandings and different meanings of situations* and how different meanings can lead to different feelings and different reactions and decisions...and you can take some time now to work out how this applies best to you and how this can help you to improve in the future…(pause for about 2 minutes)…

# REORIENTING BACK TO THE ROOM

## *Exiting hypnosis now*

Generally, I would only tell the client when to exit hypnosis if we were short of time in the session. Normally my preferred option is to allow the client to exit hypnosis when they are ready rather than because I told them to. This also allows for the therapy and the client deciding to open their eyes to be linked together so that you can suggest something like 'and when you know instinctively that all the work is complete you can drift out of hypnosis and open your eyes' this then links the eyes opening with acceptance of all the work being completed.

That's it...and you can now just take a few moments to allow yourself to get a sense of drifting back into that chair...and I don't know whether you will take 4, 5, 6 or 8 breaths to fully re-orient back to the chair...before you then start to work your way back along the route you took into hypnosis...and as you do, you can unconsciously ensure that all the new re-programming has been installed throughout the mind and body in every cell and neuron...your unconscious can *honestly and fully integrate all your new learning into that deep and instinctive part of your mind* while you continue your journey back to the here and now...and I don't know how much of what is there will be left there as you continue back and how much you will bring back with you...an it is interesting how much you know you can be aware of while you are sat there in that seat...and you can now find yourself working all the way back away from that state to the here and now becoming more aware of sounds around you...of me, of what you will be getting on with later and other random thoughts that start to cross the mind...and in a moment I'm going to count to 3 and on the count of 3 you can open your eyes and be fully back in the room...one...two...three...and open your eyes...hi now you came here to see how you are able to be helped and I asked you to close your eyes earlier...so do you have any plans for later...(have a brief chat then if you are going to set any tasks etc. you can do that before they go)...

## Allow the client to exit hypnosis when they are ready

This is my preferred option as it gives the client control over the process and allows for the success of the trance work to be contingent on the client opening their eyes.

That's it...and now as you gradually find your way back out of hypnosis you can take all the time you need to *ensure all the work is completed fully and honestly*...and only drift back out of hypnosis at the rate and speed that *all of the re-programming updates*...and when you have found your way back fully, all necessary changes will have happened on an instinctive level to allow you to open your eyes and come back to the room…(remain quiet while they take as long as they need to return to the room, once they are back in the room with their eyes open then say 'hi' and talk briefly about something irrelevant relating to before the session like how long it took them to get there then ask about if they have any plan for the rest of the day, then set any tasks and have some general chat to make sure they are very much awake now)…

## Allow the client to drift off to sleep

This ending is included for those that want to make self-hypnosis tracks for clients and feel that the client should be able to listen to the track at night and just drift off asleep. Some clients prefer this option with self-hypnosis tracks rather than being woken from hypnosis to then have to fall asleep; especially clients that already have difficulty sleeping.

That's it...and now as you gradually...*drift off to sleep*...you can take all the time you need to ensure *all the work is completed fully and honestly*...and only drift out of hypnosis and into a comfortable deep sleep at the rate and speed that *all of the re-programming updates*...and as your neurology updates you can *find your way back fully out of hypnosis and into that relaxing sleep*...and when *you drift into a dream*...all necessary changes will have happened on an instinctive level...and you can awaken at the appropriate time after your sleep...feeling refreshed and revitalised...(the client can then drift to sleep)...

# TREATMENT IDEAS

## *Gathering information*

Hypnotherapy isn't all about the scripts. It's about good quality information gathering that can be useful to help move clients on. It could be that something you say or ask a client stimulates certain mental processes that lead to future change even if these questions weren't seen as part of the 'therapy'.

Many people I work with have often moved on considerable between talking with me and having the first session. Often by the second session things have moved on tremendously with the client having insight into their situation and understanding how to move forward resiliently.

Sometimes you need to find out what purpose the current problem is serving and work with the client to find an alternative solution (not all problems are currently serving a purpose but many are so it is worth checking out). From this discussion it may turn out that the client needs to learn something like how to relax or ways to manage stress before they will be in a position to move on.

If this is the case, you can explain this to the client and how this is part of the treatment plan. If you do this you can set a goal of the session for example to be to learn to relax and practice a specific technique between now and the next session. Then you can teach them a technique or skill and just give them a brief hypnotic experience.

You can then ask them in the next session what changes they have noticed and explore any changes they report. By getting a clear understanding of the client's problem and the solution they want, you can formulate your own ideas and suggestions that are specific to that individual.

When gathering information ask 'who, what, where, when, how' questions. You want to know as much information as possible about the structure of the problem and the aspects of the problem like does it always happen around the same people or in the same situations. You also want to know about the solutions so when doesn't the problem happen, where doesn't the problem happen, who doesn't the problem happen with.

Look for exceptions as these are often where you will find the solutions. Normalise the problem for the client so that they don't feel they are the only person that has that problem or that severity of problem. Scale the problem at the beginning (E.g. from 0-10) and then at each session, or most sessions and at the end of treatment. This will allow you and the client to chart progress. Find out what the number they give means in sensory language. 'What does a three look like?' Then ask 'what stops it being one point lower and what would make it one point higher?' And where would they ideally like it to get to and what would all this look, sound, feel like, who else would notice, etc?

Ask the client for resources. Some of this would come from asking for exceptions but they may also have skills in other areas of their life like being able to be calm at work but not at home. So, you want that resource and can then explore how they can transfer it from one context to another and explore what is different that makes them able to use it in one context and not the other. Resources could also be family and friends or hobbies or interests. Things that can be used to tackle the presenting issue.

Ask hypothetical questions like 'If you woke up tomorrow and you no longer had the problem but no-one told you, what would be different? What would you see, hear, feel? What would others see and hear or notice?' From this, clients can begin to create solutions and begin to develop a mindset of noticing improvements and can also bring out more useful information and resources.

## *Task setting*

Tasks can be a good way of helping the client to take what they are getting in the session out into the real world. Many clients do well in sessions but don't do anything between sessions because they don't realise that they can.

Tasks can take on a number of forms. You can set metaphorical tasks. These are tasks that have no fixed meaning and are vague so the client finds the meaning themselves. As long as they are issued with sincerity they can be very effective. For example, you could set a task of learning about cacti as a way of teaching a client that they don't need to drink lots of alcohol (cacti can cope perfectly well in harsh environments with limited water which could be a metaphor for someone coping well in a stressful life without resorting to heavy drinking). It could be having the client find a specific shape and sized stone on a beach, carry it around with them for a week and wonder what it means and then throwing it away at the end of the week (could be a metaphor for throwing away an old habit).

Metaphorical tasks can also work well if the metaphor was used in the hypnotic work. For example, if you used a metaphor like comparing a congested city to a clean and clear countryside you could have a task where the client spends a day in a city somewhere noisy and busy and just observes and then a day in the countryside.

You can set tasks that alter the problem pattern in some way. It could be altering the time the problem takes place. So, if they always smoke when they answer the phone you can set the task of having them smoke once the phone call is finished. Any change to an established pattern begins to disrupt it and the longer the disruption goes on for the more impact it has on the pattern. In many cases if you can convince a client to alter their problem pattern and continue with this alteration, the problem often disappears.

You could alter the location the problem takes place. So, if someone smokes in a specific location you could have them smoke in a different location. You can alter the length of time the problem behaviour is carried out for. So, if someone takes three minutes to smoke a cigarette you could get them to agree to take 30 seconds or one minute or five minutes or ten minutes. This alteration is likely to become a chore and begin to add in extra feelings of not wanting to do the behaviour (the smoking, in this case). If you have got the client to agree to continue whenever they smoke then their only option is to stop smoking.

You could add in extra stages or change the order of the stages that are already there. Like having to run every time someone wants a cigarette; or having to count to twenty between each drag on the cigarette. These extra stages again create a chore and link a feeling of not wanting to do the behaviour. Even in situation where it isn't a chore it still disrupts the pattern meaning the pattern will never be the same again.

## Getting emotional needs met

We all have emotional needs that need to be met to lead an emotionally balanced life. These needs include giving and receiving attention, having a sense of control in our lives, having purpose and meaning in our lives, having stimulation and creativity; and being aware of the mind body connection.

If we don't have needs being met appropriately we may seek out alternative sources to get them met. So, for a problem like smoking it could be smoking as a way of 'breaking the ice' when socialising. Or smoking as a way of making sure we take a break (to meet our mind body connection need). Or smoking to have a sense of control in our lives as everything else seems out of our control yet we can decide to smoke and when to smoke; or smoking to give us stimulation. So just one problem can have many different ways it needs to be treated.

If you can learn what need is being met by the problem that the client is doing you can then address that need directly and as that need gets met appropriately in another healthier way, they automatically become less likely to continue with their problem and are more likely to find it easier to move on and keep their changes.

You can also set tasks that will put the client in situations where they will get their needs met appropriately and learn new ways to meet those needs. Or encourage clients to take up hobbies or interests that help them to meet their needs.

By listening out for innate emotional needs that aren't being met or are being met inappropriately you can dramatically speed up the time it takes to treat clients because you can have a greater impact on their life and on how they will continue to cope with life after therapy.

# WORKS CITED

Abdin, J. M. (2010). Imagery for sport performance : a comprehensive literature review.

Adams, S., & Allan, S. (2018). Muss' Rewind treatment for trauma: description and multi-site pilot study. *Journal of Mental Health, 27*(5).

Adams, S., & Allan, S. (2019). The effectiveness of Human Givens Rewind treatment for trauma. *Mental Health Review Journal, 24*(3).

Alladin, A., & Alibhai, A. (2007). Cognitive Hypnotherapy for Depression: An Empirical Investigation. *International Journal of Clinical and Experimental Hypnosis, 55*(2).

Bakke, A. C., Purtzer, M. Z., & Newton, P. (2002). The effect of hypnotic-guided imagery on psychological well-being and immune function in patients with prior breast cancer. *The Journal of Psychosomatic Research, 53*(6).

Bamford, C. (2006). A multifaceted approach to the treatment of phantom limb pain using hypnosis. *Contemporary Hypnosis, 23*(3).

Barnes, J., McRobbie, H., Dong, C. Y., Walker, N., & Hartmann-Boyce, J. (2019). Hypnotherapy for smoking cessation. (6).

Carmody, T., Duncan, C., Simon, J., Solkowitz, S., Huggins, J., Lee, S., & Delucchi, K. (2008, May). Hypnosis for Smoking Cessation: A Randomised Trial. *Nicotine & Tobacco Research, 10*(5).

Chamine, I., Atchley, R., & Oken, B. S. (2018). Hypnosis Intervention Effects on Sleep Outcomes: A Systematic Review. *Journal of Clinical Sleep Medicine, 14*(2).

Elkins, G., Jensen, M. P., & Patterson, D. R. (2007). Hypnotherapy for the Management of Chronic Pain. *International Journal of Clinical and Experimental Hypnosis, 55*(3).

Fisher, B., Esplin, S., Stoddard, G., & Silver, R. (2009). Randomized controlled trial of hypnobirthing versus standard childbirth classes: patient satisfaction and attitudes towards labor. *American Journal of Obstetrics & Gynecology, 201*(6).

Fried, R. G., & Hussain, S. H. (2008). Nonpharmacologic management of common skin and psychocutaneous disorders. *Dermatologic Therapy, 21*(1).

Golabadi, M., Taban, H., Yaghoubi, M., & Gholamrezaei, A. (2012). Hypnotherapy in the Treatment of Opium Addiction: A Pilot Study. *Integrative Medicine, 11*(3).

Green, J. P., & Lynn, S. J. (2000, January). Hypnosis and suggestion-based approaches to smoking cessation: An examination of the evidence. *International Journal of Clinical and Experimental Hypnosis, 48*(2), 195-224.

Hammond, D. C. (2010). Hypnosis in the treatment of anxiety- and stress-related disorders. *Expert Review of Neurotherapeutics, 10*(2).

Hasan, F. M., Zagarins, S. E., Pischke, K. M., Saiyed, S., Bettencourt, A., Beal, L., . . . McCleary, N. (2014). Hypnotherapy is more effective than nicotine replacement therapy for smoking cessation: Results of a randomized controlled trial. *Complementary Therapies in Medicine, 22*(1).

Horton-hausknecht, J. R., Mitzdorf, U., & Melchart, D. (2000). The effect of hypnosis therapy on the symptoms and disease activity in Rheumatoid Arthritis. *Psychology & Health, 14*(6).

Imannura, P. S., & Susanti, S. S. (2018). The Effectivenness of Hypnobirthing in Reducing Anxiety Level During Delivery. *The 2nd Joint International Conferences, 2*(2).

Kirsch, I., Montgomery, G., & Sapirstein, G. (1995). Hypnosis as an Adjunct to Cognitive-Behavioural Psychotherapy: A Meta-Analysis. *63*(2).

Liggett, D. R. (2000). Enhancing Imagery through Hypnosis: A Performance Aid for Athletes. *American Journal of Clinical Hypnosis, 43*(2).

Lindsay, P., Maynard, I., & Thomas, O. (2005). Effects of Hypnosis on Flow States and Cycling Performance. *Sport Psychologist, 19*(2).

Meyerson, J., & Konichezky, A. (2011). Hypnotically Induced Dissociation (HID) as a Strategic Intervention for Enhancing OCD Treatment. *American Journal of Clinical Hypnosis, 53*(3).

Milling, L. S., Gover, M. C., & Moriarty, C. L. (2018). The effectiveness of hypnosis as an intervention for obesity: A meta-analytic review. *Psychology of Consciousness: Theory, Research, and Practice, 5*(1).

Milling, L. S., Valentine, K. E., McCarley, H. S., & LoStimolo, L. M. (2018). A Meta-Analysis of Hypnotic Interventions for Depression Symptoms: High Hopes for Hypnosis? *American Journal of Clinical Hypnosis, 61*(3).

Muss, D. C. (1991). A new technique for treating post-traumatic stress disorder. *British Journal of Clinical Psychology, 30*(1).

Palsson, O. S. (2015). Hypnosis Treatment of Gastrointestinal Disorders: A Comprehensive Review of the Empirical Evidence. *American Journal of Clinical Hypnosis, 58*(2).

Pates, J., & Maynard, I. (2000). Effects of Hypnosis on Flow States and Golf Performance. *91*(3).

Pates, J., Maynard, I., & Westbury, T. (2001). An Investigation into the Effects of Hypnosis on Basketball Performance. *Journal of Applied Sport Psychology, 13*(1).

Peters, S. L., Muir, J. G., & Gibson, P. R. (2015). Review article: gut-directed hypnotherapy in the management of irritable bowel syndrome and inflammatory bowel disease. *Alimentary Pharmacology and Therapeutics, 41*(11).

Picard, P., Jusseaume, C., Boutet, M., Dualé, C., Mulliez, A., & Aublet-Cuvellier, B. (2013). Hypnosis for Management of Fibromyalgia. *International Journal of Clinical and Experimental Hypnosis, 61*(1).

Reid, D. B. (2017). Treating Panic Disorder Hypnotically. *American Journal of Clinical Hypnosis, 60*(2).

Ruzyla-Smith, P., Barabasz, A., Barabasz, M., & Warner, D. (1995). Effects of Hypnosis on the Immune Response:

B-Cells, T-Cells, Helper and Suppressor Cells. *American Journal of Clinical Hypnosis, 38*(2).

Seabrook, J. A., Gorodzinsky, F., & Freedman, S. (2005). Treatment of primary nocturnal enuresis: A randomized clinical trial comparing hypnotherapy and alarm therapy. *Paediatrics & Child Health, 10*(10).

Shestopal, I., & Bramness, J. G. (2019). Effect of Hypnotherapy in Alcohol Use Disorder Compared With Motivational Interviewing: A Randomized Controlled Trial. *Addictive Disorders and their Treatment, 18*(3).

Smith, C. A., Collins, C. T., Cyna, A. M., & Crowther, C. A. (2006). Complementary and alternative therapies for pain management in labour. *Cochrane Database of Systematic Reviews*(4).

Trakhtenberg, E. C. (2008). The Effects of Guided Imagery on the Immune System: A Critical Review. *International Journal of Neuroscience, 118*(6).